A-Level Year 2
Chemistry

Exam Board: AQA

Revising for Chemistry exams is stressful, that's for sure — even just getting your notes sorted out can leave you needing a lie down. But help is at hand...

This brilliant CGP book explains **everything you'll need to learn** (and nothing you won't), all in a straightforward style that's easy to get your head around. We've also included **exam questions** to test how ready you are for the real thing.

There's even a free Online Edition you can read on your computer or tablet!

A-Level revision? It has to be CGP!

Contents

Published by CGP

Editors:
Mary Falkner, Gordon Henderson, Emily Howe, Paul Jordin, Rachel Kordan, Sarah Pattison, Sophie Scott and Ben Train.

Contributors:
Mike Bossart, Robert Clarke, Ian H. Davis, John Duffy, Lucy Muncaster and Paul Warren.

ISBN: 978 1 78294 339 6

With thanks to Karen Wells for the proofreading.
With thanks to Jan Greenway for the copyright research.

Cover Photo **Laguna Design**/Science Photo Library

www.cgpbooks.co.uk

Clipart from Corel®
Printed by Elanders Ltd, Newcastle upon Tyne.

Based on the classic CGP style created by Richard Parsons.

Enthalpy Definitions

I'm sure that you remember enthalpies, but here's a quick reminder just in case...

First — **A Few Definitions** You Should Remember

ΔH is the symbol for **enthalpy change**.

Enthalpy change is the **heat** energy transferred in a reaction at **constant pressure**.

$\Delta H^{\ominus}$ means that the enthalpy change was measured under **standard conditions** (298 K and **100 kPa**).

Exothermic reactions have a **negative** ΔH value, because heat energy is given out.

Endothermic reactions have a **positive** ΔH value, because heat energy is absorbed.

There are **Different Types** of **Enthalpy Change**

Here are some more definitions: (you're welcome)

Enthalpy change of formation, $\Delta_f H$, is the enthalpy change when **1 mole** of a **compound** is formed from its **elements** in their standard states under standard conditions, e.g. $2C_{(s)} + 3H_{2(g)} + \frac{1}{2}O_{2(g)} \rightarrow C_2H_5OH_{(l)}$.

Bond dissociation enthalpy, $\Delta_{diss} H$, is the enthalpy change when all the **bonds of the same type** in **1 mole** of **gaseous molecules** are broken, e.g. $Cl_{2(g)} \rightarrow 2Cl_{(g)}$.

Enthalpy change of atomisation of an element, $\Delta_{at} H$, is the enthalpy change when **1 mole** of **gaseous atoms** is formed from an element in its **standard state**, e.g. $\frac{1}{2}Cl_{2(g)} \rightarrow Cl_{(g)}$.

Enthalpy change of atomisation of a compound, $\Delta_{at} H$, is the enthalpy change when **1 mole** of a compound in its **standard state** is converted to **gaseous atoms**, e.g. $NaCl_{(s)} \rightarrow Na_{(g)} + Cl_{(g)}$.

First ionisation energy, $\Delta_{ie1} H$, is the enthalpy change when **1 mole** of **gaseous 1+ ions** is formed from **1 mole** of **gaseous atoms**, e.g. $Mg_{(g)} \rightarrow Mg^+_{(g)} + e^-$.

Second ionisation energy, $\Delta_{ie2} H$, is the enthalpy change when **1 mole** of **gaseous 2+ ions** is formed from **1 mole** of **gaseous 1+ ions**, e.g. $Mg^+_{(g)} \rightarrow Mg^{2+}_{(g)} + e^-$.

First electron affinity, $\Delta_{ea1} H$, is the enthalpy change when **1 mole** of **gaseous 1– ions** is formed from **1 mole** of **gaseous atoms**, e.g. $O_{(g)} + e^- \rightarrow O^-_{(g)}$.

Second electron affinity, $\Delta_{ea2} H$, is the enthalpy change when **1 mole** of **gaseous 2– ions** is formed from **1 mole** of **gaseous 1– ions**, e.g. $O^-_{(g)} + e^- \rightarrow O^{2-}_{(g)}$.

Enthalpy change of hydration, $\Delta_{hyd} H$, is the enthalpy change when **1 mole** of **aqueous ions** is formed from **1 mole** of **gaseous ions**, e.g. $Na^+_{(g)} \rightarrow Na^+_{(aq)}$.

Enthalpy change of solution, $\Delta_{solution} H$, is the enthalpy change when **1 mole of solute** is dissolved in **enough solvent** that no further enthalpy change occurs on further dilution, e.g. $NaCl_{(s)} \rightarrow NaCl_{(aq)}$.

Practice Questions

Q1   Do exothermic reactions have positive or negative enthalpy changes?

Q2   Give the definition of bond dissociation enthalpy.

Q3   Write the equation representing the enthalpy change of atomisation for $NaCl_{(s)}$.

Q4   Define first ionisation energy and first electron affinity.

My eyes, MY EYES — the definitions make them hurt...

Well, isn't this a lovely way to begin — a whole barrage of definitions to learn. It's not all that bad though — once you're happy with a few of them, the rest should make a lot more sense. And by the way, don't think you won't need to learn this stuff just because there are no exam questions on this page. You WILL need to understand these definitions...

Lattice Enthalpy and Born-Haber Cycles

Now you know all your enthalpy change definitions, here's how to use them... enjoy.

Lattice Enthalpy is a Measure of Ionic Bond Strength

Lattice enthalpy, $\Delta_{lattice}H$, can be defined in two ways:

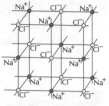

Part of the sodium
chloride lattice

1 **Lattice enthalpy of formation:** the enthalpy change when **1 mole** of a **solid ionic compound** is **formed** from its **gaseous ions** under standard conditions.

Example: $Na^+_{(g)} + Cl^-_{(g)} \rightarrow NaCl_{(s)}$ $\Delta_{lattice}H = -787$ kJ mol^{-1} **(exothermic)**

$Mg^{2+}_{(g)} + 2Cl^-_{(g)} \rightarrow MgCl_{2(s)}$ $\Delta_{lattice}H = -2526$ kJ mol^{-1} **(exothermic)**

2 **Lattice enthalpy of dissociation:** the enthalpy change when **1 mole** of a **solid ionic compound** is completely **dissociated** into its **gaseous ions** under standard conditions.

Example: $NaCl_{(s)} \rightarrow Na^+_{(g)} + Cl^-_{(g)}$ $\Delta_{lattice}H = +787$ kJ mol^{-1} **(endothermic)**

$MgCl_{2(s)} \rightarrow Mg^{2+}_{(g)} + 2Cl^-_{(g)}$ $\Delta_{lattice}H = +2526$ kJ mol^{-1} **(endothermic)**

Notice that lattice formation enthalpy and lattice dissociation enthalpy are exact opposites.

Born-Haber Cycles can be Used to Calculate Lattice Enthalpies

Hess's law says that the **total enthalpy change** of a reaction is always the **same**, no matter which route is taken. You can't calculate a lattice enthalpy **directly**, so you have to use a **Born-Haber cycle** to figure out what the enthalpy change would be if you took **another, less direct, route**.

Here's a Born-Haber cycle you could use to calculate the lattice enthalpy of **NaCl**:

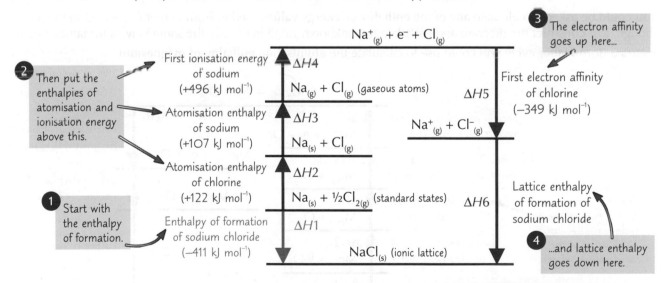

2 Then put the enthalpies of atomisation and ionisation energy above this.

First ionisation energy of sodium (+496 kJ mol^{-1}) — $\Delta H4$

Atomisation enthalpy of sodium (+107 kJ mol^{-1}) — $\Delta H3$

Atomisation enthalpy of chlorine (+122 kJ mol^{-1}) — $\Delta H2$

1 Start with the enthalpy of formation.

Enthalpy of formation of sodium chloride (−411 kJ mol^{-1}) — $\Delta H1$

$Na^+_{(g)} + e^- + Cl_{(g)}$

$Na_{(g)} + Cl_{(g)}$ (gaseous atoms)

$Na_{(s)} + Cl_{(g)}$

$Na_{(s)} + \frac{1}{2}Cl_{2(g)}$ (standard states)

$NaCl_{(s)}$ (ionic lattice)

3 The electron affinity goes up here...

First electron affinity of chlorine (−349 kJ mol^{-1}) — $\Delta H5$

$Na^+_{(g)} + Cl^-_{(g)}$

$\Delta H6$ Lattice enthalpy of formation of sodium chloride

4 ...and lattice enthalpy goes down here.

There are **two routes** you can follow to get from the elements in their **standard states** to the **ionic lattice**. The green arrow shows the **direct route** and the purple arrows show the **indirect route**. The enthalpy change for each is the **same**.

From **Hess's law:** $\Delta H6 = -\Delta H5 - \Delta H4 - \Delta H3 - \Delta H2 + \Delta H1$
$= -(-349) - (+496) - (+107) - (+122) + (-411) = -787$ **kJ mol^{-1}**

You need a minus sign if you go the wrong way along an arrow.

So the **lattice enthalpy of formation** of sodium chloride is **−787 kJ mol^{-1}**.

Lattice Enthalpy and Born-Haber Cycles

Calculations Involving Group 2 Elements are a Bit Different

Born-Haber cycles for compounds containing **Group 2 elements** have at least one **extra step** compared to the one on the previous page. Make sure you understand what's going on so you can handle whatever compound they throw at you. Here's the Born-Haber cycle for calculating the lattice enthalpy of **magnesium chloride** ($MgCl_2$).

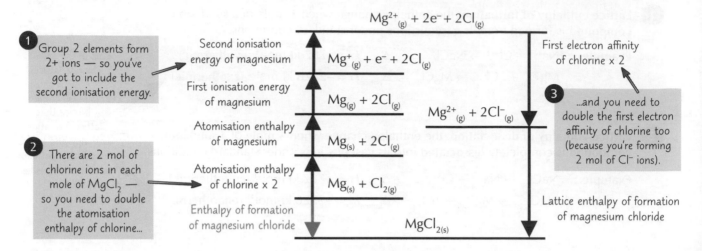

If the formation of a compound involves ions with **charges** of **more than 1**, you just have to add the **extra ionisation energies** and possibly **electron affinities** (see the example below) to the Born-Haber cycle. So you can **adapt** this method to any compound if you have all the information needed.

Born-Haber Cycles can be Used to Calculate Different Values

You could be asked to calculate **any** of the **enthalpy or energy values** used in Born-Haber cycles. Don't worry though, just construct the diagram and calculate the unknown value in exactly **the same way** as for lattice enthalpy.

Here's a Born-Haber cycle you could use to calculate the **atomisation enthalpy of magnesium**:

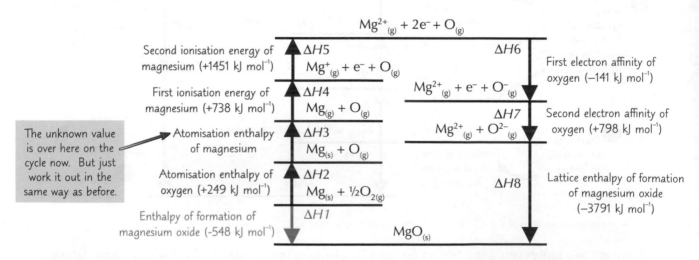

Work your way round the arrows, just like the example on the previous page. Since you're calculating the **atomisation enthalpy of magnesium**, move from [$Mg_{(s)} + O_{(g)}$] to [$Mg_{(g)} + O_{(g)}$] by the **indirect route**.

$$\Delta H3 = -\Delta H2 + \Delta H1 - \Delta H8 - \Delta H7 - \Delta H6 - \Delta H5 - \Delta H4$$
$$= -(+249) + (-548) - (-3791) - (+798) - (-141) - (+1451) - (+738) = \textbf{+148 kJ mol}^{-1}$$

Lattice Enthalpy and Born-Haber Cycles

Theoretical Lattice Enthalpies are Often Different from Experimental Values

You can work out a **theoretical lattice enthalpy** by doing some calculations based on the **purely ionic model** of a lattice. The purely ionic model of a lattice assumes that all the ions are **spherical**, and have their charge **evenly distributed** around them.

But if you find the **lattice enthalpy experimentally**, the value that you get is often different. This is **evidence** that most ionic compounds have some **covalent character**.

The positive and negative ions in a lattice **aren't** usually exactly spherical. Positive ions **polarise** neighbouring negative ions to different extents, and the **more polarisation** there is, the **more covalent** the bonding will be.

unpolarised ions — purely ionic bonding

polarised ions — partial covalent bonding

Comparing Lattice Enthalpies Can Tell You 'How Ionic' an Ionic Lattice Is

Here are experimental and theoretical lattice enthalpy values for some **magnesium halides** and some **sodium halides**.

Compound	Lattice Enthalpy of Formation (kJ mol^{-1})	
	From experimental values	From theory
$MgCl_2$	−2526	−2326
$MgBr_2$	−2440	−2097
MgI_2	−2327	−1944
NaCl	−787	−766
NaBr	−742	−731
NaI	−698	−686

The differences between experimental and theoretical lattice enthalpies are **much bigger** for the **magnesium halides** than for the **sodium halides**. This shows that the bonding in **magnesium halides** is **stronger** than the **ionic model** predicts, so the bonds are **strongly polarised** and have quite a lot of **covalent character.** The bonding in the **sodium halides** is **similar** to the predictions of the **ionic model**, so the compounds are close to being **purely ionic**.

Practice Questions

Q1 Is lattice formation an exothermic or endothermic process?

Q2 Explain why theoretical lattice enthalpies are often different from experimentally determined lattice enthalpies.

Exam Questions

Q1 Using this data:

Δ_fH [potassium bromide] = −394 kJ mol^{-1} $\Delta_{at}H$ [bromine] = +112 kJ mol^{-1} $\Delta_{at}H$ [potassium] = +89 kJ mol^{-1}

$\Delta_{ie1}H$ [potassium] = +419 kJ mol^{-1} $\Delta_{ea1}H$ [bromine] = −325 kJ mol^{-1}

a) Construct a Born-Haber cycle for potassium bromide (KBr).   [3 marks]

b) Use your Born-Haber cycle to calculate the lattice formation enthalpy of potassium bromide.   [2 marks]

Q2 Using this data:

Δ_fH [aluminium chloride] = −706 kJ mol^{-1} $\Delta_{at}H$ [chlorine] = +122 kJ mol^{-1} $\Delta_{at}H$ [aluminium] = +326 kJ mol^{-1}

$\Delta_{ea1}H$ [chlorine] = −349 kJ mol^{-1} $\Delta_{ie2}H$ [aluminium] = +1817 kJ mol^{-1}

$\Delta_{ie3}H$ [aluminium] = +2745 kJ mol^{-1} $\Delta_{lattice}H$ [aluminium chloride] = −5491 kJ mol^{-1}

a) Construct a Born-Haber cycle for aluminium chloride (AlCl$_3$).   [3 marks]

b) Use your Born-Haber cycle to calculate the first ionisation energy of aluminium.   [2 marks]

Using Born-Haber cycles — it's just like riding a bike...

All this energy going in and out can get a bit confusing. Remember these simple rules: 1) It takes energy to break bonds, but energy is given out when bonds are made. 2) A negative ΔH means energy is given out (it's exothermic). 3) A positive ΔH means energy is taken in (it's endothermic). 4) Never return to a firework once lit.

Enthalpies of Solution

Once you know what's happening when you stir sugar into your tea, your cuppa'll be twice as enjoyable.

Dissolving Involves Enthalpy Changes

When a solid **ionic lattice** dissolves in water, these **two** things happen:

1) The bonds between the ions **break** to give free ions — this is **endothermic**.
2) Bonds between the ions and the water are **made** — this is **exothermic**.
3) The **enthalpy change of solution** is the overall effect on the enthalpy of these two things.

Ionic lettuce.

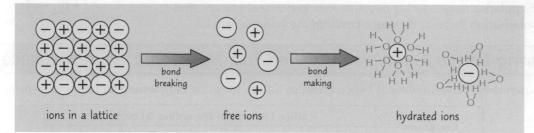

| ions in a lattice | free ions | hydrated ions |

4) Water molecules can bond to the ions because oxygen is more **electronegative** than hydrogen, so it draws electrons towards itself, creating a **dipole**. The dipole means the **positively charged hydrogen** atoms can form bonds with **negative ions** and **negatively charged oxygen** atoms can form bonds with **positive ions**.

> Substances generally **only** dissolve if the energy released is roughly the same, or **greater than** the energy taken in. So soluble substances tend to have **exothermic** enthalpies of solution.

Enthalpy Change of Solution can be Calculated

1) You can work out the **enthalpy change of solution** using a Born-Haber cycle.
2) Imagine that, instead of dissolving the compound directly, you are going to break the lattice into separate **gaseous** ions and then dissolve the gaseous ions in water.
3) Both of these are standard enthalpy changes that you can look up — the **lattice dissociation enthalpy** and the **enthalpies of hydration** of the ions. So you can use them to construct a Born-Haber cycle to find the enthalpy change of solution.

In reality, of course, you don't turn the ions into gases. But the net effect is the same (you start with a solid lattice and end with dissolved ions), so the energy change is the same too.

Here's how to draw the Born-Haber cycle for working out the **enthalpy change of solution** for **sodium chloride**.

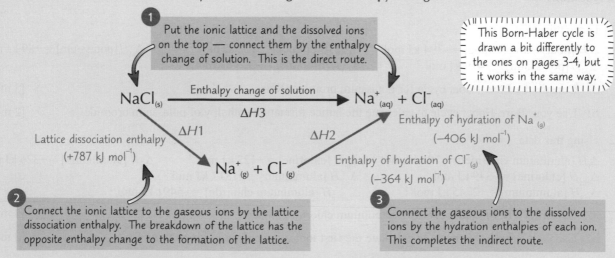

This Born-Haber cycle is drawn a bit differently to the ones on pages 3-4, but it works in the same way.

1 Put the ionic lattice and the dissolved ions on the top — connect them by the enthalpy change of solution. This is the direct route.

2 Connect the ionic lattice to the gaseous ions by the lattice dissociation enthalpy. The breakdown of the lattice has the opposite enthalpy change to the formation of the lattice.

3 Connect the gaseous ions to the dissolved ions by the hydration enthalpies of each ion. This completes the indirect route.

From Hess's law: $\Delta H3 = \Delta H1 + \Delta H2 = +787 + (-406 + -364) = +17 \text{ kJ mol}^{-1}$

The enthalpy change of solution is **slightly endothermic**. (But, in case you're wondering, there are other factors at work here that mean that sodium chloride will still dissolve in water — there's more about this on page 8).

Enthalpies of Solution

Here's another. This one's for working out the **enthalpy change of solution** for **silver chloride**:

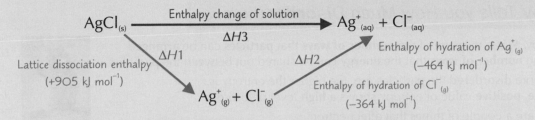

From Hess's law: $\Delta H3 = \Delta H1 + \Delta H2 = +905 + (-464 + -364) = +77 \text{ kJ mol}^{-1}$

This is much **more endothermic** than the enthalpy change of solution for sodium chloride. As such, silver chloride is **insoluble** in water.

As long as there's only one unknown enthalpy value, you can use these cycles to work out any value on the arrows. For example, if you know the enthalpy change of solution and the enthalpy changes of hydration, you can use those values to work out the lattice dissociation enthalpy.

Practice Questions

Q1 Describe the two steps that occur when an ionic lattice dissolves in water.

Q2 Do soluble substances have exothermic or endothermic enthalpies of solution, in general?

Q3 Sketch a Born-Haber cycle to calculate the enthalpy change of solution of magnesium chloride.

Exam Questions

Q1 a) Draw a Born-Haber cycle for the enthalpy change of solution of $AgF_{(s)}$. Label each enthalpy change.   [2 marks]

b) Calculate the enthalpy change of solution for AgF, using the data below.   [1 mark]

$\Delta_{lattice}H\,[AgF_{(s)}] = +960 \text{ kJ mol}^{-1}$, $\Delta_{hyd}H\,[Ag^+_{(g)}] = -464 \text{ kJ mol}^{-1}$, $\Delta_{hyd}H\,[F^-_{(g)}] = -506 \text{ kJ mol}^{-1}$.

Q2 Use this Born-Haber cycle to calculate the enthalpy change of solution for SrF_2.   [2 marks]

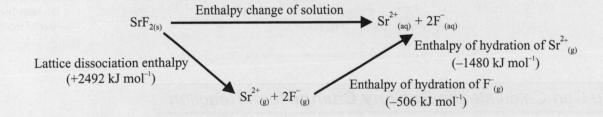

Q3 Show that the enthalpy of hydration of $Cl^-_{(g)}$ is -364 kJ mol^{-1}, given that: [3 marks]

$\Delta_{lattice}H\,[MgCl_{2(s)}] = -2526 \text{ kJ mol}^{-1}$, $\Delta_{hyd}H\,[Mg^{2+}_{(g)}] = -1920 \text{ kJ mol}^{-1}$, $\Delta_{sol}H\,[MgCl_{2(s)}] = -122 \text{ kJ mol}^{-1}$.

N A Chloride & dissociates — attorneys at Hess's Law...

Compared to the ones on pages 3-4, these Born-Haber cycles are a breeze. You do need to make sure that you've got the relevant enthalpy change definitions fixed in your mind. But once you know the lattice dissociation enthalpy of a compound and the enthalpy of hydration of its ions, you're well on your way to finding its enthalpy change of solution.

Entropy

Entropy sounds a bit like enthalpy (to start with at least), but they're not the same thing at all. Read on...

Entropy Tells you How Much Disorder there is

1) Entropy, *S*, is a measure of the **number of ways** that **particles** can be **arranged** and the **number of ways** that the **energy** can be shared out between the particles.

2) The more **disordered** the particles are, the higher the entropy is. A **large**, **positive** value of entropy shows a **high** level of disorder.

3) There are a couple of things that affect entropy:

Squirrels do not teach Chemistry. But if they did, this is what a demonstration of increasing entropy would look like.

Physical State affects Entropy

You have to go back to the good old **solid-liquid-gas** particle explanation thingy to understand this.

Solid particles just wobble about a fixed point — there's **hardly any** disorder, so they have the **lowest entropy**.

Gas particles whizz around wherever they like. They've got the most **disordered arrangements** of particles, so they have the **highest entropy**.

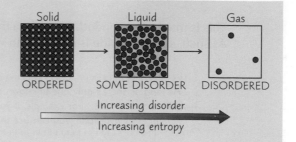

Solid — ORDERED Liquid — SOME DISORDER Gas — DISORDERED

Increasing disorder
Increasing entropy

More Particles means More Entropy

It makes sense — the more particles you've got, the **more ways** they and their energy can be **arranged** — so in a reaction like $N_2O_{4(g)} \rightarrow 2NO_{2(g)}$, entropy increases because the **number of moles** increases.

More Arrangements Means More Stability

1) Substances always tend towards disorder — they're actually more **energetically stable** when there's more disorder. So particles will move to **increase their entropy**.

2) This is why some reactions are **feasible** (they just happen by themselves — without the addition of energy) even when the enthalpy change is **endothermic**.

Feasible reactions are sometimes called spontaneous reactions.

Example: The reaction of sodium hydrogencarbonate with hydrochloric acid is an **endothermic reaction** — but it is **feasible**. This is due to an **increase in entropy** as the reaction produces carbon dioxide gas and water. Liquids and gases are **more disordered** than solids and so have a **higher entropy**. This increase in entropy **overcomes** the change in enthalpy.

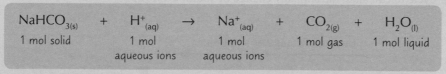

$$NaHCO_{3(s)} \quad + \quad H^+_{(aq)} \quad \rightarrow \quad Na^+_{(aq)} \quad + \quad CO_{2(g)} \quad + \quad H_2O_{(l)}$$

1 mol solid | 1 mol aqueous ions | 1 mol aqueous ions | 1 mol gas | 1 mol liquid

The reaction is also favoured because it increases the number of moles.

You Can Calculate the Entropy Change for a Reaction

1) During a reaction, there's an entropy change, ΔS, between the **reactants and products**.

2) You can calculate ΔS using this formula:

This is just the difference between the entropies of the products and reactants. $\longrightarrow$ $\Delta S = S_{products} - S_{reactants}$

The units of entropy are $J\,K^{-1}\,mol^{-1}$.

3) You can find $S_{products}$ by adding up the **standard entropy** of all of the products, and $S_{reactants}$ by adding up the standard entropy of all of the reactants.

4) The **standard entropy** of a substance, $S^{\ominus}$, is the entropy of 1 mole of that substance under standard conditions (at a pressure of 100 kPa and a temperature of 298 K).

Entropy

Example: Use the data given below to calculate the entropy change
of the reaction between ammonia and hydrogen chloride: $NH_{3(g)} + HCl_{(g)} \rightarrow NH_4Cl_{(s)}$

$S^{\ominus}[NH_{3(g)}] = 192$ J K^{-1} mol^{-1}, $S^{\ominus}[HCl_{(g)}] = 187$ J K^{-1} mol^{-1}, $S^{\ominus}[NH_4Cl_{(s)}] = 94.6$ J K^{-1} mol^{-1}.

$S_{products} = S^{\ominus}[NH_4Cl_{(s)}] = 94.6$ J K^{-1} mol^{-1}

$S_{reactants} = S^{\ominus}[NH_{3(g)}] + S^{\ominus}[HCl_{(g)}] = 192 + 187 = 379$ J K^{-1} mol^{-1}

$\Delta S = S_{products} - S_{reactants} = 94.6 - 379 = \mathbf{-284.4}$ **J K^{-1} mol^{-1}**

This shows a negative change in entropy. It's not surprising as 2 moles of gas have combined to form 1 mole of solid.

If the balanced equation for the reaction contains more than one mole of a reactant or product,
you'll need to multiply the entropy value for that substance by the same number.

Example: Nitrogen gas reacts with hydrogen gas to form ammonia: $3H_{2(g)} + N_{2(g)} \rightarrow 2NH_{3(g)}$
Use the data given below to calculate the entropy change associated with this reaction.

$S^{\ominus}[NH_{3(g)}] = 192$ J K^{-1} mol^{-1}, $S^{\ominus}[H_{2(g)}] = 131$ J K^{-1} mol^{-1}, $S^{\ominus}[N_{2(g)}] = 192$ J K^{-1} mol^{-1}.

$S_{products} = 2 \times S^{\ominus}[NH_{3(g)}] = 2 \times 192 = 384$ J K^{-1} mol^{-1}

$S_{reactants} = (3 \times S^{\ominus}[H_{2(g)}]) + S^{\ominus}[N_{2(g)}] = (3 \times 131) + 192 = 585$ J K^{-1} mol^{-1}

$\Delta S = S_{products} - S_{reactants} = 384 - 585 = \mathbf{-201}$ **J K^{-1} mol^{-1}**

An increase in total entropy means that it is **feasible** for a reaction to occur, but it's not a **guarantee** that it will
— **enthalpy**, **temperature** and **kinetics** also play a part in whether or not a reaction occurs.

There's more about this on the next page...

Practice Questions

Q1 What does the term 'entropy' mean?

Q2 In each of the following pairs, say which one will have the greater entropy.
   a) 1 mole of $NaCl_{(aq)}$ and 1 mole of $NaCl_{(s)}$ b) 1 mole of $Br_{2(l)}$ and 1 mole of $Br_{2(g)}$
   c) 1 mole of $Br_{2(g)}$ and 2 moles of $Br_{2(g)}$

Q3 Write down the formula used for finding the entropy change of a reaction.

Exam Questions

Q1   Zinc carbonate breaks down when heated to give zinc oxide and carbon dioxide: $ZnCO_{3(s)} \rightarrow ZnO_{(s)} + CO_{2(g)}$

Would you expect the entropy change for this reaction to be positive or negative? Explain your answer.   [2 marks]

Q2   Magnesium burns in oxygen according to the following equation:

$Mg_{(s)} + \frac{1}{2}O_{2(g)} \rightarrow MgO_{(s)}$

Use the data on the right to calculate
the entropy change for this reaction.   [2 marks]

Substance	$S^{\ominus}$ (J K^{-1} mol^{-1})
$Mg_{(s)}$	32.7
$O_{2(g)}$	205
$MgO_{(s)}$	26.9

Q3   Hydrogen peroxide decomposes to give water and oxygen gas:

$2H_2O_{2(l)} \rightarrow 2H_2O_{(l)} + O_{2(g)}$

Use the data given below to calculate the entropy change for this reaction.

$S^{\ominus}[H_2O_{2(l)}] = 110$ J K^{-1} mol^{-1}, $S^{\ominus}[O_{2(g)}] = 205$ J K^{-1} mol^{-1}, $S^{\ominus}[H_2O_{(l)}] = 69.9$ J K^{-1} mol^{-1}.   [2 marks]

Being neat and tidy is against the laws of nature...

Well, there you go. Entropy in all its glory. You haven't seen the back of it yet though, oh no. There's more where this came from. Which is why, if random disorder has left you in a spin, I'd suggest reading it again and making sure you've got your head round this lot before you turn over. You'll thank me for it, you will... Chocolates are always welcome...

Free Energy Change

Free energy — I could definitely do with a bit of that. My gas bill is astronomical.

For a Reaction to be **Feasible** ΔG must be **Negative** or **Zero**

Free energy change, ΔG, is a measure used to predict whether a reaction is **feasible**.
If ΔG is **negative or equal to zero**, then the reaction might happen by itself.

Free energy change takes into account the changes in **enthalpy** and **entropy** in the system. And of course, there's a formula for it:

ΔG = free energy change (in J mol^{-1})

$$\Delta G = \Delta H - T\Delta S$$

ΔH = enthalpy change (in J mol^{-1})
T = temperature (in K)
ΔS = entropy change (in J K^{-1} mol^{-1}) (see pages 8-9)

Even if ΔG shows that a reaction is theoretically feasible, it might have a very high activation energy or be so slow that you wouldn't notice it happening at all.

Example: Calculate the free energy change for the following reaction at 298 K.

$$MgCO_{3(g)} \rightarrow MgO_{(s)} + CO_{2(g)} \qquad \Delta H^\ominus = +117\ 000\ \text{J mol}^{-1}, \quad \Delta S^\ominus = +175\ \text{J K}^{-1}\ \text{mol}^{-1}$$

$$\Delta G = \Delta H - T\Delta S = +117\ 000 - (298 \times (+175)) = \mathbf{+64\ 900\ J\ mol^{-1}}\ (3\ \text{s.f.})$$

ΔG is positive — so the reaction isn't feasible at this temperature.

The **Feasibility** of Some Reactions Depends on **Temperature**

If a reaction is exothermic (**negative ΔH**) and has a **positive** entropy change, then ΔG is **always negative** since $\Delta G = \Delta H - T\Delta S$. These reactions are feasible at any temperature.

If a reaction is endothermic (**positive ΔH**) and has a **negative** entropy change, then ΔG is **always positive**. These reactions are not feasible at any temperature.

But for other combinations, temperature has an effect.

1) If ΔH is **positive** (endothermic) and ΔS is **positive** then the reaction won't be feasible at some temperatures but will be at a high enough temperature.

   For example, the decomposition of calcium carbonate is **endothermic** but results in an **increase in entropy** (the number of molecules increases and CO_2 is a gas).

$$CaCO_{3(s)} \rightarrow CaO_{(s)} + CO_{2(g)}$$

   The reaction will only occur when $CaCO_3$ is heated — it isn't feasible at 298 K.

After her surgery, Anne found that a reaction wasn't feasible.

   Example: $\Delta H = +10\ \text{kJ mol}^{-1}$, $\Delta S = +10\ \text{J K}^{-1}\ \text{mol}^{-1}$

at **300 K**	$\Delta G = \Delta H - T\Delta S = +10 \times 10^3 - (300 \times 10) = +7000\ \text{J mol}^{-1}$
at **1500 K**	$\Delta G = \Delta H - T\Delta S = +10 \times 10^3 - (1500 \times 10) = -5000\ \text{J mol}^{-1}$

So a reaction with these enthalpy and entropy changes is feasible at 1500 K, but not at 300 K...

2) If ΔH is **negative** (exothermic) and ΔS is **negative** then the reaction will be feasible at lower temperatures but won't be feasible at higher temperatures.

   For example, the process of turning water from a liquid to a solid is **exothermic** but results in a **decrease in entropy** (a solid is more ordered than a liquid), which means it will only occur at certain temperatures (i.e. at 0 °C or below).

   Example: $\Delta H = -10\ \text{kJ mol}^{-1}$, $\Delta S = -10\ \text{J K}^{-1}\ \text{mol}^{-1}$

at **300 K**	$\Delta G = \Delta H - T\Delta S = -10 \times 10^3 - (300 \times -10) = -7000\ \text{J mol}^{-1}$
at **1500 K**	$\Delta G = \Delta H - T\Delta S = -10 \times 10^3 - (1500 \times -10) = +5000\ \text{J mol}^{-1}$

...and this one is feasible at 300 K, but not at 1500 K.

Free Energy Change

You can **Calculate** the **Temperature** at which a Reaction **Becomes Feasible**

When ΔG is zero, a reaction is **just feasible**.
You can find the **temperature** when ΔG is zero by rearranging the free energy equation from the previous page.

$\Delta G = \Delta H - T\Delta S$. When $\Delta G = 0$, $T\Delta S = \Delta H$.
So you can find the temperature at which a reaction becomes feasible using the formula:

$$T = \frac{\Delta H}{\Delta S}$$

T = temperature at which a reaction becomes feasible (in K)
ΔH = enthalpy change (in J mol^{-1})
ΔS = entropy change (in J K^{-1} mol^{-1})

Example: Tungsten, W, can be extracted from its ore, WO$_3$, by reduction using hydrogen:

$$WO_{3(s)} + 3H_{2(g)} \rightarrow W_{(s)} + 3H_2O_{(g)} \qquad \Delta H^{\ominus} = +110 \text{ kJ mol}^{-1}$$

Use the data in the table to find the minimum temperature at which the reaction becomes feasible.

Substance	$S^{\ominus}$/J K^{-1} mol^{-1}
WO$_{3(s)}$	76
H$_{2(g)}$	65
W$_{(s)}$	33
H$_2$O$_{(g)}$	189

First, convert the **enthalpy change**, ΔH, to joules per mole:

$$\Delta H = 110 \times 10^3 = \mathbf{110\ 000 \text{ J mol}^{-1}}$$

Then find the **entropy change**, ΔS:

$$\Delta S = S_{products} - S_{reactants} = [33 + (3 \times 189)] - [76 + (3 \times 65)] = \mathbf{+329 \text{ J K}^{-1} \text{ mol}^{-1}}$$

See page 8 for more on the entropy change formula.

Then divide ΔH by ΔS to find the temperature at which the reaction just becomes feasible:

$$T = \frac{\Delta H}{\Delta S} = \frac{110\ 000}{329} = \mathbf{334 \text{ K}}$$

Practice Questions

Q1 What does ΔG stand for? What is it used for?

Q2 State whether each of the following reactions are feasible, feasible at certain temperatures or not feasible:

Reaction A: positive ΔH and negative ΔS Reaction B: negative ΔH and positive ΔS

Q3 Write down the formula for calculating the temperature at which a reaction becomes feasible.

Exam Questions

Q1 Magnesium carbonate decomposes to form magnesium oxide and carbon dioxide:

$$MgCO_{3(s)} \rightarrow MgO_{(s)} + CO_{2(g)} \qquad \Delta H = +117 \text{ kJ mol}^{-1} \qquad \Delta S = +175 \text{ J K}^{-1} \text{ mol}^{-1}$$

a) Calculate the free energy change of this reaction at the following temperatures:

i) 500 K   ii) 760 K   [2 marks]

b) At which of the temperatures in part a) is the reaction feasible? Explain your answer.   [2 marks]

Q2 a) Use the equation below and the table on the right to calculate the free energy change for the complete combustion of methane at 298 K.   [2 marks]

$$CH_{4(g)} + 2O_{2(g)} \rightarrow CO_{2(g)} + 2H_2O_{(l)} \qquad \Delta H^{\ominus} = -730 \text{ kJ mol}^{-1}$$

b) What is the maximum temperature at which the reaction is feasible?   [2 marks]

Substance	$S^{\ominus}$(J K^{-1} mol^{-1})
CH$_{4(g)}$	186
O$_{2(g)}$	205
CO$_{2(g)}$	214
H$_2$O$_{(l)}$	69.9

The feasibility of revision depends on what's on the telly...

These pages are a bit tricky if you ask me — so make sure you've properly understood them before you move on. The most important bit to learn is the formula for ΔG. If you know that, then you can always work out whether a reaction is feasible even if you can't remember the rules about positive and negative enthalpy and entropy.

Rate Equations

Sorry — this section gets a bit mathsy. Just take a deep breath, dive in, and don't bash your head on the bottom.

Reaction Rate tells you How Fast Reactants are Converted to Products

You should remember from Year 1 that **reaction rate** is the **change in amount** of reactant or product **per unit time**. E.g. if the reactants are in solution, the rate could be **change in concentration per second** (in units of **mol dm^{-3} s^{-1}**).

You can Work out Reaction Rate from the Gradient of a Graph

If you draw a graph of the **amount of reactant or product** (on the *y* axis) against **time** (on the *x* axis), then the reaction rate is just the **gradient** of the graph. You can work out the gradient of a line using this formula:

> gradient = change in *y* ÷ change in *x*

Example: The data on this graph came from measuring the volume of gas given off during a chemical reaction.

Draw a line of best fit through the data points.

Pick two points on the line that are easy to read.

Then draw a vertical line down from one point and a horizontal line across from the other to make a triangle.

change in *y* = 3.6 – 1.4 = 2.2 cm³
change in *x* = 5.0 – 2.0 = 3.0 minutes
gradient = 2.2 ÷ 3.0 = 0.73 cm³ min⁻¹

So the rate of reaction = **0.73 cm³ min⁻¹**

You may need to Work out the Gradient from a Curved Graph

When the points on a graph lie in a **curve**, you can't draw a straight line of best fit through them. But you can still work out the gradient, and so the rate, at a **particular point** in the reaction by working out the **gradient of a tangent**.

A tangent is a line that just touches a curve and has the same gradient as the curve does at that point.

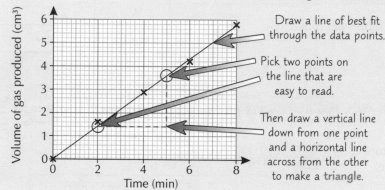

1 Find the point on the curve that you need to look at. For example, if you want to find the rate of reaction at 3 minutes, find 3 on the *x*-axis and go up to the curve from there.

2 Place a ruler at that point so that it's just touching the curve. Position the ruler so that you can see the whole curve.

3 Adjust the ruler until the space between the ruler and the curve is equal on both sides of the point.

4 Draw a line along the ruler to make the tangent. Extend the line right across the graph — it'll help to make your gradient calculation easier as you'll have more points to choose from.

5 Calculate the gradient of the tangent to find the rate:
gradient = change in *y* ÷ change in *x*
= (0.46 – 0.22) ÷ (5.0 – 1.4)
= 0.24 mol dm⁻³ ÷ 3.6 mins = 0.067 mol dm⁻³ min⁻¹
So, the rate of reaction at 3 mins is **0.067 mol dm⁻³ min⁻¹**.

Pick two points on the tangent that are easy to read.

Don't forget the units — you've divided mol dm⁻³ by mins, so it's mol dm⁻³ min⁻¹.

Rate Equations

The **Rate Equation** links **Reaction Rate** to **Reactant Concentrations**

Rate equations look scary, but all they're telling you is how the **rate** is affected by the **concentrations of reactants**. For a general reaction **A + B → C + D**, the **rate equation** is:

The units of rate are $mol\,dm^{-3}\,s^{-1}$.

$$Rate = k[A]^m[B]^n$$

Remember — square brackets mean the concentration of whatever's inside them.

m and **n** are the orders of reaction and **k** is the rate constant. If you want to know what all that means then read on...

Orders of Reaction Tell You How the **Reactant Concentrations** Affect the **Rate**

1) **m** and **n** are the **orders of the reaction** with respect to reactant A and reactant B. An order of reaction is defined as the **power** to which the **concentration** of a reactant is raised in the rate equation.

2) **m** tells you how the **concentration of reactant A** affects the **rate** and **n** tells you the same for **reactant B**.

> If [A] changes and the rate **stays the same**, the order of reaction with respect to A is **0**.
> So if [A] doubles, the rate will stay the same. If [A] triples, the rate will stay the same.
>
> If the rate is **proportional to [A]**, then the order of reaction with respect to A is **1**.
> So if [A] doubles, the rate will double. If [A] triples, the rate will triple.
>
> If the rate is **proportional to $[A]^2$**, then the order of reaction with respect to A is **2**.
> So if [A] doubles, the rate will be $2^2 = 4$ times faster. If [A] triples, the rate will be $3^2 = 9$ times faster.

3) The **overall order of the reaction** is **m + n**.

4) You can only find **orders of reaction** from **experiments**. You **can't** work them out from chemical equations.

k Relates the **Reactant Concentrations** to the **Rate** at a **Particular Temperature**

1) **k** is the **rate constant** — a number that links the rate of the reaction to the concentration of the reactants. The bigger the value of **k** is, the **faster** the reaction.

2) The rate constant is **always the same** for a certain reaction at a **particular temperature** — but if you **increase** the temperature, the rate constant rises too.

> When you **increase** the **temperature** of a reaction, the **rate of reaction increases** — you're increasing the **number of collisions** between reactant molecules, and also the **energy** of each collision. But the **concentrations** of the reactants and the **orders of reaction** stay the same. So the value of **k** must **increase** for the rate equation to balance.

Pages 20-21 deal with the equation that links k with temperature.

If You Know the **Rate Constant** and **Orders**, You can Calculate the **Rate**

Example: Propanone will react with iodine in the presence of an acid-catalyst: $CH_3COCH_{3(aq)} + I_{2(aq)} \xrightarrow{H^+_{(aq)}} CH_3COCH_2I_{(aq)} + H^+_{(aq)} + I^-_{(aq)}$

This reaction is first order with respect to propanone and $H^+_{(aq)}$ and zero order with respect to iodine. At a certain temperature, k was found to be $520\,mol^{-1}\,dm^3\,s^{-1}$ when $[CH_3COCH_3] = [I_2] = [H^+] = 1.50 \times 10^{-3}\,mol\,dm^{-3}$. Calculate the rate at this temperature.

1) The **rate equation** is: rate = $k[CH_3COCH_3]^1[H^+]^1[I_2]^0$
[X]^1 is usually written as [X]. [X]^0 equals **1**.
So you can **simplify** it to: **rate** = $k[CH_3COCH_3][H^+]$

Even though H$^+$ is a catalyst, rather than a reactant, it can still be in the rate equation.

2) Now you have the rate equation, calculating the **rate** is as simple as putting in the values:
rate = $k[CH_3COCH_3][H^+] = 520 \times (1.50 \times 10^{-3}) \times (1.50 \times 10^{-3}) = \textbf{1.17} \times \textbf{10}^{-3}$

3) You can find the **units** for the rate by putting the other units into the rate equation.
The units for the rate are $mol^{-1}\,dm^3\,s^{-1} \times mol\,dm^{-3} \times mol\,dm^{-3} = \textbf{mol}\,\textbf{dm}^{-3}\,\textbf{s}^{-1}$.

mol and mol^{-1} cancel each other out, as do dm^3 and dm^{-3}.

So the answer is: rate = $\textbf{1.17} \times \textbf{10}^{-3}\,\textbf{mol}\,\textbf{dm}^{-3}\,\textbf{s}^{-1}$

Rate Equations

You can Calculate the Rate Constant from the Orders and Rate of Reaction

Once the rate and the orders of the reaction have been found by experiment, you can work out the **rate constant**, k. The **units of k vary**, so you'll need to work them out too.

> **Example:** The reaction below is second order with respect to NO and zero order with respect to CO and O_2.
>
> $$NO_{(g)} + CO_{(g)} + O_{2(g)} \rightarrow NO_{2(g)} + CO_{2(g)}$$
>
> At a certain temperature, when $[NO_{(g)}] = [CO_{(g)}] = [O_{2(g)}] = 2.00 \times 10^{-3} \ mol \, dm^{-3}$ the rate is
> $1.76 \times 10^{-3} \ mol \, dm^{-3} s^{-1}$. Find the value of the rate constant, k, at this temperature.
>
> 1) First write out the **rate equation**: $\quad$ Rate $= k[NO]^2[CO]^0[O_2]^0 = k[NO]^2$
>
> 2) Next insert the **concentration** and the **rate**. **Rearrange** the equation and calculate the value of k:
>
> $$\text{Rate} = k[NO]^2, \text{ so } 1.76 \times 10^{-3} = k \times (2.00 \times 10^{-3})^2 \Rightarrow k = \frac{1.76 \times 10^{-3}}{(2.00 \times 10^{-3})^2} = 440$$
>
> 3) Find the **units of k** by putting the other units in the rate equation:
>
> $$\text{Rate} = k[NO]^2, \text{ so } mol \, dm^{-3} s^{-1} = k \times (mol \, dm^{-3})^2 \Rightarrow k = \frac{mol \, dm^{-3} s^{-1}}{(mol \, dm^{-3})(mol \, dm^{-3})} = \frac{s^{-1}}{(mol \, dm^{-3})} = dm^3 \, mol^{-1} s^{-1}$$
>
> So the answer is: $k = 440 \ dm^3 \ mol^{-1} \ s^{-1}$

Practice Questions

Q1 Write the general rate equation for the reaction $A + B \rightarrow C + D$.

Q2 Explain what is meant by the term 'order of reaction'.

Q3 How would the value of k change if you decreased the temperature of a chemical reaction?

Exam Questions

Q1 Compounds X and Y react as in the equation below.

$$X + Y \rightarrow Z$$

a) From the graph on the right, work out the rate of reaction at 3 minutes. **[3 marks]**

b) The reaction above is first order with respect to X and first order with respect to Y. Write the rate equation for this reaction in terms of k, the rate constant. **[1 mark]**

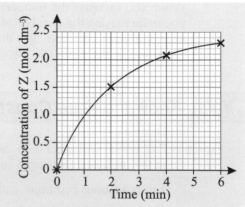

Q2 The following reaction is second order with respect to NO and first order with respect to H_2.

$$2NO_{(g)} + 2H_{2(g)} \rightarrow 2H_2O_{(g)} + N_{2(g)}$$

a) Write a rate equation for the reaction in terms of k, the rate constant. **[1 mark]**

b) The rate of the reaction at 800 °C was determined to be $0.00267 \ mol \, dm^{-3} s^{-1}$ when $[H_2] = 0.00200 \ mol \, dm^{-3}$ and $[NO] = 0.00400 \ mol \, dm^{-3}$. Calculate a value for the rate constant at 800 °C, including units. **[2 marks]**

Rate of Chemistry Revision = k [Student] [Tea]...

These rate equations might look a bit odd, but knowing how to use them can be really handy. Learn what all the different bits of the equation mean, and how to use it to find the overall order of reaction. Practise drawing some tangents to curved graphs and working out their gradients too — we're not through with all that graph stuff yet...

Rate Experiments

Told you, didn't I? Here are some more pages on rates and graphs for you to get your head around...

The **Initial Rates Method** can be used to work out **Rate Equations**

The **initial rate of a reaction** is the rate right at the **start** of the reaction. You can find this from a **concentration-time** graph by calculating the **gradient** of the **tangent** at time = 0.

Initial rate = $\frac{y}{x}$

Here's a quick explanation of how to use the **initial rates method**:

1) Repeat an experiment several times using **different initial concentrations** of the reactants. You should usually only change **one** of the concentrations at a time, keeping the rest constant.

   You might get exam questions where they change more than one concentration though — handily, there's an example of this below.

2) Calculate the **initial rate** for each experiment using the method above.

3) Finally, see how the **initial concentrations** affect the **initial rates** and figure out the **order** for each reactant. The example below shows you how to do this. Once you know the **orders**, you can work out the rate equation.

Example:
The table on the right shows the results of a series of initial rate experiments for the reaction:

$$NO_{(g)} + CO_{(g)} + O_{2(g)} \rightarrow NO_{2(g)} + CO_{2(g)}$$

The experiments were carried out at a constant temperature.
Write down the rate equation for the reaction.

Experiment number	[NO] (mol dm⁻³)	[CO] (mol dm⁻³)	[O₂] (mol dm⁻³)	Initial rate (mol dm⁻³ s⁻¹)
1	2.0×10^{-2}	1.0×10^{-2}	1.0×10^{-2}	0.17
2	6.0×10^{-2}	1.0×10^{-2}	1.0×10^{-2}	1.53
3	2.0×10^{-2}	2.0×10^{-2}	1.0×10^{-2}	0.17
4	4.0×10^{-2}	1.0×10^{-2}	2.0×10^{-2}	0.68

1) Look at experiments 1 and 2 — when [NO] **triples** (and all the other concentrations stay constant) the rate is **nine times** faster, and $9 = 3^2$. So the reaction is **second order** with respect to NO.

2) Look at experiments 1 and 3 — when [CO] **doubles** (but all the other concentrations stay constant), the rate **stays the same**. So the reaction is **zero order** with respect to CO.

3) Look at experiments 1 and 4 — the rate of experiment 4 is **four times faster** than experiment 1. The reaction is **second order** with respect to [NO], so the rate will **quadruple** when you **double** [NO]. But in experiment 4, [O₂] has also been **doubled**. As doubling [O₂] hasn't had any additional effect on the rate, the reaction must be **zero order** with respect to O₂.

4) Now that you know the order with respect to each reactant you can write the rate equation: **rate = k[NO]²**.

You can calculate k at this temperature by putting the concentrations and the initial rate from one of the experiments into the rate equation (see page 14).

You Can Also **Measure** *the* **Initial Reaction Rate**

For some reactions there is a **sudden colour change** when a product reaches a certain concentration. The **rate of reaction** can be worked out from measuring the **time** it takes for the colour change to happen — the **shorter** the time, the **faster** the rate.

1) In an **iodine clock reaction**, the reaction you're monitoring is: $H_2O_{2(aq)} + 2I^-_{(aq)} + 2H^+_{(aq)} \rightarrow 2H_2O_{(l)} + I_{2(aq)}$

   A small amount of **sodium thiosulfate solution** and **starch** are added to the reaction mixture. The sodium thiosulfate reacts instantly with the iodine that's being formed. But once all of the sodium thiosulfate has been used up, any more iodine that's formed stays in solution. This turns the starch indicator blue-black.

   Varying the **concentration** of iodide or hydrogen peroxide while keeping everything else **constant** will give **different times** for the colour change. These can be used to work out the reaction order.

2) For reactions that produce a **precipitate** that clouds the solution, you can measure the **time** it takes for a **mark** underneath the reaction vessel to **disappear** from view.

3) For other reactions, you can work out the initial reaction rate by measuring the **time** taken for a **small amount of product** to be formed. E.g. the catalytic decomposition of hydrogen peroxide produces O_2, so you could measure the time it takes for 5 cm³ of O_2 to be released.

Rate Experiments

You Can **Measure** the Rate of Reaction by **Continuous Monitoring**

Instead of working out the initial rate of several reactions. you can follow a reaction all the way though to its end by recording the **amount of product** (or **reactant**) you have at **regular time intervals** — this is called **continuous monitoring**.

The results can be used to work out how the **rate changes** over **time**.

There are **Loads** of Ways to **Follow the Rate of a Reaction**

Although there are a lot of ways to follow reactions, not every method works for every reaction. You've got to **pick a property** that **changes** as the reaction goes on. You can then use your results to calculate the **concentrations** of reactants at different time points.

Gas volume

If a **gas** is given off, you could **collect it** in a gas syringe and record how much you've got at **regular time intervals** (e.g. every 15 seconds). For example, this would work for the reaction between an **acid** and a **carbonate** in which **carbon dioxide gas** is given off.

To find the concentration of a reactant at each time point, use the **ideal gas equation** to work out how many moles of gas you've got, then use the **molar ratio** to work out the concentration of the reactant.

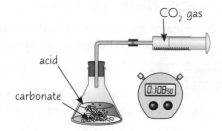

Loss of mass

If a **gas** is given off, the system will **lose mass**. You can measure this at regular intervals with a **balance**.

Use mole calculations to work out how much gas you've lost, and therefore how many moles of reactants are left.

Colour change

You can sometimes track the colour change of a reaction using a gadget called a **colorimeter**. A colorimeter measures **absorbance** (the amount of light absorbed by the solution). The **more concentrated** the **colour** of the solution, the **higher** the **absorbance** is.

For example, in the reaction between propanone and iodine, the **brown** colour fades. So the absorbance of the solution will **decrease**.

$$CH_3COCH_{3(aq)} + I_{2(aq)} \rightarrow CH_3COCH_2I_{(aq)} + H^+_{(aq)} + I^-_{(aq)}$$
colourless   brown   colourless

You measure the change in absorbance like this:

1) Plot a **calibration curve** — a graph of **known concentrations** of the coloured solution (in this case I_2) plotted against absorbance. (There's more about calibration curves on page 51.)

2) During the experiment, take a **small sample** from your reaction solution at **regular intervals** and read the **absorbance**.

3) Use your calibration curve to **convert** the absorbance at each time point into a **concentration**.

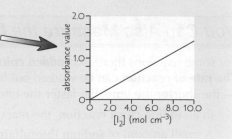

Change in pH

If the reaction produces or uses up H^+ ions, the pH of the solution will change. So you could measure the **pH** of the solution at **regular intervals** and calculate the **concentration of H^+**.

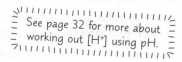

See page 32 for more about working out [H^+] using pH.

You can use the data you've gathered from your rate of reaction experiment to draw a **concentration–time graph**. This'll help you work out the orders of reaction — more about that on the next page...

Rate Experiments

The **Shape** of a **Rate-Concentration Graph** Tells You the **Order**

You can use data from a **concentration–time graph** to construct a **rate-concentration graph**, which can tell you the **reaction order**. Here's how...

1) Find the **gradient** at various points on the graph. This will give you the **rate** at that particular **concentration**. With a **straight-line graph**, this is easy, but if it's a **curve**, you need to draw **tangents** and find their gradients.

2) Now plot each point on a new graph with the axes **rate** and **concentration**. Then draw a smooth line or curve through the points. The shape of the line will tell you the order of the reaction with respect to that reactant.

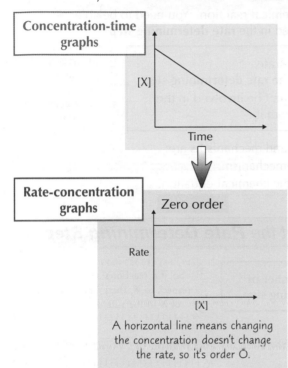

Concentration-time graphs

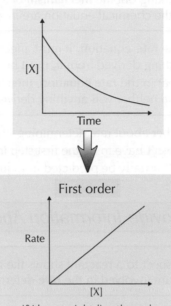

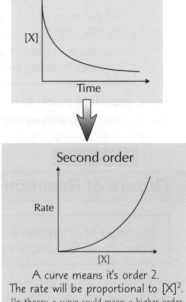

Rate-concentration graphs

Zero order

A horizontal line means changing the concentration doesn't change the rate, so it's order 0.

First order

If it's a straight line through the origin, the rate is proportional to [X], and it's order 1.

Second order

A curve means it's order 2. The rate will be proportional to $[X]^2$. (In theory, a curve could mean a higher order than 2 but you won't be asked about them.)

Practice Questions

Q1 How could you find the initial reaction rate from a concentration-time graph?

Q2 A solid carbonate is added to an acid to produce carbon dioxide gas. Describe how you could follow the rate of reaction for this reaction.

Q3 Sketch rate-concentration graphs for zero, first and second order reactions.

Exam Question

Q1 This table shows the results of a series of initial rate experiments for the reaction between substances D and E at a constant temperature:

Experiment	[D] (mol dm^{-3})	[E] (mol dm^{-3})	Initial rate × 10^{-3} (mol dm^{-3} s^{-1})
1	0.2	0.2	1.30
2	0.4	0.2	2.60
3	0.1	0.1	0.65
4	0.6	0.1	

a) Find the order of reaction with respect to reactant D. [1 mark]

b) Find the order of reaction with respect to reactant E. [1 mark]

c) Work out the initial rate for experiment 4. [1 mark]

Describe the link between concentration and rate, soldier — that's an order...

Picking a way to measure the rate of reaction is easy enough once you figure out what physical changes are going to happen, like a colour changing or a gas being produced. But if you need to draw a graph, don't forget that to work out the reaction order you need to plot concentrations, not volumes or pH — so you may have to do some maths first.

The Rate Determining Step

If you want to work out the mechanism of a reaction then you're going to have to know about the rate determining step...

The **Rate Determining Step** is the **Slowest Step** in a Multi-Step Reaction

Mechanisms can have **one step** or a **series of steps**. In a series of steps, each step can have a **different rate**.
The **overall rate** is decided by the step with the **slowest** rate — the **rate determining step**.

Otherwise known as the rate-limiting step.

Reactants in the **Rate Equation** Affect the **Rate**

The rate equation is handy for working out the **mechanism** of a chemical reaction. You need to be able
to pick out which reactants from the chemical equation are involved in the **rate determining step**:

> If a reactant appears in the **rate equation**, it must affect the **rate**.
> So this reactant, or something derived from it, must be in the **rate determining step**.
> If a reactant **doesn't** appear in the **rate equation**, then it **won't** be involved in the
> **rate determining step** (and neither will anything derived from it).

Catalysts can appear in rate equations, so they can be in rate determining steps too.

Some **important points** to remember about rate determining steps and mechanisms are:
1) The rate determining step **doesn't** have to be the first step in a mechanism.
2) The reaction mechanism **can't** usually be predicted from **just** the chemical equation.

Orders of Reaction Provide Information About the **Rate Determining Step**

> The **order of a reaction** with respect to a reactant shows the **number of
> molecules** of that reactant that are involved in the **rate determining step**.

So, if a reaction's second order with respect to X, there'll be two molecules of X in the rate determining step.

For example, the mechanism for the reaction between **chlorine free radicals** and **ozone**, O_3, consists of **two steps**:

$$Cl \bullet_{(g)} + O_{3(g)} \rightarrow ClO \bullet_{(g)} + O_{2(g)} \text{ — slow (rate determining step)}$$

$$ClO \bullet_{(g)} + O \bullet_{(g)} \rightarrow Cl \bullet_{(g)} + O_{2(g)} \text{ — fast}$$

The O• radical is formed when O_2 is broken down by UV light. (If you don't remember this reaction, have a look back at your Year 1 notes.)

$Cl \bullet$ and O_3 must both be in the rate equation, so the rate equation will be: **rate = $k[Cl \bullet]^m[O_3]^n$**.
There's only **one** $Cl \bullet$ radical and **one** O_3 molecule in the rate determining step,
so the **orders**, m and n, are both **1**.

So the rate equation is **rate = $k[Cl \bullet][O_3]$**.

The rate determining step can sometimes involve an **intermediate** that isn't in the full equation.

Example: The reaction $2NO + O_2 \rightarrow 2NO_2$ has a two-step mechanism:
Step 1 — $NO + NO \rightarrow N_2O_2$
Step 2 — $N_2O_2 + O_2 \rightarrow 2NO_2$
The rate equation for this reaction is: **rate = $k[NO]^2[O_2]$**.
What is the rate determining step of this reaction?

1) From the rate equation, you know that the **rate determining step**
must involve **2 molecules of NO** and **1 molecule of O_2**.
2) So the rate determining step can't be step 1, as step 1 does not involve O_2.
3) Step 2 doesn't contain all the molecules you'd expect from the rate equation, but it does
contain N_2O_2. N_2O_2 is an **intermediate** molecule **derived from** 2 molecules of NO.
4) So **step 2** must be the rate determining step.

Geoffrey's rate determining steps were all out of sync with his partner's.

The Rate Determining Step

The **Rate Determining Step** Can Help You Work Out the **Reaction Mechanism**

Knowing which reactants are in the **rate determining step** can help you to work out the **reaction mechanism**.

Example:
There are two possible mechanisms for the nucleophile **OH⁻** substituting for **Br** in 2-bromo-2-methylpropane:

$$CH_3-\underset{\underset{CH_3}{|}}{\overset{\overset{CH_3}{|}}{C}}-Br + OH^- \rightarrow CH_3-\underset{\underset{CH_3}{|}}{\overset{\overset{CH_3}{|}}{C}}-OH + Br^-$$

or

$$CH_3-\underset{\underset{CH_3}{|}}{\overset{\overset{CH_3}{|}}{C}}-Br \rightarrow CH_3-\underset{\underset{CH_3}{|}}{\overset{\overset{CH_3}{|}}{C}}{}^+ + Br^- \text{ — slow}$$
(rate determining step)

This involves breaking strong carbon-bromine bonds, so this will be a <u>slow</u> change.

$$CH_3-\underset{\underset{CH_3}{|}}{\overset{\overset{CH_3}{|}}{C}}{}^+ + OH^- \rightarrow CH_3-\underset{\underset{CH_3}{|}}{\overset{\overset{CH_3}{|}}{C}}-OH \text{ — fast}$$

If the OH⁻ concentration is high, the positive ion has a good chance of colliding with one. So this step will be <u>fast</u>.

The actual **rate equation** was worked out using rate experiments. It was found to be: **rate = $k[(CH_3)_3CBr]$**
OH⁻ isn't in the **rate equation**, so it **can't** be involved in the rate determining step.
The **second mechanism** is correct because OH⁻ **isn't** in the rate determining step.

Practice Questions

Q1 What is meant by the 'rate determining step' of a reaction?
Q2 Explain how knowing the rate equation for a reaction can help you to predict a reaction mechanism.
Q3 For a reaction between three reactants, X, Y and Z, the rate determining step is X + 2Y → M + N.
What will the order of reaction be with respect to: a) reactant X? b) reactant Y? c) reactant Z?

Exam Questions

Q1 For the reaction $CH_3COOH_{(aq)} + C_2H_5OH_{(aq)} \rightarrow CH_3COOC_2H_{5(aq)} + H_2O_{(l)}$, the rate equation is:
rate = $k[CH_3COOH][H^+]$

What can you deduce about the role that H⁺ plays in the reaction? Explain your answer. [2 marks]

Q2 Hydrogen reacts with iodine monochloride as in the equation $H_{2(g)} + 2ICl_{(g)} \rightarrow I_{2(g)} + 2HCl_{(g)}$.
The rate equation for this reaction is: rate = $k[H_2][ICl]$.

a) The mechanism for the reaction consists of two steps.
Identify the molecules that are in the rate determining step. Justify your answer. [3 marks]

b) A chemist suggested the following mechanism for the reaction:

$2ICl_{(g)} \rightarrow I_{2(g)} + Cl_{2(g)}$ slow
$H_{2(g)} + Cl_{2(g)} \rightarrow 2HCl_{(g)}$ fast

Suggest, with reasons, whether this mechanism is likely to be correct. [2 marks]

I found rate determining step aerobics a bit on the slow side...

These pages show you how rate equations, orders of reaction, and reaction mechanisms all tie together and how each actually means something in the grand scheme of A-Level Chemistry. It's all very profound. So get it all learnt, answer the questions and then you'll have plenty of time to practise the quickstep for your Strictly Come Dancing routine.

The Arrhenius Equation

The Arrhenius Equation. As the name suggests, it's a bit heinous to learn I'm afraid, but super useful. It links together reaction constants, activation energies and temperatures — all pretty important in the world of reaction rates.

The **Arrhenius Equation** Links **k** with **Temperature** and **Activation Energy**

The **Arrhenius equation** (nasty-looking thing in the green box) shows how the **rate constant** (k) varies with **temperature** (T) and **activation energy** (E_a, the minimum amount of kinetic energy particles need to react).

This is probably the **worst** equation you're going to meet. Luckily, it'll be given to you in your exams if you need it, so you don't have to learn it off by heart. But you do need to know what all the different bits **mean**, and how it works. Here it is:

What be a pirate's favourite part of chemistry? The ARR-henius equation!

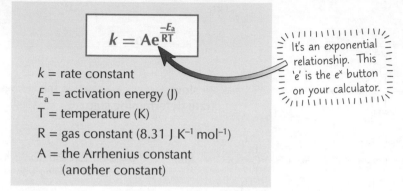

$$k = Ae^{\frac{-E_a}{RT}}$$

k = rate constant
E_a = activation energy (J)
T = temperature (K)
R = gas constant (8.31 J K^{-1} mol^{-1})
A = the Arrhenius constant (another constant)

It's an exponential relationship. This 'e' is the e^x button on your calculator.

1) As the activation energy, E_a, gets **bigger**, k gets **smaller**.
   You can **test** this out by trying **different numbers** for E_a in the equation... ahh go on, have a go.

2) So, a **large E_a** will mean a **slow rate**. This **makes sense** when you think about it — if a reaction has a **high activation energy**, then not many of the reactant particles will have enough energy to react. So only a **few** of the collisions will result in the reaction actually happening, and the rate will be **slow**.

3) The equation also shows that as the temperature **rises**, **k increases**.
   (You can **test** this out by trying **different numbers** for T as well. Will the fun never cease?)

4) The **temperature dependence** makes sense too. **Higher temperatures** mean reactant particles move around **faster** and with **more energy** so they're more likely to **collide** and more likely to collide with at least the **activation energy**, so the **reaction rate increases**.

Use the **Arrhenius Equation** to Calculate the **Rate Constant** or **E_a**

You might be given four of the five values from the Arrhenius equation and asked to use the equation to find the value of the fifth. Here's how you'd go about getting the answer...

Example: The decomposition of N_2O_5 at 308 K has a rate constant of 1.35×10^{-4} s^{-1}. The Arrhenius constant for this reaction is 4.79×10^{13} s^{-1}. Calculate the activation energy of this reaction. (R = 8.31 J K^{-1} mol^{-1})

First it's a good idea to get the Arrhenius equation into a **simpler** form so it's easier to use. That means getting rid of the nasty exponential bit — so you need to take the **natural log (ln)** of everything in the equation:

$$k = Ae^{\frac{-E_a}{RT}} \longrightarrow \ln k = \ln A - \frac{E_a}{RT}$$

Thankfully there should be a handy 'ln' button on your calculator for taking natural logs.

Now **rearrange** the equation to get **E_a** on the **left hand side**: $\quad \frac{E_a}{RT} = \ln A - \ln k$

And another quick rearrangement to get **E_a** on its **own**: $\quad E_a = (\ln A - \ln k) \times RT$

Now you can just pop the numbers from the question into this formula:

$E_a = (\ln (4.79 \times 10^{13}) - \ln (1.35 \times 10^{-4})) \times (8.31 \times 308)$

$= (31.5... - (-8.91...)) \times (8.31 \times 308) = 103\,429.54$ J mol^{-1} = **103 kJ mol^{-1}** (3 s.f.)

The Arrhenius Equation

Use an **Arrhenius Plot** to Find the **E_a** and the **Arrhenius Constant**

1) As you saw on the previous page, putting the **Arrhenius equation** into **logarithmic form** generally makes it a bit easier to use. $\implies$

$$\ln k = -\frac{E_a}{RT} + \ln A$$

2) You can use the equation in this form to create an **Arrhenius plot** by plotting **ln k** against $\frac{1}{T}$.

3) The line of best fit for the points on the Arrhenius plot will be a straight line graph with a **gradient** of $\frac{-E_a}{R}$.

4) Once you know the gradient, you can use it to find both the **activation energy** and the **Arrhenius constant**.

Example: The graph below shows an Arrhenius plot for the decomposition of hydrogen iodide. Calculate the activation energy and the Arrhenius constant for this reaction. $R = 8.31$ J K^{-1} mol^{-1}.

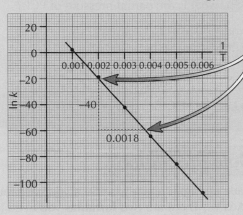

To find the gradient, pick two points on the line with 'nice' coordinates, e.g. (0.002, –20) and (0.0038, –60).

gradient = $\frac{-40}{0.0018}$ = –22 222. So $\frac{-E_a}{R}$ = –22 222

E_a = –(–22 222 × 8.31) = 184 666 J mol^{-1}
= **185 kJ mol^{-1}** (3 s.f.)

1 kJ = 1000 J

To find ln A, substitute the gradient and the coordinates of any point on the line into $\ln k = -\frac{E_a}{RT} + \ln A$

$-\frac{E_a}{R} \times \frac{1}{T} = -\frac{E_a}{RT}$

At (0.002, –20): –20 = ($\frac{-40}{0.0018}$ × 0.002) + ln A
–20 = –44.4 + ln A
ln A = 24.4, so A = $e^{24.4}$ = **4 × 10^{10} dm^3 mol^{-1} s^{-1}**

The values of k and T used to draw the Arrhenius plot come from experiments. To gather the data you repeat the same experiment at several different temperatures.

The value of ln A is given to one decimal place here, so you should give this answer to one significant figure.

Practice Questions

Q1 In the Arrhenius equation, what do the terms k, T and R represent?

Q2 How does increasing the temperature of a reaction affect the value of k?

Q3 The Arrhenius equation is $k = Ae^{-E_a/RT}$. Which one of the following answers is true as E_a increases?
A k increases and rate of reaction increases.   B k increases and rate of reaction decreases.
C k decreases and rate of reaction increases.   D k decreases and rate of reaction decreases.

Q4 Describe how you would find activation energy from a graph of ln k against 1/T.

Exam Question

Q1 The table on the right gives values for the rate constant of the reaction between hydroxide ions and bromoethane at different temperatures.

a) Complete the table.   [2 marks]

b) Use the table to plot a graph that would allow you to calculate the activation energy of the reaction.   [3 marks]

c) Calculate the activation energy of the reaction. (R = 8.31 J K^{-1} mol^{-1})   [2 marks]

d) Calculate the value of the Arrhenius constant, A.   [1 mark]

T (K)	k	1/T (K^{-1})	ln k
305	0.181	0.00328	–1.709
313	0.468		
323	1.34		
333	3.29	0.00300	1.191
344	10.1		
353	22.7	0.00283	3.122

Who knew rates of reaction could be such a pain in the ar...

...rhenius? You don't need to learn the Arrhenius equation, but you do need to know how to use it. There's some vicious-looking maths here, but the best way to get your head around it is to do loads of practice questions. Then, if any of the different rearrangements of the equation pop up in the exam, you can look them in the eye without panicking.

Gas Equilibria and K_p

It's easier to talk about gases in terms of their pressures rather than their molar concentrations. If you're dealing with an equilibrium where all the reactants and products are gases, you use a special equilibrium constant called K_p.

The **Total Pressure** of a Gas is **Equal** to the **Sum** of the **Partial Pressures**

In a mixture of gases, each individual gas exerts its own pressure — this is called its **partial pressure**.

> The **total pressure** of a gas mixture is the **sum** of all the **partial pressures** of the individual gases.

You might have to put this fact to use in pressure calculations:

Example: When 3.00 moles of the gas PCl_5 is heated, it decomposes into PCl_3 and Cl_2: $PCl_{5(g)} \rightleftharpoons PCl_{3(g)} + Cl_{2(g)}$

In a sealed vessel at 500 K, the equilibrium mixture contains chlorine with a partial pressure of 263 kPa. If the total pressure of the mixture is 714 kPa, what is the partial pressure of PCl_5?

From the equation you know that PCl_3 and Cl_2 are produced in equal amounts, so the partial pressures of these two gases are the **same** at equilibrium — they're both 263 kPa.

Total pressure = $p_{PCl_5} + p_{PCl_3} + p_{Cl_2}$

714 = $p_{PCl_5} + 263 + 263$ ← p_X just means 'partial pressure of X'.

So the partial pressure of PCl_5 = 714 – 263 – 263 = **188 kPa**

Partial Pressures can be Worked Out from **Mole Fractions**

A '**mole fraction**' is just the **proportion** of a gas mixture that is a made up of particular gas. So if you have four moles of gas in total and two of them are gas A, the mole fraction of gas A is ½. There are **two formulas** you need to know:

1) Mole fraction of a gas in a mixture = $\dfrac{\text{number of moles of gas}}{\text{total number of moles of gas in the mixture}}$

2) Partial pressure of a gas = **mole fraction of gas × total pressure of the mixture**

Example: When 3.00 mol of PCl_5 is heated in a sealed vessel, the equilibrium mixture contains 1.75 mol of chlorine. If the total pressure of the mixture is 714 kPa, what is the partial pressure of PCl_5?

From the equation, PCl_3 and Cl_2 are produced in equal amounts, so there'll be **1.75 moles** of PCl_3 too.

1.75 moles of PCl_5 must have decomposed so (3.00 – 1.75) = **1.25 moles** of PCl_5 must be left at equilibrium.

This means that the total number of moles of gas at equilibrium = 1.75 + 1.75 + 1.25 = **4.75**.

So the mole fraction of PCl_5 = $\dfrac{1.25}{4.75}$ = **0.263**

The partial pressure of PCl_5 = mole fraction × total pressure = 0.263 × 714 = **188 kPa**

The **Equilibrium Constant K_p** is Calculated from **Partial Pressures**

1) K_p is the equilibrium constant for a reversible reaction where all the reactants and products are **gases**.

2) The **expression** for K_p is just like the one for K_c, except you use **partial pressures** instead of concentrations. (If you can't remember how K_c works, have a look back at your Year 1 notes.)

For the equilibrium

$aA_{(g)} + bB_{(g)} \rightleftharpoons dD_{(g)} + eE_{(g)}$ $K_p = \dfrac{(p_D)^d (p_E)^e}{(p_A)^a (p_B)^b}$

3) To calculate K_p you put the partial pressures in the expression. Then you work out the **units**, as you did for K_c.

Example: Find the value of K_p for the decomposition of PCl_5 gas at 500 K (as described above).

The partial pressures of each gas are: p_{PCl_5} = 188 kPa, p_{PCl_3} = 263 kPa, p_{Cl_2} = 263 kPa

$K_p = \dfrac{p_{Cl_2} \times p_{PCl_3}}{p_{PCl_5}} = \dfrac{263 \times 263}{188} = 368$

Find the units by putting the units for the partial pressures in the expression instead of the numbers and cancelling: $K_p = \dfrac{kPa \times kPa}{kPa} = kPa$. So, K_p = **368 kPa**

Gas Equilibria and K_p

Temperature Changes Alter K_p

1) In Year 1, you saw how changes in pressure and temperature affect the equilibrium position. The effects of **Le Chatelier's principle** still apply to gas equilibria. Remember:

> If you **increase** the **pressure**, the equilibrium shifts to the side with **fewer moles of gas**.
> If you **decrease** the **pressure**, the equilibrium shifts to the side with **more moles of gas**.

> If you **increase** the **temperature**, the equilibrium shifts in the **endothermic (positive ΔH) direction**.
> If you **decrease** the **temperature**, the equilibrium shifts in the **exothermic (negative ΔH) direction**.

2) Just like K_c, the value of K_p is affected by **temperature**. A particular value of K_p is only valid for a **given temperature**. Changing the **temperature** changes how much product is formed at equilibrium. This changes the **mole fractions** of the gases present, which changes their **partial pressures**. For example:

The reaction on the right is exothermic in the forward direction. If the temperature is **increased**, the equilibrium shifts to the **left** to counteract the change. This means that **less product** is formed.

Exothermic $\Longrightarrow$
$2SO_{2(g)} + O_{2(g)} \rightleftharpoons 2SO_{3(g)} \quad \Delta H = -197 \text{ kJ mol}^{-1}$
$\Longleftarrow$ Endothermic

$$K_p = \frac{(p_{SO_3})^2}{(p_{SO_2})^2 \times p_{O_2}}$$ ← The partial pressure of SO_3 will be reduced.
← The partial pressures of SO_2 and O_2 will increase.

As the temperature **increases**, p_{SO_3} will **decrease** and p_{SO_2} and p_{O_2} will **increase**, so K_p will **decrease**.

3) Just as changing concentration doesn't change K_c, **changing pressure doesn't affect K_p** — the equilibrium will **shift** to keep it the same.

4) And, like K_c, adding a **catalyst won't affect K_p** — it just gets the system to equilibrium more quickly.

Practice Questions

Q1 If you knew the partial pressures of all the gases in a mixture, how would you find the total pressure?

Q2 How do you work out the mole fraction of a gas?

Q3 Write the expression for K_p for this equilibrium: $N_{2(g)} + 3H_{2(g)} \rightleftharpoons 2NH_{3(g)}$*

*Answer on page 117.

Exam Questions

Q1 At high temperatures, SO_2Cl_2 dissociates according to the equation $SO_2Cl_{2(g)} \rightleftharpoons SO_{2(g)} + Cl_{2(g)}$ ($\Delta H = +67 \text{ kJ mol}^{-1}$)
When 1.50 moles of SO_2Cl_2 dissociates at 700 K, the equilibrium mixture contains SO_2 with a partial pressure of 60.2 kPa. The mixture has a total pressure of 141 kPa.

a) Write an expression for K_p for this reaction. [1 mark]

b) Calculate the partial pressure of Cl_2 and the partial pressure of SO_2Cl_2 in the equilibrium mixture. [2 marks]

c) Calculate a value for K_p for this reaction and give its units. [2 marks]

d) Describe and explain the effect that increasing the temperature would have on the value of K_p. [3 marks]

Q2 When nitric oxide and oxygen were mixed in a 2:1 mole ratio at a constant temperature in a sealed flask, an equilibrium was set up according to the equation $2NO_{(g)} + O_{2(g)} \rightleftharpoons 2NO_{2(g)}$. The partial pressure of the nitric oxide (NO) at equilibrium was 36 kPa and the total pressure in the flask was 99 kPa.

a) Deduce the partial pressure of oxygen in the equilibrium mixture. [1 mark]

b) Calculate the partial pressure of nitrogen dioxide in the equilibrium mixture. [1 mark]

c) Write an expression for the equilibrium constant, K_p, for this reaction and calculate its value at this temperature. State its units. [3 marks]

Pressure pushing down on me, pressing down on you... Under pressure...

Partial pressures are just like concentrations, but for gases. The more of a substance you've got in a solution, the higher its concentration — and the more of a gas that you've got squashed into a container, the higher its partial pressure.

Electrode Potentials

There are electrons toing and froing in redox reactions. And when electrons move, you get electricity.

Electrochemical Cells Make Electricity

An electrochemical cell can be made from **two different metals** dipped in salt solutions of their **own ions** and connected by a wire (the **external circuit**).

There are always **two** reactions within an electrochemical cell — one's an oxidation and one's a reduction — so it's a **redox process**.

Here's what happens in the **zinc/copper** electrochemical cell on the right:

1) Zinc **loses electrons** more easily than copper. So in the half-cell on the left, zinc (from the zinc electrode) is **oxidised** to form $Zn^{2+}_{(aq)}$ ions. This releases electrons into the external circuit.

2) In the other half-cell, the **same number of electrons** are taken from the external circuit, **reducing** the Cu^{2+} ions to copper atoms.

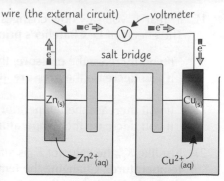

The solutions are connected by a **salt bridge** made from filter paper soaked in $KNO_{3(aq)}$. This allows ions to flow through and balance out the charges.

Electrons flow through the wire from the more reactive metal to the less reactive one.

A voltmeter in the external circuit shows the **voltage** between the two half-cells. This is the **cell potential** or **EMF** (which stands for electromotive force), also known as E_{cell}.

You can also have half-cells involving **solutions of two aqueous ions of the same element**, such as $Fe^{2+}_{(aq)}/Fe^{3+}_{(aq)}$. The conversion from Fe^{2+} to Fe^{3+} or vice versa happens on the surface of a platinum **electrode**. The electrode is made of **platinum** because it is an **inert metal**, so it won't react with the ions.

The Reactions Happening at Each Electrode are Reversible

1) The reactions that occur at each of the electrodes in an electrochemical cell are **reversible**.

Example: The reactions that are taking place at the electrodes in the zinc/copper cell above are:

$$Zn^{2+}_{(aq)} + 2e^- \rightleftharpoons Zn_{(s)}$$
$$Cu^{2+}_{(aq)} + 2e^- \rightleftharpoons Cu_{(s)}$$

The 'reversible' arrows show that both reactions can go in **either direction**.

2) These equations are **half-equations**. When you write half-equations for electrochemical cells, they're always written with the **reduction reaction** going in the **forward** direction (with the **electrons** on the **left-hand side**).

3) When two half-cells are joined to make a cell, which direction each reaction will actually go in depends on how easily each metal **loses electrons** (i.e. how easily it's **oxidised**).

4) How easily a metal is oxidised is measured using **electrode potentials**. A metal that's easy to oxidise has a **very negative** electrode potential. One that's harder to oxidise has a **less negative** (or **positive**) electrode potential.

Example: The table below shows the electrode potentials for the copper and zinc half-cells:

Half-cell	Electrode potential $E^{\ominus}$ (V)
$Zn^{2+}_{(aq)}/Zn_{(s)}$	−0.76
$Cu^{2+}_{(aq)}/Cu_{(s)}$	+0.34

There's more about how these values are worked out coming up on the next page.

The zinc half-cell has a **more negative** electrode potential than the copper half-cell.
So in a zinc/copper cell: • zinc is **oxidised** (the half-equation shown above goes **backwards**).
• copper is **reduced** (the half-equation shown above goes **forwards**).

5) Once you know which direction each of the half-equations will go in, you can write the equation for the **overall reaction** that will happen in the cell:

$$Cu^{2+}_{(aq)} + Zn_{(s)} \rightleftharpoons Cu_{(s)} + Zn^{2+}_{(aq)}$$

Electrode Potentials

Electrode Potentials are Measured Against Standard Hydrogen Electrodes

You measure the electrode potential of a half-cell against a **standard hydrogen electrode**.
The cell potential is **affected** by the conditions (**temperature**, **pressure** and **concentration**).
To get around this, **standard conditions** are used to measure electrode potentials.

> The **standard electrode potential**, $E^\ominus$, of a half-cell is the **voltage measured** under
> **standard conditions** when the **half-cell** is connected to a **standard hydrogen electrode**.

Standard conditions are:

1) Any solutions must have a concentration of **1.00 mol dm^{-3}**.

2) The temperature must be **298 K (25 °C)**.

3) The pressure must be **100 kPa**.

For example, this cell would allow you to find the standard electrode potential of the Zn^{2+}/Zn half-cell:

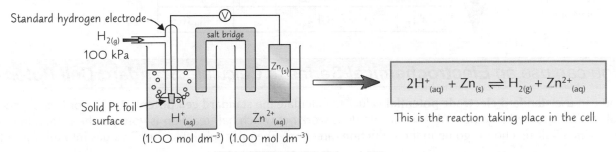

$$2H^+_{(aq)} + Zn_{(s)} \rightleftharpoons H_{2(g)} + Zn^{2+}_{(aq)}$$

This is the reaction taking place in the cell.

If **standard conditions** are maintained, the **reading on the voltmeter** when a half-cell is connected to the
standard hydrogen electrode will be the **standard electrode potential** of that half-cell.

Practice Questions

Q1 Sketch a diagram showing how you would set up an electrochemical cell using zinc and copper electrodes
and solutions containing zinc and copper ions.

Q2 Here are the half-equations for the reactions taking place at the electrodes in a zinc/copper cell:
$Zn^{2+}_{(aq)} + 2e^- \rightleftharpoons Zn_{(s)}$, $E^\circ = -0.76$ V $Cu^{2+}_{(aq)} + 2e^- \rightleftharpoons Cu_{(s)}$, $E^\circ = +0.34$ V
When the cell is operating, which of these reactions will be moving backwards (in the oxidation direction)?

Q3 Why are standard conditions used to measure standard electrode potentials?

Exam Questions

Q1 A cell is made up of a lead and an iron plate, dipped in solutions of lead(II) nitrate and iron(II) nitrate, respectively.
The two half-cells are connected using wires and a salt bridge. The electrode potentials for the two electrodes are:

$Fe^{2+}_{(aq)} + 2e^- \rightleftharpoons Fe_{(s)}$, $E^\ominus = -0.44$ V $Pb^{2+}_{(aq)} + 2e^- \rightleftharpoons Pb_{(s)}$, $E^\ominus = -0.13$ V

Which metal is oxidised in this cell? Explain your answer.   [2 marks]

Q2 An electrochemical cell containing a zinc half-cell and a silver half-cell was set up.
The two half-cells were connected using wires and a salt bridge..

$Zn^{2+}_{(aq)} + 2e^- \rightleftharpoons Zn_{(s)}$, $E^\ominus = -0.76$ V $Ag^+_{(aq)} + e^- \rightleftharpoons Ag_{(s)}$, $E^\ominus = +0.80$ V

a) Write an equation for the overall cell reaction.   [1 mark]

b) Which half-cell accepts electrons from the circuit? Explain your answer.   [1 mark]

My mam always said I had potential...

OK, so this stuff is tricky, but don't panic. The most important thing to remember here is that in the half-cell with the
more negative electrode potential the half-equation will go in the oxidation direction (and vice versa). And don't forget
to learn what the standard hydrogen electrode is (and what it's used for) too. Then take a deep breath and relax...

The Electrochemical Series

Elements have different standard electrode potentials. So what do chemists do — they write a list of them all in order.

The **Electrochemical Series** Shows You What's **Reactive** and What's Not

An electrochemical series is basically a **list** of **standard electrode potentials** for different electrochemical **half-cells**. They look something like this:

This isn't the whole series. You might see different lists. Every list works the same way though.

Half-reaction	$E^{\ominus}/V$
$Mg^{2+}_{(aq)} + 2e^- \rightleftharpoons Mg_{(s)}$	-2.37
$Zn^{2+}_{(aq)} + 2e^- \rightleftharpoons Zn_{(s)}$	-0.76
$2H^+_{(aq)} + 2e^- \rightleftharpoons H_{2(g)}$	0.00
$Cu^{2+}_{(aq)} + 2e^- \rightleftharpoons Cu_{(s)}$	$+0.34$
$Fe^{3+}_{(aq)} + e^- \rightleftharpoons Fe^{2+}_{(aq)}$	$+0.77$
$Br_{2(aq)} + 2e^- \rightleftharpoons 2Br^-_{(aq)}$	$+1.07$
$Cl_{2(aq)} + 2e^- \rightleftharpoons 2Cl^-_{(aq)}$	$+1.36$

More positive electrode potentials mean that:
1. The left-hand substances are more easily reduced.
2. The right-hand substances are more stable.

More negative electrode potentials mean that:
1. The right-hand substances are more easily oxidised.
2. The left-hand substances are more stable.

You can use an **Electrochemical Series** to Calculate **Standard Cell Potentials**

You can use **standard electrode potential** values to calculate the **standard cell potential**, E°_{cell} (or EMF), when two half-cells are joined together. All you have to do is work out which half-reaction is going in the **oxidation** direction and which half-reaction is going in the **reduction** direction. Then just substitute the E° values into this formula:

$$E^{\circ}_{cell} = E^{\circ}_{reduced} - E^{\circ}_{oxidised}$$

Example: Calculate the standard cell potential of a Mg/Fe electrochemical cell using the two redox reaction equations shown in the series above.

First write the two **half-equations** down as reduction reactions:

$$Mg^{2+}_{(aq)} + 2e^- \rightleftharpoons Mg_{(s)} \quad\quad E^{\circ} = -2.37\ V$$
$$Fe^{3+}_{(aq)} + e^- \rightleftharpoons Fe^{2+}_{(aq)} \quad\quad E^{\circ} = +0.77\ V$$

The **Mg/Mg^{2+}** half-cell has the **more negative electrode potential**, so this half reaction will go in the direction of **oxidation**. The **Fe^{2+}/Fe^{3+}** half-cell has the **more positive electrode potential**, so this half reaction will go in the direction of **reduction**. The overall reaction is:

$$2Fe^{3+}_{(aq)} + Mg_{(s)} \rightleftharpoons 2Fe^{2+}_{(aq)} + Mg^{2+}_{(aq)}$$

So, $E^{\circ}_{cell} = E^{\circ}_{reduced} - E^{\circ}_{oxidised} = +0.77 - (-2.37) = \mathbf{+3.14\ V}$

There's a **Convention** for **Drawing** Electrochemical Cells

It's a bit of a faff drawing pictures of electrochemical cells. There's a **shorthand** way of representing them though:

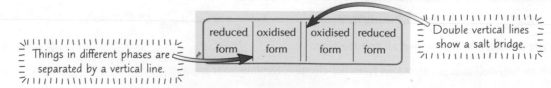

Things in different phases are separated by a vertical line.

| reduced form | oxidised form | oxidised form | reduced form |

Double vertical lines show a salt bridge.

There are a couple of important **conventions** when drawing cells:

1) The **half-cell** with the **more negative** potential goes on the **left**.
2) The **oxidised forms** go in the **centre** of the cell diagram.

So for the Zn/Cu cell (see page 24), the diagram would look like this:

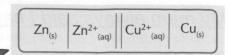

$$Zn_{(s)} \mid Zn^{2+}_{(aq)} \parallel Cu^{2+}_{(aq)} \mid Cu_{(s)}$$

The Electrochemical Series

Use **Electrode Potentials** to **Predict** Whether a Reaction Will Happen

To figure out if a metal will react with the aqueous ions of another metal, you can use their E° values.

Example: Predict whether zinc metal reacts with aqueous copper(II) ions.

First write down the two **half-equations** as reduction reactions:

$$Zn^{2+}_{(aq)} + 2e^- \rightleftharpoons Zn_{(s)} \qquad E^\circ = -0.76\,V$$
$$Cu^{2+}_{(aq)} + 2e^- \rightleftharpoons Cu_{(s)} \qquad E^\circ = +0.34\,V$$

The half-reactions are written as reduction reactions but one will always have to move in the direction of oxidation. Zn^{2+}/Zn has a more negative electrode potential than Cu^{2+}/Cu, so the zinc will be oxidised.

Then look at the standard electrode potentials.

The half-equation with the **more negative** electrode potential will move to the **left**: $Zn_{(s)} \rightarrow Zn^{2+}_{(aq)} + 2e^-$

The half-equation with the **more positive** electrode potential will move to the **right**: $Cu^{2+}_{(aq)} + 2e^- \rightarrow Cu_{(s)}$

The two half-equations combine to give: $Zn_{(s)} + Cu^{2+}_{(aq)} \rightarrow Zn^{2+}_{(aq)} + Cu_{(s)}$

This is the **feasible** direction of the overall reaction. It matches the reaction described in the question, so zinc **will** react with aqueous copper ions.

For any **feasible reaction** E°_{cell} is **positive** — E°_{cell} for this reaction is $+0.34 - (-0.76) = \mathbf{+1.10\,V}$.

Practice Questions

Q1 Copper is less reactive than magnesium. Predict which of these half-reactions has the more negative standard electrode potential: A $Mg^{2+}_{(aq)} + 2e^- \rightleftharpoons Mg_{(s)}$ B $Cu^{2+}_{(aq)} + 2e^- \rightleftharpoons Cu_{(s)}$

Q2 Use electrode potentials to show that magnesium will reduce Zn^{2+} ions.

Q3 Use the table on the previous page to predict whether or not Zn^{2+} ions can oxidise Fe^{2+} ions to Fe^{3+} ions.

Exam Questions

Q1 Use the $E^{\ominus}$ values in the table on the right and on the previous page to determine the outcome of mixing the following solutions. If there is a reaction, determine the overall $E^{\ominus}$ value and write the equation. Explain how you know whether or not the reaction takes place.

Half-reaction	$E^{\ominus}/V$
$Ni^{2+}_{(aq)} + 2e^- \rightleftharpoons Ni_{(s)}$	-0.25
$Sn^{4+}_{(aq)} + 2e^- \rightleftharpoons Sn^{2+}_{(aq)}$	$+0.14$
$Cr_2O_7^{2-}_{(aq)} + 14H^+_{(aq)} + 6e^- \rightleftharpoons 2Cr^{3+}_{(aq)} + 7H_2O_{(l)}$	$+1.33$
$MnO_4^-_{(aq)} + 8H^+_{(aq)} + 5e^- \rightleftharpoons Mn^{2+}_{(aq)} + 4H_2O_{(l)}$	$+1.51$

   a) Zinc metal and Ni^{2+} ions.   [2 marks]

   b) Acidified MnO_4^- ions and Sn^{2+} ions.   [2 marks]

   c) $Br_{2(aq)}$ and acidified $Cr_2O_7^{2-}$ ions.   [2 marks]

Q2 Potassium manganate(VII), $KMnO_4$, and potassium dichromate $K_2Cr_2O_7$, are both used as oxidising agents. From their electrode potentials (given in the table above), which would you predict is the stronger oxidising agent? Explain why.   [2 marks]

Q3 Use the following data to answer the questions below.

$$O_{2(g)} + 2H_2O_{(l)} + 4e^- \rightleftharpoons 4OH^-_{(aq)} \qquad E^\circ = +0.40\,V$$

$$Fe^{2+}_{(aq)} + 2e^- \rightleftharpoons Fe_{(s)} \qquad E^\circ = -0.44\,V$$

   a) i) Draw a cell diagram for the reaction using the conventional representation.   [1 mark]

      ii) Calculate the EMF for the cell.   [1 mark]

   b) Use electrode potentials to explain why iron is oxidised in the presence of oxygen and water.   [1 mark]

Why so series? Let's put a smile on that face...

To see if a reaction will happen, you basically find the two half-equations in the electrochemical series and check that the one you are predicting will go backwards is the one with the more negative electrode potential. Alternatively, you could calculate the cell potential for the reaction — if it's negative, it's never going to happen.

Batteries and Fuel Cells

It turns out that electrochemical cells aren't just found in the lab — they're all over your house too... whoa.

Electrochemical Cells Are Used as Batteries

1) **Batteries** are types of **electrochemical cell** which provide the **electricity** we use to power things like watches and mobile phones. Some types of cell are **rechargeable** while others can only be used until they **run out**.

2) **Non-rechargeable** batteries are **cheaper** than rechargeable ones. But since you can just **recharge** and **re-use** rechargeable batteries, they **last longer** and work out **cheaper** in the **long run**.

Lithium Batteries are Rechargeable

Rechargeable batteries are found in loads of devices, such as **mobile phones**, **laptops** and **cars**. For example:

Lithium cells are used in mobile phones and laptops. One type of lithium cell is made up of a **lithium cobalt oxide ($LiCoO_2$) electrode** and a **graphite electrode**. The **electrolyte** is a **lithium salt** in an **organic solvent**.

The **half-equations** are:

$Li^+ + e^- \rightleftharpoons Li$ $E^\circ = -3.04\,V$

$Li^+ + CoO_2 + e^- \rightleftharpoons Li^+[CoO_2]^-$ $E^\circ = +0.56\,V$

The **Li^+/ Li** half-cell has the **more negative** E° value so goes in the direction of **oxidation** (backwards).

So the reactions which happen when the battery supplies power are:

At the **negative** electrode: $Li \rightarrow Li^+ + e^-$

At the **positive** electrode: $Li^+ + CoO_2 + e^- \rightarrow Li^+[CoO_2]^-$

Learn these two half-reactions — you could be asked to give them in the exams.

The EMF of this type of cell is: $E^\circ_{cell} = E^\circ_{reduced} - E^\circ_{oxidised} = +0.56 - (-3.04) = \textbf{+3.60 V}$

To recharge these batteries, a **current** is supplied to force **electrons** to flow in the **opposite direction** around the circuit and **reverse the reactions**. The reactions that take place in **non-rechargeable** batteries are **difficult** or **impossible to reverse** in this way.

Fuel Cells can Generate Electricity From Hydrogen and Oxygen

In most cells the **chemicals** that generate the electricity are contained in the **electrodes** and the **electrolyte** that form the cell. In a **fuel cell** the chemicals are **stored separately** outside the cell and fed in when electricity is required. One example of this is the **alkaline hydrogen-oxygen fuel cell**, which can be used to **power electric vehicles**. **Hydrogen and oxygen gases** are fed into two separate platinum-containing electrodes. The electrodes are separated by an **anion-exchange membrane** that **allows anions** (OH^-) and water to pass through it, but **not hydrogen and oxygen gas**. The **electrolyte** is an aqueous alkaline (KOH) solution.

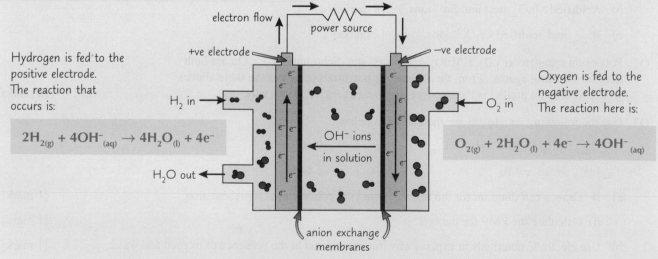

Hydrogen is fed to the positive electrode. The reaction that occurs is:

$2H_{2(g)} + 4OH^-_{(aq)} \rightarrow 4H_2O_{(l)} + 4e^-$

electron flow — power source

+ve electrode — −ve electrode

H_2 in OH^- ions in solution O_2 in

H_2O out

anion exchange membranes

Oxygen is fed to the negative electrode. The reaction here is:

$O_{2(g)} + 2H_2O_{(l)} + 4e^- \rightarrow 4OH^-_{(aq)}$

The **electrons** flow from the **positive electrode** through an **external circuit** to the **negative electrode**. The OH^- ions pass through the **anion-exchange membrane** towards the positive electrode.

The **overall effect** is that H_2 and O_2 react to make **water**: $2H_{2(g)} + O_{2(g)} \rightarrow 2H_2O_{(g)}$

Batteries and Fuel Cells

Fuel Cells Have some Big Advantages

The **major advantage** of using **fuel cells** in cars, rather than the **internal combustion engine**, is that fuel cells are **more efficient** — they **convert more** of their **available energy** into **kinetic** energy to get the car moving. Internal combustion engines **waste** a lot of their **energy** producing **heat**. Other benefits are

- The only **waste product** is **water**, so there are **no nasty toxic chemicals** to dispose of and **no CO_2 emissions** from the cell itself.
- Fuel cells don't need to be recharged like batteries. As long as **hydrogen** and **oxygen** are supplied, the cell will continue to **produce electricity**.

The **downside** is that you **need energy** to produce a supply of **hydrogen** and **oxygen**. They can be produced from the **electrolysis of water**, i.e. by **reusing the waste product** from the fuel cell, but this requires **electricity** — and this **electricity** is normally generated by **burning fossil fuels**. So the whole process isn't usually carbon neutral. **Hydrogen** is also **highly flammable** so it needs to be handled carefully when it is **stored** or **transported**.

Practice Questions

Q1 Give one advantage and one disadvantage of non-rechargeable batteries.

Q2 Name a metal that is used in the electrodes in an alkaline hydrogen-oxygen fuel cell.

Q3 What electrolyte is used in an alkaline hydrogen-oxygen fuel cell?

Exam Questions

Q1 The diagram below shows the structure of an alkaline hydrogen-oxygen fuel cell.

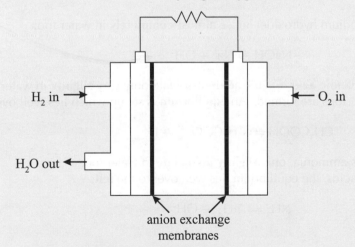

H₂ in →

← O₂ in

H₂O out ←

anion exchange membranes

a) i)   Label the site of oxidation and the site of reduction on the diagram. [1 mark]

ii) Draw an arrow to show the direction of the flow of electrons. [1 mark]

b) Write a half-equation for the reaction at each electrode. [2 marks]

c) Explain the purpose of the anion exchange membrane in the fuel cell. [1 mark]

Q2 a) Write the half-equations that take place in a lithium battery cell. [2 marks]

b) How is a lithium battery recharged? [1 mark]

c) What happens to the half-equations from part a) when the cell is being recharged? [1 mark]

Been charged with a salt in battery? Don't worry, it's reversible...

You've got to love batteries — they sit there in their shiny metal cases all ready to release the energy stored inside them just when you need it most. So, have some respect for batteries and don't just throw them in the bin when they go flat, recharge them if you can, and if not recycle them. Oh, and you'd probably best learn those half-equations too.

Acids, Bases and K_w

Remember this stuff? Well, it's all down to Brønsted and Lowry — they've got a lot to answer for.

An Acid **Releases** Protons — a Base **Accepts** Protons

Brønsted-Lowry acids are **proton donors** — they release **hydrogen ions** (H^+) when they're mixed with water. You never get H^+ ions by themselves in water though — they're always combined with H_2O to form **hydroxonium ions**, H_3O^+.

HA is any old acid.

$$HA_{(aq)} + H_2O_{(l)} \rightarrow H_3O^+_{(aq)} + A^-_{(aq)}$$

Brønsted-Lowry bases are **proton acceptors**.
When they're in solution, they grab **hydrogen ions** from water molecules.

B is just a random base.

$$B_{(aq)} + H_2O_{(l)} \rightarrow BH^+_{(aq)} + OH^-_{(aq)}$$

You might see the term 'alkali' being used instead of 'base'. Don't panic though — an alkali is just a soluble base.

Brønsted laid down the base.
Lowry rocked the flow.
That's just how chemists roll.

Acids and Bases can be **Strong** or **Weak**

1) **Strong acids dissociate** (or ionise) **almost completely** in water — **nearly all the H^+ ions** will be released. **Hydrochloric acid** is a strong acid:

$$HCl \rightarrow H^+ + Cl^-$$

Strong bases (like sodium hydroxide) **ionise almost completely** in water too:

$$NaOH \rightarrow Na^+ + OH^-$$

These are really both reversible reactions, but the equilibrium lies extremely far to the right.

2) **Weak acids** (e.g. **ethanoic acid** or citric acid) dissociate only very **slightly** in water — so only small numbers of H^+ ions are formed. An **equilibrium** is set up which lies well over to the **left**:

$$CH_3COOH \rightleftharpoons CH_3COO^-_{(aq)} + H^+_{(aq)}$$

Weak bases (such as ammonia) **only slightly dissociate** in water too.
Just like with weak acids, the equilibrium lies well over to the **left**:

$$NH_3 \rightleftharpoons NH_4^+ + OH^-$$

Protons are **Transferred** when **Acids** and **Bases** React

Acids can't just throw away their protons — they can only get rid of them if there's a **base** to accept them.
In this reaction the **acid**, HA, **transfers** a proton to the **base**, B:

$$HA_{(aq)} + B_{(aq)} \rightleftharpoons BH^+_{(aq)} + A^-_{(aq)}$$

It's an **equilibrium**, so if you add more **HA** or **B**, the position of equilibrium moves to the **right**.
But if you add more **BH+** or **A−**, the equilibrium will move to the **left**.
(Have a look back at your Year 1 notes if you need a reminder about how equilibria work.)

When an acid is added to **water**, water acts as the **base** and accepts the proton:

$$HA_{(aq)} + H_2O_{(l)} \rightleftharpoons H_3O^+_{(aq)} + A^-_{(aq)}$$

The equilibrium's far to the left for weak acids, and far to the right for strong acids.

Acids, Bases and K_w

Water Dissociates Slightly

Water dissociates into **hydroxonium ions** and **hydroxide ions**.

So this **equilibrium** exists in water:

$$H_2O + H_2O \rightleftharpoons H_3O^+ + OH^-$$ or more simply $$H_2O \rightleftharpoons H^+ + OH^-$$

And, just as for any other equilibrium reaction, you can apply the equilibrium law and write an expression for the **equilibrium constant**:

$$K_c = \frac{[H^+][OH^-]}{[H_2O]}$$

Water only dissociates a **tiny amount**, so the equilibrium lies well over to the **left**. There's so much water compared to the amounts of H^+ and OH^- ions that the concentration of water is considered to have a **constant** value.

So if you multiply the expression you wrote for K_c (which is a constant) by $[H_2O]$ (another constant), you get a **constant**. This new constant is called the **ionic product of water** and it's given the symbol K_w.

$$K_w = K_c \times [H_2O] = [H^+][OH^-] \implies \boxed{K_w = [H^+][OH^-]}$$

The units of K_w are always $mol^2 \, dm^{-6}$.

K_w always has the **same value** for an aqueous solution at a **given temperature**. For example, at 298 K (25 °C), K_w has a value of $1.00 \times 10^{-14} \, mol^2 \, dm^{-6}$. The value of K_w changes as temperature changes.

In **pure water**, there is always **one H^+ ion** for **each OH^- ion**. So $[H^+] = [OH^-]$. That means if you are dealing with **pure water**, then you can say that $K_w = [H^+]^2$.

Practice Questions

Q1 Explain what is meant by the term 'strong acid' and give an example of one.
Q2 Which substance is acting as a Brønsted-Lowry base in the equation on the right? $HA + H_2O \rightleftharpoons H_3O^+ + A^-$
Q3 Define K_w and give its value at 298 K.

Exam Questions

Q1 Show, by writing appropriate equations, how HSO_4^- can behave as:

  a) a Brønsted-Lowry acid,   b) a Brønsted-Lowry base. [2 marks]

Q2 Hydrocyanic acid (HCN) is a weak acid.

  a) Define the term 'weak acid'. [1 mark]

  b) Write a balanced equation for the equilibrium that occurs when HCN dissolves in water. [1 mark]

Q3 A solution contains 2.50 g dm^{-3} of sodium hydroxide.
  What is the molar concentration of the hydroxide ions in this solution? [2 marks]

Alright, this is a stick-up — hand over your protons and nobody gets hurt...

Don't confuse strong acids with concentrated acids, or weak acids with dilute acids. Strong and weak are to do with how much an acid ionises, whereas concentrated and dilute are to do with the concentration of the acid. You can have a strong dilute acid, or a weak concentrated acid. And it works just the same way with bases too.

pH Calculations

Just when you thought it was safe to turn the page, there's even more about acids and bases.
This page is positively swarming with calculations and constants...

The **pH Scale** is a Measure of the **Hydrogen Ion Concentration**

The **concentration of hydrogen ions** in a solution can vary enormously, so those
wise chemists of old decided to express the concentration on a **logarithmic scale**.

$$pH = -\log_{10} [H^+]$$

$[H^+]$ is the concentration of hydrogen ions
in a solution, measured in mol dm^{-3}.

The pH scale normally goes from **0** (very acidic) to **14** (very basic). **pH 7** is regarded as being **neutral**.

You Can **Calculate pH** from **Hydrogen Ion Concentration**...

If you know the **hydrogen ion concentration** of a solution,
you can calculate its **pH** by sticking the numbers into the **formula**.

> **Example:** A solution of hydrochloric acid has a hydrogen ion
> concentration of 0.01 mol dm^{-3}. What is the pH of this solution?
>
> $$pH = -\log_{10} [H^+] = -\log_{10} (0.01) = \textbf{2.0}$$
>
> Use the 'log' button on
> your calculator for this.

Pippa's an expert at finding logs.

...Or **Hydrogen Ion Concentration** From **pH**

If you've got the **pH** of a solution, and you want to know its
hydrogen ion concentration, then you need the **inverse** of the pH formula:

$$[H^+] = 10^{-pH}$$

Now you can use this formula to find $[H^+]$.

> **Example:** A solution of sulfuric acid has a pH of 1.5.
> What is the hydrogen ion concentration of this solution?
>
> $$[H^+] = 10^{-pH} = 10^{-1.5} = 0.03 \text{ mol } dm^{-3} = \textbf{3} \times \textbf{10}^{-2} \text{ mol } dm^{-3}$$

For Strong **Monoprotic** Acids, **[H⁺] = [Acid]**

1) **Strong acids** such as hydrochloric acid and nitric acid **ionise fully** in solution.

2) Hydrochloric acid (HCl) and nitric acid (HNO_3) are also **monoprotic**, which means that **each molecule** of acid
will release **one proton** when it dissociates. This means **one mole of acid** produces **one mole of hydrogen ions**.
So the H^+ concentration is the **same** as the acid concentration.

> **E.g.** For **0.10 mol dm^{-3} HCl**, $[H^+]$ is also 0.10 mol dm^{-3}. So the **pH** $= -\log_{10} [H^+] = -\log_{10} (0.10) = \textbf{1.00}$.
> Or for **0.050 mol dm^{-3} HNO_3**, $[H^+]$ is also 0.050 mol dm^{-3}, giving **pH** $= -\log_{10} (0.050) = \textbf{1.30}$.

For Strong **Diprotic** Acids, **[H⁺] = 2[Acid]**

There's more about
diprotic acids on page 38.

1) Each molecule of a **strong diprotic acid** releases **2 protons** when it dissociates.
So, diprotic acids produce **2 mol of hydrogen ions** for **each mole of acid**.

2) Sulfuric acid is an example of a **strong diprotic acid**: $H_2SO_{4(l)} + \text{water} \rightarrow 2H^+_{(aq)} + SO_4^{2-}{}_{(aq)}$

> **E.g.** For **0.10 mol dm^{-3} H_2SO_4**, $[H^+]$ is 0.20 mol dm^{-3}. So the **pH** $= -\log_{10} [H^+] = -\log_{10} (0.20) = \textbf{0.70}$.

pH Calculations

Use K_w to Find the pH of a Strong Base

1) Sodium hydroxide (NaOH) and potassium hydroxide (KOH) are **strong bases** that **fully ionise** in water:

$$NaOH \rightarrow Na^+ + OH^-$$ $$KOH \rightarrow K^+ + OH^-$$

2) They donate **one mole of OH⁻ ions** per mole of base.
This means that the concentration of OH⁻ ions is the **same** as the **concentration of the base**.
So for 0.02 mol dm⁻³ sodium hydroxide solution, [OH⁻] is also **0.02 mol dm⁻³**.

3) But to work out the **pH** you need to know **[H⁺]**
— luckily this is linked to **[OH⁻]** through the **ionic product of water**, K_w: $K_w = [H^+][OH^-]$

4) So if you know K_w and [OH⁻] for a **strong aqueous base** at a certain temperature, you can work out **[H⁺]** and then the **pH**.

Example: Find the pH of 0.10 mol dm⁻³ NaOH at 298 K, given that K_w at 298 K is 1.0×10^{-14} mol² dm⁻⁶.

1) First put all the values you know into the expression for the ionic product of water, K_w:

$$1.0 \times 10^{-14} = [H^+] \times 0.10$$

2) Now rearrange the expression to find [H⁺]:

$$[H^+] = \frac{1.0 \times 10^{-14}}{0.10} = 1.0 \times 10^{-13} \text{ mol dm}^{-3}$$

3) Use your value of [H⁺] to find the pH of the solution:

$$pH = -\log_{10}[H^+] = -\log_{10}(1.0 \times 10^{-13}) = \textbf{13.00}$$

Practice Questions

Q1 Write the formula for calculating the pH of a solution.
Q2 What can you assume about [H⁺] for a strong monoprotic acid?
Q3 Explain how you'd find the pH of a strong base.

Exam Questions

Q1 a) What's the pH of a solution of the strong acid, hydrobromic acid (HBr), if it has a concentration of 0.32 mol dm⁻³? [1 mark]

b) Hydrobromic acid is a stronger acid than ethanoic acid.
Explain what that means in terms of hydrogen ions and pH. [1 mark]

Q2 Nitric acid, HNO_3, is a strong monoprotic acid.

a) Explain what is meant by a monoprotic acid. [1 mark]

b) Find the concentration of a solution of nitric acid that has a pH value of 0.55. [1 mark]

Q3 A solution contains 11.22 g dm⁻³ of potassium hydroxide. K_w at 298 K is 1.0×10^{-14} mol² dm⁻⁶.

a) What is the molar concentration of the hydroxide ions in this solution? [2 marks]

b) Calculate the pH of this solution. [2 marks]

James and the Giant pH — a bit too basic for me if I'm being honest...

You know things are getting serious when maths stuff like logs start appearing. It's fine really though, just practise a few questions and make sure you know how to use the log button on your calculator. And make sure you've learned the equation for K_w and both pH equations. And while you're up, go and make me a nice cup of tea, lots of milk, no sugar.

More pH Calculations

More acid calculations to come, so you'll need to get that calculator warmed up... Either hold it for a couple of minutes in your armpit, or even better, sit on it for a while. OK, done that? Good stuff...

K_a is the **Acid Dissociation Constant**

1) Weak acids (like CH_3COOH) and weak bases **dissociate only slightly** in aqueous solution, so the [H+] **isn't** the same as the acid concentration. This makes it a **bit trickier** to find their pH. You have to use yet another **equilibrium constant**, K_a (the acid dissociation constant).

- For a weak aqueous acid, HA, you get the following equilibrium: $HA_{(aq)} \rightleftharpoons H^+_{(aq)} + A^-_{(aq)}$

- As only a **tiny amount** of HA dissociates, you can assume that $[HA_{(aq)}]_{equilibrium} \approx [HA_{(aq)}]_{start}$.

- So if you apply the equilibrium law, you get: $K_a = \dfrac{[H^+][A^-]}{[HA]_{start}}$

- You can also assume that dissociation of the **acid** is much greater than dissociation of **water**. This means you can assume that all the H+ ions in solution come from the **acid**, so $[H^+_{(aq)}] \approx [A^-_{(aq)}]$.

  So, for a weak acid: $K_a = \dfrac{[H^+]^2}{[HA]}$ ⬅ The units of K_a are mol dm^{-3}.

2) The assumptions made above to find K_a only work for **weak acids**, because strong acids dissociate almost completely in solution. (So for a strong acid, $[HA_{(aq)}]_{equilibrium}$ is not equal to $[HA_{(aq)}]_{start}$.)

To Find the **pH** of a **Weak Acid**, You Use K_a

K_a is an **equilibrium constant** just like K_c or K_w. It applies to a particular acid at a **specific temperature**, regardless of the **concentration**. You can use this fact to find the **pH** of a known concentration of a weak acid.

Example: Calculate the hydrogen ion concentration and the pH of a 0.0200 mol dm^{-3} solution of propanoic acid (CH_3CH_2COOH) at 298 K. K_a for propanoic acid at 298 K is 1.30×10^{-5} mol dm^{-3}.

First, write down your expression for K_a and rearrange to find [H+].

$K_a = \dfrac{[H^+]^2}{[CH_3CH_2COOH]}$ ⟹ $[H^+]^2 = K_a[CH_3CH_2COOH] = 1.30 \times 10^{-5} \times 0.0200 = 2.60 \times 10^{-7}$

⟹ $[H^+] = \sqrt{(2.60 \times 10^{-7})} = \mathbf{5.10 \times 10^{-4}}$ **mol dm^{-3}**

You can now use your value for [H+] to find pH: pH = $-\log_{10}(5.10 \times 10^{-4})$ = **3.292**

You Might Have to Find the **Concentration** or K_a of a **Weak Acid**

You don't need to know anything new for this type of calculation. You usually just have to find **[H+]** from the pH, then fiddle around with the K_a **expression** to find the missing bit of information.

This bunny may look cute, but he can't help Horace with his revision.

Example: The pH of an ethanoic acid (CH_3COOH) solution was 3.02 at 298 K. Calculate the molar concentration of this solution. K_a of ethanoic acid is 1.75×10^{-5} mol dm^{-3} at 298 K.

First, use the pH to find [H+]: $[H^+] = 10^{-pH} = 10^{-3.02} = \mathbf{9.55 \times 10^{-4}}$ **mol dm^{-3}**

Then rearrange the expression for K_a and plug in your values to find $[CH_3COOH]$:

$K_a = \dfrac{[H^+]^2}{[CH_3COOH]}$ ⟹ $[CH_3COOH] = \dfrac{[H^+]^2}{K_a} = \dfrac{(9.55 \times 10^{-4})^2}{1.75 \times 10^{-5}} = \mathbf{0.0521}$ **mol dm^{-3}**

More pH Calculations

$pK_a = -\log_{10} K_a$ and $K_a = 10^{-pK_a}$

pK_a is calculated from K_a in exactly the same way as pH is calculated from $[H^+]$ — and vice versa.

Example: i) If an acid has a K_a value of 1.50×10^{-7} mol dm³, what is its pK_a?

$$pK_a = -\log_{10}(1.50 \times 10^{-7}) = 6.824$$

ii) What is the K_a value of an acid if its pK_a is 4.32?

$$K_a = 10^{-4.32} = 4.8 \times 10^{-5} \text{ mol dm}^{-3}$$

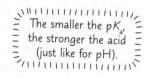
The smaller the pK_a, the stronger the acid (just like for pH).

Just to make things that bit more complicated, you might be given a **pK_a** value in a question to work out concentrations or pH. If so, you just need to convert it to K_a so that you can use the **K_a expression**.

Example: Calculate the pH of 0.0500 mol dm⁻³ methanoic acid (HCOOH).
Methanoic acid has a pK_a of 3.75 at this temperature.

$$K_a = 10^{-pK_a} = 10^{-3.75} = 1.8 \times 10^{-4} \text{ mol dm}^{-3} \quad \longleftarrow \text{First you have to convert the } pK_a \text{ to } K_a.$$

$$K_a = \frac{[H^+]^2}{[HCOOH]} \longrightarrow [H^+]^2 = K_a \times [HCOOH] = 1.78 \times 10^{-4} \times 0.0500 = 8.90 \times 10^{-6}$$

$$[H^+] = \sqrt{(8.90 \times 10^{-6})} = 2.98 \times 10^{-3} \text{ mol dm}^{-3}$$

$$pH = -\log_{10}(2.98 \times 10^{-3}) = 2.526$$

You might also be asked to work out a **pK_a** value from concentrations or pH. In this case, you just work out the K_a value as usual and then convert it to **pK_a** — and Bob's your revision goat.

Bob the revision goat.

Practice Questions

Q1 What are the units of K_a?

Q2 What assumptions do you have to make when calculating K_a for a weak acid?
Why aren't these assumptions true for a strong acid?

Q3 Would you expect strong acids to have higher or lower pK_a values than weak acids?

Exam Questions

Q1 The value of K_a for the weak acid HA, at 298 K, is 5.60×10^{-4} mol dm⁻³.

a) Write an expression for K_a for HA. [1 mark]

b) Calculate the pH of a 0.280 mol dm⁻³ solution of HA at 298 K. [2 marks]

Q2 The pH of a 0.150 mol dm⁻³ solution of a weak monoprotic acid, HX, is 2.64 at 298 K.

a) Calculate the value of K_a for the acid HX at 298 K. [2 marks]

b) Using your answer from part a), calculate pK_a for this acid. [1 mark]

Q3 Benzoic acid is a weak acid that is used as a food preservative. It has a pK_a of 4.2 at 298 K.
Find the pH of a 1.6×10^{-4} mol dm⁻³ solution of benzoic acid at 298 K. [3 marks]

Fluffy revision animals... aaawwwww...

Strong acids have high K_a values and weak acids have low K_a values. For pK_a values, it's the other way round — the stronger the acid, the lower the pK_a. If something's got p in front of it, like pH, pK_w or pK_a, it'll mean $-\log_{10}$ of whatever. Oh and did you like the cute animals? Did they really make your day? Good, I'm really pleased about that.

pH Curves and Indicators

If you add a base to an acid, the pH changes in a squiggly sort of way.

Use **Titration** to Find the **Concentration** of an **Acid** or **Base**

Acid-base titration was covered in detail in Year 1, so if it's a little hazy in your mind, best to go back and brush up on it first. Here's a reminder of the basics:

1) In **acid-base** titrations, you add a **standard solution** of acid to a **measured quantity** of base (or vice versa).

2) **Pipettes** and **burettes** are used so that you know **precisely** how much acid and base is used.

3) An **indicator** is added to the base to show you **exactly** when it's **neutralised** by the acid.

4) When you know how much acid it takes to neutralise the base, you can work out the **concentration of the base**. (Remember, you could swap it round and titrate an acid with a standard solution of a base instead — then you'd be working out the **concentration of the acid**.)

pH Curves Plot **pH** Against **Volume** of **Acid** or **Base** Added

The graphs below show the pH curves for the different combinations of **strong and weak** monoprotic acids and bases.

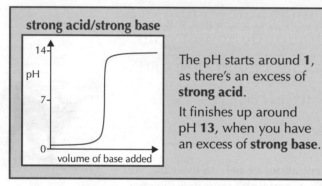

strong acid/strong base

The pH starts around **1**, as there's an excess of **strong acid**.

It finishes up around pH **13**, when you have an excess of **strong base**.

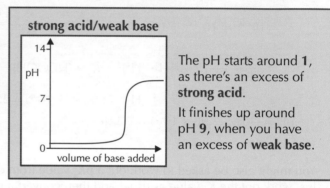

strong acid/weak base

The pH starts around **1**, as there's an excess of **strong acid**.

It finishes up around pH **9**, when you have an excess of **weak base**.

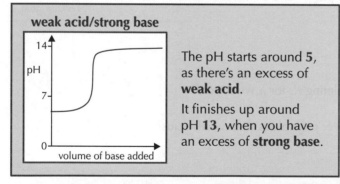

weak acid/strong base

The pH starts around **5**, as there's an excess of **weak acid**.

It finishes up around pH **13**, when you have an excess of **strong base**.

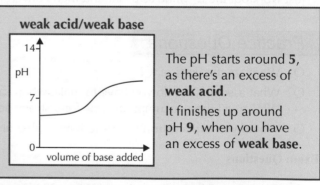

weak acid/weak base

The pH starts around **5**, as there's an excess of **weak acid**.

It finishes up around pH **9**, when you have an excess of **weak base**.

All the graphs, apart from the weak acid/weak base graph, have a bit that's vertical — this is the **equivalence point** or **end point**. At this point, a tiny amount of base causes a sudden, big change in pH — it's here that all the acid is just **neutralised**.

You don't get such a sharp change in a **weak acid/weak base** titration.
If you used an indicator for this type of titration, its colour would change very **gradually**, and it would be very tricky to see the exact end point. So you're usually better off using a **pH meter** for this type of titration.

If you titrate a **base** with an **acid** instead, the **shapes** of the curves **stay the same**, but they **flip** over:

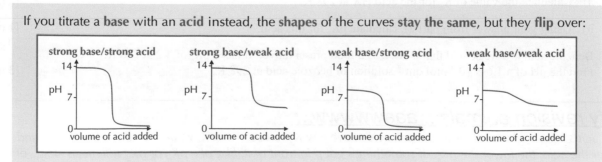

pH Curves and Indicators

pH Curves can Help you Decide which Indicator to Use

When you use an **indicator**, you need it to change colour exactly at the **end point** of your titration. So you need to pick one that changes colour over a **narrow pH range** that lies **entirely** on the **vertical part** of the **pH curve**.

E.g. For this titration, the curve is vertical between **pH 8** and **pH 11** — so a very small amount of base will cause the pH to **change** from 8 to 11.

So you want an indicator that changes **colour** somewhere between pH 8 and pH 11.

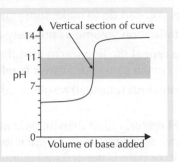

Methyl orange and **phenolphthalein** are **indicators** that are often used for acid-base titrations. They each change colour over a **different pH range**:

- For a **strong acid/strong base** titration, you can use **either** of these indicators — there's a rapid pH change over the range for **both** indicators.

- For a **strong acid/weak base** only **methyl orange** will do. The pH changes rapidly across the range for methyl orange, but not for phenolphthalein.

Name of indicator	Colour at low pH	Approx. pH of colour change	Colour at high pH
Methyl orange	red	3.1 – 4.4	yellow
Phenolphthalein	colourless	8.3 – 10	pink

- For a **weak acid/strong base**, **phenolphthalein** is the stuff to use. The pH changes rapidly over phenolphthalein's range, but not over methyl orange's.

- For **weak acid/weak base** titrations there's no sharp pH change, so **neither** of these indicators works. In fact, there aren't **any** indicators you can use in weak acid/weak base titrations, so you should just use a pH meter.

Practice Questions

Q1 Sketch the pH curve for a strong acid/weak base titration.

Q2 What indicator should you use for a strong acid/weak base titration — methyl orange or phenolphthalein?

Q3 What colour is methyl orange at low pH?

Exam Questions

Q1 NaOH (a strong base) is added separately to samples of nitric acid (a strong acid) and ethanoic acid (a weak acid). Sketch the pH curves for each of these titrations. [2 marks]

Q2 A sample of ethanoic acid (a weak acid) was added to a solution of potassium hydroxide (a strong base).

From the table on the right, select the best indicator for this titration, and explain your choice. [2 marks]

Name of indicator	pH range
bromophenol blue	3.0 – 4.6
methyl red	4.2 – 6.3
bromothymol blue	6.0 – 7.6
thymol blue	8.0 – 9.6

Q3 Ethanoic acid (a weak acid) was added to ammonia (a weak base).

a) Sketch the pH curve for this titration. [1 mark]

b) Explain why an indicator can't be used to accurately determine the end point of this titration. [2 marks]

My face turns luminous red when I reach my end point with revision...

Titrations involve playing with big bits of glassware that you're told not to break as they're really expensive — so you instantly become really clumsy. If you manage not to smash the burette, you'll find it easier to get accurate results if you use a dilute acid or base — drops of dilute acid and base contain fewer particles so you're less likely to overshoot.

Titration Calculations

OK, so you can carry out titrations like a boss, but here's what you can do with the results...

You Can Use **Titration Results** to Calculate **Concentrations**

When you've done a titration you can use your results to calculate the **concentration** of your acid or base.

There are a few things you can do to make sure your titration **results** are as **accurate** as possible:

1) Measure the neutralisation volume as precisely as you possibly can (this will usually be to the **nearest 0.05 cm³**).

2) It's a good idea to **repeat** the titration at least three times and take a **mean** titre value.
That'll help you to make sure your answer is **reliable**.

3) Don't use any **anomalous** (unusual) results — all your results should be within 0.1 cm³ of each other.

If you use a **pH meter**, rather than an indicator, you can draw a pH curve of the titration and use it to work out how much acid or base is needed for neutralisation.

You do this by finding the **equivalence point** (the mid-point of the line of rapid pH change) and drawing a **vertical line downwards** until it meets the x-axis. The value at this point on the x-axis is the volume of acid or base needed.

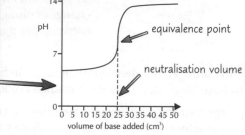

Here's an **Example Calculation**...

You should have seen these types of calculations before but it never hurts to refresh the important stuff.

Example: 40 cm³ of 0.75 mol dm⁻³ HNO_3 was needed to neutralise 60 cm³ of KOH solution.
Calculate the concentration of the potassium hydroxide solution.

$$HNO_3 + KOH \rightarrow KNO_3 + H_2O$$

Work out how many **moles of HNO_3** you have:

$$\text{Number of moles of } HNO_3 = \frac{\text{conc.} \times \text{volume (cm}^3)}{1000} = \frac{0.75 \times 40}{1000} = 0.030 \text{ mol}$$

You should remember this formula — you divide by 1000 to get the volume from cm³ to dm³.

From the equation, you know 1 mol of HNO_3 neutralises 1 mol of KOH.
So 0.030 mol of HNO_3 must neutralise **0.030** mol of KOH.

This is just the formula above, rearranged.

$$\text{Concentration of KOH} = \frac{\text{moles of } HNO_3 \times 1000}{\text{volume (cm}^3)} = \frac{0.030 \times 1000}{60} = 0.50 \text{ mol dm}^3$$

A **Diprotic Acid** Releases **Two Protons** When it Dissociates

A **diprotic acid** is one that can release **two protons** when it's in solution. **Ethanedioic acid** (HOOC-COOH) is diprotic. When ethanedioic acid reacts with a **base** like sodium hydroxide, it's **neutralised**.
But the reaction happens in **two stages**, because the **two protons** are removed from the acid **separately**.

This means that when you titrate **ethanedioic acid** with a **strong base** you get a pH curve with two **equivalence points**:

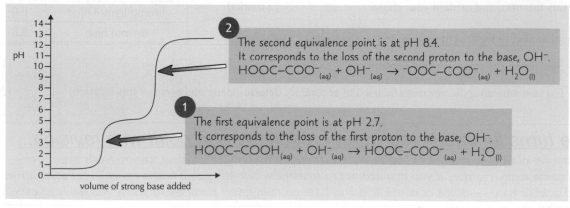

2 The second equivalence point is at pH 8.4.
It corresponds to the loss of the second proton to the base, OH^-.
$HOOC-COO^-_{(aq)} + OH^-_{(aq)} \rightarrow {}^-OOC-COO^-_{(aq)} + H_2O_{(l)}$

1 The first equivalence point is at pH 2.7.
It corresponds to the loss of the first proton to the base, OH^-.
$HOOC-COOH_{(aq)} + OH^-_{(aq)} \rightarrow HOOC-COO^-_{(aq)} + H_2O_{(l)}$

UNIT 1: SECTION 9 — ACIDS, BASES AND pH

Titration Calculations

You Can Find the *Concentration* of a *Diprotic Acid* From Titration Results Too

You can calculate the concentration of a **diprotic** acid from titration data in the same way as you did for a monoprotic acid.

Example: 25 cm³ of ethanedioic acid, $C_2H_2O_4$, was completely neutralised by 20 cm³ of 0.10 mol dm⁻³ NaOH solution. Calculate the concentration of the ethanedioic acid solution.

Write a **balanced equation** and decide what you know and what you **need to know**:

$$C_2H_2O_4 + 2NaOH \rightarrow Na_2C_2O_4 + 2H_2O$$
25 cm³   20 cm³
?   0.10 mol dm⁻³

Because it's a diprotic acid, you need twice as many moles of base as moles of acid.

Now work out how many **moles of NaOH** you have:

$$\text{Number of moles of NaOH} = \frac{\text{conc.} \times \text{volume (cm}^3)}{1000} = \frac{0.10 \times 20}{1000} = 0.0020 \text{ mol}$$

You know from the equation that you need 2 mol of NaOH to neutralise 1 mol of $C_2H_2O_4$.

So 0.0020 mol of NaOH must neutralise (0.002 ÷ 2) = **0.0010 mol of $C_2H_2O_4$**.

Now find the **concentration of $C_2H_2O_4$**.

$$\text{Concentration of } C_2H_2O_4 = \frac{\text{moles of } C_2H_2O_4 \times 1000}{\text{volume (cm}^3)} = \frac{0.0010 \times 1000}{25} = \textbf{0.040 mol dm}^3$$

Practice Questions

Q1 What is a diprotic acid?

Q2 How many moles of NaOH would you need to neutralise one mole of a diprotic acid?

Exam Questions

Q1 A student performed a titration with 25 cm³ of hydrochloric acid, adding 0.10 mol dm⁻³ sodium hydroxide from a burette. The student's results are shown in the table below.

	Titration 1	Titration 2	Titration 3
Titre volume (cm³ of NaOH)	25.60	25.65	25.55

a) Write a balanced equation for the reaction. [1 mark]

b) i) Calculate the average titre of sodium hydroxide needed to neutralise the hydrochloric acid. [1 mark]

   ii) Use this to find the number of moles of sodium hydroxide that were needed to neutralise the acid. [1 mark]

c) Find the concentration of the hydrochloric acid. [1 mark]

Q2 Sulfuric acid is a diprotic acid.
25.0 cm³ of this acid is needed to neutralise 35.6 cm³ of 0.100 mol dm⁻³ sodium hydroxide.

a) Write a balanced equation for the reaction. [1 mark]

b) Calculate:

   i) the number of moles of sodium hydroxide present in the 35.6 cm³ sample. [1 mark]

   ii) the number of moles of sulfuric acid needed to neutralise the sodium hydroxide. [1 mark]

   iii) the concentration of the sulfuric acid used. [1 mark]

Diprotic acids — double the protons, double the fun...

Don't forget, if it's a diprotic acid that you're using, you need twice as many moles of NaOH to neutralise it as you would for a monoprotic acid. But when it comes down to it, it's just the same story as any other chemistry calculation — write out the equation, compare the number of moles, and put the values into the right formula.

Buffer Action

Some solutions resist becoming more acidic if you add acid to them. Why would they want to? Read on to find out...

Buffers Resist Changes in pH

A **buffer** is a solution that **resists** changes in pH when **small** amounts of acid or base are added, or when it's **diluted**.

A buffer **doesn't** stop the pH from changing completely — it does make the changes **very slight** though.
Buffers only work for small amounts of acid or base. You get **acidic buffers** and **basic buffers**.

Acidic Buffers are Made from a Weak Acid and one of its Salts

Acidic buffers have a pH of less than 7 — they're made by mixing a **weak acid** with one of its **salts**.
Ethanoic acid and **sodium ethanoate** ($CH_3COO^- Na^+$) is a good example:

The ethanoic acid is a **weak acid**, so it only **slightly** dissociates: $CH_3COOH_{(aq)} \rightleftharpoons H^+_{(aq)} + CH_3COO^-_{(aq)}$.

But the salt **fully** dissociates into its ions when it dissolves: $CH_3COONa_{(s)} + water \rightarrow CH_3COO^-_{(aq)} + Na^+_{(aq)}$.

So in the solution you've got lots of **undissociated ethanoic acid molecules**, and lots of **ethanoate ions** from the salt.

When you alter the **concentration** of H^+ or OH^- **ions** in the buffer solution, the **equilibrium position** moves
to **counteract** the change (this is down to **Le Chatelier's principle**). Here's how it all works:

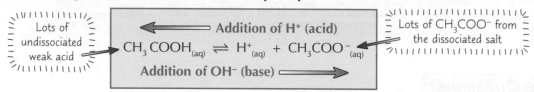

1) If you add a **small** amount of **acid**, the H^+ **concentration** increases. Most of the extra H^+ ions combine with CH_3COO^- ions to form CH_3COOH. This shifts the equilibrium to the **left**, reducing the H^+ concentration to close to its original value. So the **pH** doesn't change.

2) If a **small** amount of **base** (e.g. NaOH) is added, the OH^- **concentration** increases. Most of the extra OH^- ions react with H^+ ions to form water — removing H^+ ions from the solution. This causes more CH_3COOH to **dissociate** to form H^+ ions — shifting the equilibrium to the **right**. The H^+ concentration increases until it's close to its original value, so the **pH** doesn't change.

Basic Buffers are Made from a Weak Base and one of its Salts

Basic buffers have a pH greater than 7 — and they're made by mixing a **weak base** with one of its **salts**.
A solution of **ammonia** (NH_3, a weak base) and **ammonium chloride** (NH_4Cl, a salt of ammonia) acts as a **basic** buffer.

The **salt** fully dissociates in solution: $NH_4Cl_{(aq)} \rightarrow NH_4^+_{(aq)} + Cl^-_{(aq)}$.

Some of the NH_3 molecules will also react with water molecules: $NH_{3\,(aq)} + H_2O_{(aq)} \rightleftharpoons NH_4^+_{(aq)} + OH^-_{(aq)}$.

So the solution will contain loads of **ammonium ions** (NH_4^+), and lots of **ammonia** molecules too.

The **equilibrium position** of this reaction
can move to **counteract** changes in pH:

$$\text{Addition of } H^+ \text{ (acid)} \Longrightarrow$$
$$NH_{3(aq)} + H_2O_{(l)} \rightleftharpoons NH_4^+_{(aq)} + OH^-_{(aq)}$$
$$\Longleftarrow \text{Addition of } OH^- \text{ (base)}$$

1) If a small amount of **base** is added, the OH^- concentration **increases**, making the solution more **basic**. Most of the extra OH^- ions will react with the NH_4^+ ions, to form NH_3 and H_2O. So the equilibrium will shift to the **left**, removing OH^- ions from the solution, and stopping the pH from changing much.

2) If a small amount of **acid** is added, the H^+ concentration **increases**, making the solution more **acidic**. Some of the H^+ ions react with OH^- ions to make H_2O. When this happens the equilibrium position **moves to the right** to replace the OH^- ions that have been used up. Some of the H^+ ions react with NH_3 molecules to form NH_4^+: $NH_3 + H^+ \rightleftharpoons NH_4^+$. These reactions will **remove** most of the extra H^+ ions that were added — so the pH **won't** change much.

Buffer Action

Here's How to Calculate the pH of a Buffer Solution

Calculating the **pH** of an acidic buffer isn't too tricky. You just need to know the K_a of the weak acid and the **concentrations** of the weak acid and its salt. Here's how to go about it:

Example: A buffer solution contains 0.40 mol dm^{-3} methanoic acid, HCOOH, and 0.60 mol dm^{-3} sodium methanoate, $HCOO^- Na^+$. For methanoic acid, $K_a = 1.6 \times 10^{-4}$ mol dm^{-3}. What is the pH of this buffer?

First, write the expression for K_a of the weak acid:

$$HCOOH_{(aq)} \rightleftharpoons H^+_{(aq)} + HCOO^-_{(aq)} \longrightarrow K_a = \frac{[H^+_{(aq)}] \times [HCOO^-_{(aq)}]}{[HCOOH_{(aq)}]}$$

Remember — these are all equilibrium concentrations.

Then rearrange the expression and stick in the data to calculate $[H^+_{(aq)}]$:

$$[H^+_{(aq)}] = K_a \times \frac{[HCOOH_{(aq)}]}{[HCOO^-_{(aq)}]}$$

$$[H^+_{(aq)}] = 1.6 \times 10^{-4} \times (0.40 \div 0.60) = 1.07 \times 10^{-4} \text{ mol dm}^{-3}$$

You have to make a **few assumptions** here:
- $HCOO^- Na^+$ is fully dissociated, so assume that the equilibrium concentration of $HCOO^-$ is the same as the initial concentration of $HCOO^- Na^+$.
- HCOOH is only slightly dissociated, so assume that its equilibrium concentration is the same as its initial concentration.

Finally, convert $[H^+_{(aq)}]$ to pH:

$$pH = -\log_{10}[H^+_{(aq)}] = -\log_{10}(1.07 \times 10^{-4}) = \textbf{3.971}$$

Buffers are Really Handy

Most **shampoos** contain a pH 5.5 buffer. Human hair becomes rougher if it's exposed to alkaline conditions — the buffer in the shampoo stops this from happening, keeping hair smooth and shiny.

Biological washing powders also contain buffers. They keep the pH at the right level for the enzymes to work most efficiently.

There are lots of **biological buffer** systems in our bodies too, making sure our tissues are kept at the **right pH**. For example, it's vital that **blood** stays at a pH close to 7.4, so it contains a buffer system.

Ed resolved to use a champoo with a buffer in future.

Practice Questions

Q1 What's a buffer solution? Give two uses of buffer solutions.

Q2 How can a mixture of ethanoic acid and sodium ethanoate act as a buffer?

Q3 Describe how to make a basic buffer.

Exam Questions

Q1 A buffer solution contains 0.40 mol dm^{-3} propanoic acid, CH_3CH_2COOH, and 0.20 mol dm^{-3} sodium propanoate, $CH_3CH_2COO^- Na^+$. At 25 °C, K_a for propanoic acid is 1.3×10^{-5} mol dm^{-3}.

   a) Calculate the pH of the buffer solution.   [3 marks]

   b) Explain the effect on the buffer of adding a small quantity of dilute sulfuric acid.   [2 marks]

Q2 A buffer was prepared by mixing solutions of butanoic acid, $CH_3(CH_2)_2COOH$, and sodium butanoate, $CH_3(CH_2)_2COO^- Na^+$, so that they had the same concentration.

   a) Write a chemical equation to show butanoic acid acting as a weak acid.   [1 mark]

   b) Given that K_a for butanoic acid is 1.5×10^{-5} mol dm^{-3}, calculate the pH of the buffer solution.   [3 marks]

Old buffers are often resistant to change...

So that's how buffers work. There's a pleasing simplicity and neatness about it that I find rather elegant. Like a fine glass of red wine with a nose of berry and undertones of raspberries, oak and... OK, I'll shut up now.

UNIT 1: SECTION 9 — ACIDS, BASES AND pH

Period 3 Elements and Oxides

Period 3's the third row down on the periodic table — the one that starts with sodium and ends with argon.

Sodium is More Reactive Than Magnesium

1) **Sodium** and **magnesium** are the first two elements in **Period 3**. Sodium is in **Group 1**, and magnesium is in **Group 2**. When they react, sodium **loses one electron** to form an **Na⁺** ion, while **magnesium loses two electrons** to form **Mg²⁺**.

2) Sodium is **more reactive** than **magnesium** because it takes **less energy** to lose **one electron** than to lose two. So **more energy** (usually **heat**) is needed for magnesium to react. This is shown in their reactions with **water**.

Sodium will react **vigorously** with **cold water**, forming a molten ball on the surface, fizzing and producing H_2 gas. This reaction produces **sodium hydroxide**, so it creates a strongly **alkaline** solution (pH 12 – 14).

$$2Na_{(s)} + 2H_2O_{(l)} \rightarrow 2NaOH_{(aq)} + H_{2(g)}$$

Magnesium reacts **very slowly** with **cold water**. It forms a **weakly alkaline** solution (pH 9 – 10) and a thin coating of magnesium hydroxide forms on the surface of the metal. The solution is only weakly alkaline because magnesium hydroxide is **not very soluble** in water, so relatively **few hydroxide ions** are produced.

$$Mg_{(s)} + 2H_2O_{(l)} \rightarrow Mg(OH)_{2(aq)} + H_{2(g)}$$

Magnesium reacts much faster with **steam** (i.e. when there is **more energy**), to form **magnesium oxide**.

$$Mg_{(s)} + H_2O_{(g)} \rightarrow MgO_{(s)} + H_{2(g)}$$

Most Period 3 Elements React Readily With Oxygen

Period 3 elements form **oxides** when they react with **oxygen**. They're usually oxidised to their **highest** oxidation states — the same as their **group numbers**. Sulfur is the exception to this — it forms **SO₂**, in which it's only got a **+4** oxidation state (a **high temperature** and a **catalyst** are needed to make **SO₃**, where sulfur has an oxidation state of +6).

The equations are all **really similar** — element + oxygen → oxide:

$$2Na_{(s)} + \tfrac{1}{2}O_{2(g)} \rightarrow Na_2O_{(s)} \quad \text{sodium oxide}$$
$$2Al_{(s)} + 1\tfrac{1}{2}O_{2(g)} \rightarrow Al_2O_{3(s)} \quad \text{aluminium oxide}$$
$$P_{4(s)} + 5O_{2(g)} \rightarrow P_4O_{10(s)} \quad \text{phosphorus(V) oxide}$$

$$Mg_{(s)} + \tfrac{1}{2}O_{2(g)} \rightarrow MgO_{(s)} \quad \text{magnesium oxide}$$
$$Si_{(s)} + O_{2(g)} \rightarrow SiO_{2(s)} \quad \text{silicon dioxide}$$
$$S_{(s)} + O_{2(g)} \rightarrow SO_{2(g)} \quad \text{sulfur dioxide}$$

SO₂ reacts with oxygen and a vanadium catalyst to form SO₃ (see p.58).

The **more reactive metals** (Na, Mg) and the **non-metals** (P, S) react **readily** in air, while **Al** and **Si** react **slowly**.

Element	Na	Mg	Al	Si	P	S
Formula of oxide	Na_2O	MgO	Al_2O_3	SiO_2	P_4O_{10}	SO_2
Reaction of element in air	Vigorous	Vigorous	Slow (faster if powdered)	Slow	Spontaneously combusts	Burns steadily

Bonding and Structure Affect Melting Points

1) **Na₂O, MgO** and **Al₂O₃** are metal oxides. They have **high melting points** because they form **giant ionic lattices**. The **strong forces of attraction** between each ion mean it takes a lot of heat energy to **break the bonds** and melt them.

2) MgO has a **higher melting point** than Na₂O because Mg forms **2+ ions**, so bonds more strongly than the 1+ Na ions in Na₂O.

3) Al₂O₃ has a **lower melting point** than you might expect because the highly charged Al³⁺ ions distort the oxygen's electron cloud making the bonds **partially covalent**.

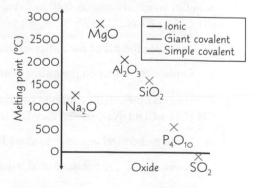

4) **SiO₂** has a **higher melting point** than the other non-metal oxides because it has a **giant macromolecular** structure. In order to melt, the strong covalent bonds between atoms need to be broken, and this requires a lot of energy.

5) **P₄O₁₀** and **SO₂** have relatively **low melting points** because they form **simple molecular** structures. The molecules are bound by **weak intermolecular forces** (dipole-dipole and van der Waals), which take little energy to break.

Period 3 Elements and Oxides

Ionic Oxides are Alkaline, Covalent Oxides are Acidic

1) The **ionic oxides** of the **metals** Na and Mg both contain oxide ions (O^{2-}). When they dissolve in water, the O^{2-} ions accept protons from the water molecules to form hydroxide ions. The solutions are both **alkaline**, but **sodium hydroxide** is more soluble in water, so it forms a **more alkaline** solution than magnesium hydroxide.

$$Na_2O_{(s)} + H_2O_{(l)} \rightarrow 2NaOH_{(aq)} \quad \textbf{pH 12 - 14} \qquad MgO_{(s)} + H_2O_{(l)} \rightarrow Mg(OH)_{2(aq)} \quad \textbf{pH 9 - 10}$$

2) The **simple covalent oxides** of the **non-metals** phosphorus and sulfur form **acidic** solutions. All of the acids are **strong** and so the pH of their solutions is about **0 – 2** (for solutions with a concentration of at least 1 mol dm^{-3}). They will **dissociate** (split up into ions) in solution, forming hydrogen ions and a negative ion (sometimes called a **conjugate base**).

$$P_4O_{10(s)} + 6H_2O_{(l)} \rightarrow 4H_3PO_{4(aq)} \qquad \text{phosphoric(V) acid} \qquad H_3PO_{4(aq)} \rightarrow 3H^+_{(aq)} + PO_4^{3-}_{(aq)}$$
$$SO_{2(g)} + H_2O_{(l)} \rightarrow H_2SO_{3(aq)} \qquad \text{sulfurous acid (or sulfuric(IV) acid)} \qquad H_2SO_{3(aq)} \rightarrow 2H^+_{(aq)} + SO_3^{2-}_{(aq)}$$
$$SO_{3(l)} + H_2O_{(l)} \rightarrow H_2SO_{4(aq)} \qquad \text{sulfuric(VI)acid} \qquad H_2SO_{4(aq)} \rightarrow 2H^+_{(aq)} + SO_4^{2-}_{(aq)}$$

3) The **giant covalent structure** of **silicon dioxide** means that it is **insoluble** in water. However, it will **react with bases** to form salts so it is classed as **acidic**.

4) **Aluminium oxide**, which is partially **ionic** and partially **covalently** bonded, is also **insoluble** in water. But, it will react with **acids and bases** to form salts — i.e. it can act as an acid or a base, so it's classed as **amphoteric**.

Acid + Base → Salt + Water

The equation for **neutralising** an **acid** with a **base** is a classic (**acid + base → salt + water**) and it's no different for the Period 3 oxides. You may be asked to **write equations** for these reactions, so here are some examples:

1) Basic oxides neutralise acids:

$$Na_2O_{(s)} + 2HCl_{(aq)} \rightarrow 2NaCl_{(aq)} + H_2O_{(l)}$$
$$MgO_{(s)} + H_2SO_{4(aq)} \rightarrow MgSO_{4(aq)} + H_2O_{(l)}$$

2) Acidic oxides neutralise bases:

$$SiO_{2(s)} + 2NaOH_{(aq)} \rightarrow Na_2SiO_{3(aq)} + H_2O_{(l)}$$
$$P_4O_{10(s)} + 12NaOH_{(aq)} \rightarrow 4Na_3PO_{4(aq)} + 6H_2O_{(l)}$$
$$SO_{2(g)} + 2NaOH_{(aq)} \rightarrow Na_2SO_{3(aq)} + H_2O_{(l)}$$
$$SO_{3(g)} + 2NaOH_{(aq)} \rightarrow Na_2SO_{4(aq)} + H_2O_{(l)}$$

3) Amphoteric oxides neutralise acids and bases:

$$Al_2O_{3(s)} + 3H_2SO_{4(aq)} \rightarrow Al_2(SO_4)_{3(aq)} + 3H_2O_{(l)}$$
$$Al_2O_{3(s)} + 2NaOH_{(aq)} + 3H_2O_{(l)} \rightarrow 2NaAl(OH)_{4(aq)}$$

An ironic ox-side?

Practice Questions

Q1 Why is Na more reactive than Mg with water?

Q2 What type of bonding is in the following oxides: a) Na_2O,   b) P_4O_{10}.

Q3 Write an equation for the reaction of Na_2O with water.

Q4 Explain why MgO forms a less alkaline solution than Na_2O.

Exam Question

Q1 X and Y are oxides of Period 3 elements. The element in X has an oxidation state of +6 and X forms an acidic solution in water. The element in Y has an oxidation state of +1 and Y has a high melting point.

    a) Identify compound X and write an equation for its reaction with water.   [2 marks]

    b) i) Identify compound Y and write an equation for its reaction with water.   [2 marks]

         ii) Explain why compound Y has a high melting point.   [2 marks]

These pages have got more trends than a school disco...

Hang on a minute, I hear you cry — what about chlorine and argon? Aren't they in Period 3 too? Well, yes, they are, but you don't need to know about them. Argon's a noble gas, anyway, so it doesn't really react with anything... yawn.

Transition Metals — The Basics

This section's all about transition metals — and there's a lot of it. It's obviously important stuff in the Chemistry world.

Transition Elements are Found in the d-Block

The **d-block** is the block of elements in the middle of the periodic table. Most of the elements in the d-block are **transition elements** (or transition metals).

You mainly need to know about the ones in the first row of the d-block. These are the elements from **titanium to copper**.

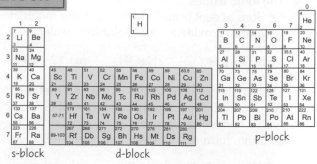

Transition Metals Have Partially Filled d Sub-levels in their Atoms or Ions

Here's the definition of a transition metal:

> A **transition metal** is a metal that can form **one or more stable ions** with a **partially filled d sub-level**.

A d-orbital can contain **up to 10** electrons. So transition metals must form **at least one ion** that has **between 1 and 9 electrons** in the d-orbital. All the Period 4 d-block elements are transition metals apart from **scandium** and **zinc**. Here are their electron configurations:

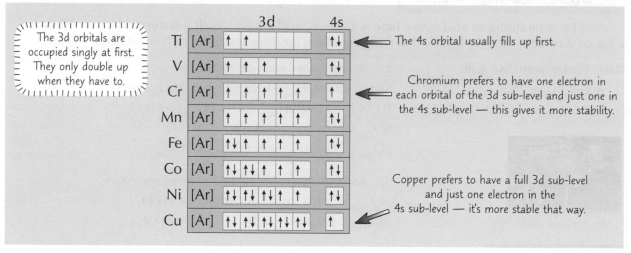

It's the **incomplete** d sub-level that causes the **special chemical properties** of transition metals on the next page.

Sc and Zn Aren't Transition Metals

1) **Scandium** only forms one ion, Sc^{3+}, which has an **empty d sub-level**. Scandium has the electron configuration $[Ar]3d^1 4s^2$, so when it loses three electrons to form Sc^{3+}, it ends up with the electron configuration [Ar].

2) **Zinc** only forms one ion, Zn^{2+}, which has a **full d sub-level**. Zinc has the electron configuration $[Ar]3d^{10} 4s^2$. When it forms Zn^{2+} it loses 2 electrons, both from the 4s sub-level. This means it keeps its full 3d sub-level.

When Ions are Formed, the s Electrons are Removed First

Transition metal atoms form **positive** ions. When this happens, the **s electrons** are removed **first**, **then** the d electrons.

> **Example:** Iron forms both Fe^{2+} and Fe^{3+} ions. What are the electron configurations of these ions?

When iron forms 2+ ions, it loses **both its 4s electrons**. $Fe = [Ar]3d^6 4s^2 \rightarrow Fe^{2+} = [Ar]3d^6$

Only once the 4s electrons are removed can a **3d electron** be removed. E.g. $Fe^{2+} = [Ar]3d^6 \rightarrow Fe^{3+} = [Ar]3d^5$

Transition Metals — The Basics

The Transition Metals All Have Similar Physical Properties

The transition elements don't gradually change across the periodic table like you might expect.
They're all typical metals and have **similar physical properties**:

> 1) They all have a **high density**.
> 2) They all have **high melting** and **high boiling points**.
> 3) Their **ionic radii** are more or less the same.

Transition Metals Have Special Chemical Properties

1) They can form **complex ions** — see pages 46-49. E.g. iron forms a **complex ion with water** — $[Fe(H_2O)_6]^{2+}$.

2) They form **coloured ions** — see pages 50-51. E.g. Fe^{2+} ions are **pale green** and Fe^{3+} ions are **yellow**.

3) They're **good catalysts** — see pages 58-59. E.g. iron is the catalyst used in the **Haber process**.

4) They can exist in **variable oxidation states** — see pages 54-55.
   E.g. iron can exist in the **+2** oxidation state as Fe^{2+} ions and in the **+3** oxidation state as Fe^{3+} ions.

Some common **coloured** ions and **oxidation states** are shown below. The colours refer to the **aqueous ions**.

oxidation state	+7	+6	+5	+4	+3	+2
			VO_2^+ (yellow)	VO^{2+} (blue)	V^{3+} (green)	V^{2+} (violet)
		$Cr_2O_7^{2-}$ (orange)			Cr^{3+} (green/violet)	
	MnO_4^- (purple)					Mn^{2+} (pale pink)
					Fe^{3+} (yellow)	Fe^{2+} (pale green)
						Co^{2+} (pink)
						Ni^{2+} (green)
						Cu^{2+} (blue)

> When Cr^{3+} ions are surrounded by 6 water ligands (see page 60) they're violet. But the water ligands are often substituted (see page 52), so this solution usually looks green instead.

These elements show **variable** oxidation states because the **energy levels** of the 4s and the 3d sub-levels are **very close** to one another. So different numbers of electrons can be gained or lost using fairly **similar** amounts of energy.

Practice Questions

Q1 What is the definition of a transition metal?

Q2 Give the electron arrangement of: a) a vanadium atom, b) a V^{2+} ion.

Q3 State four chemical properties which are characteristic of transition elements.

Exam Question

Q1 When solid copper(I) sulfate is added to water, a blue solution forms with a red-brown precipitate of copper metal.

a) Give the electron configuration of copper(I) ions. [1 mark]

b) Does the formation of copper(I) ions show copper acting as a transition metal? Explain your answer. [2 marks]

c) Identify the blue solution. [1 mark]

s electrons — like rats leaving a sinking ship...

Definitely have a quick read of your Year 1 notes on electron configurations if it's been pushed to a little corner of your mind labelled, "Well, I won't be needing that again in a hurry". It should come flooding back pretty quickly. This page is just an overview of the properties of transition metals. They're all covered in lots more detail in the coming pages...

Complex Ions

Transition metals are always forming complex ions. These aren't as complicated as they sound, though. Honest.

Complex Ions are Metal Ions Surrounded by Ligands

> A **complex** is a central **metal atom** or **ion** surrounded by **co-ordinately bonded ligands**.

1) A **co-ordinate bond** (or dative covalent bond) is a covalent bond in which **both electrons** in the shared pair come from the **same atom**. In a complex, they come from the **ligands**.

2) So, a **ligand** is an atom, ion or molecule that **donates a pair of electrons** to a central **transition metal ion** to form a **co-ordinate bond**.

3) The **co-ordination number** is the **number** of **co-ordinate bonds** that are formed with the central metal ion.

4) The usual co-ordination numbers are **6** and **4**. If the ligands are **small**, like H_2O or NH_3, **6** can fit around the central metal ion. But if the ligands are **larger**, like Cl^-, **only 4** can fit around the central metal ion.

6 CO-ORDINATE BONDS MEAN AN OCTAHEDRAL SHAPE

Here are a few examples.

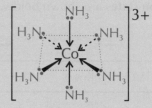

$[Fe(H_2O)_6]^{2+}_{(aq)}$

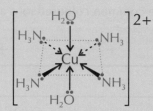

$[Co(NH_3)_6]^{3+}_{(aq)}$

$[Cu(NH_3)_4(H_2O)_2]^{2+}_{(aq)}$

The **bond angles** are all **90°**.

> The ligands don't have to be all the same.

4 CO-ORDINATE BONDS USUALLY MEAN A TETRAHEDRAL SHAPE...

E.g. the $[CuCl_4]^{2-}$ complex, which is yellow, and the $[CoCl_4]^{2-}$ complex ion, which is blue.

The **bond angles** are **109.5°**.

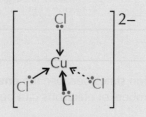

> Make sure you learn the shapes of these complexes.

The Thomson family were proud of their colour co-ordination.

...BUT CAN FORM A SQUARE PLANAR SHAPE

In a **few** complexes, e.g. **cisplatin** (shown on the right), **4 co-ordinate bonds** form a **square planar** shape. The **bond angles** are **90°**.

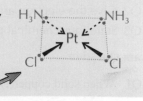

> This compound is called cisplatin. It's used as an anti cancer drug (see page 93).

SOME SILVER COMPLEXES HAVE 2 CO-ORDINATE BONDS AND FORM A LINEAR SHAPE

$[Ag(NH_3)_2]^+$ forms a **linear shape**, as shown. The bond angles are **180°**.

$$[H_3N\!:\!\rightarrow\!Ag\!\leftarrow\!:\!NH_3]^+$$

> $[Ag(NH_3)_2]^+$ is also called Tollens' reagent — have a look at page 66 to see how it's used.

The different types of **bond arrow** used in the examples above show that the complexes are **3D**. The **wedge-shaped arrows** represent bonds coming **towards you** and the **dashed arrows** represent bonds **sticking out behind** the molecule.

Complex Ions

Complex Ions Have an *Overall Charge* or *Total Oxidation State*

The **overall charge** on the complex ion is its **total oxidation state**. It's put **outside** the **square** brackets.
For example:

$[Cu(H_2O)_6]^{2+}_{(aq)}$ ⟵ Overall charge is 2+.

You can work out the **oxidation state of the metal**:

The oxidation state of the metal ion = **the total oxidation state – the sum of the oxidation states of the ligands**

Example: Give the oxidation state of the metal ions in the following complexes:

a) The cobalt ion in $[CoCl_4]^{2-}$.

The total oxidation state is **–2** and each Cl^- ligand has an oxidation state of **–1**.
So in this complex, cobalt's oxidation state = $-2 - (4 \times -1) = +2$.

b) The chromium ion in $[CrCl_2(H_2O)_4]^+$.

The total oxidation state is **+1**. Each Cl^- ligand has an oxidation state of **–1**,
and each H_2O ligand has an oxidation state of **0**.
So in this complex, cobalt's oxidation state = $+1 - (2 \times -1) - (4 \times 0) = +3$.

Practice Questions

Q1 What is meant by the term 'complex ion'?
Q2 Describe how a ligand, such as ammonia, bonds to a central metal ion.
Q3 Draw the shape of the complex ion $[Co(NH_3)_6]^{3+}$. Name the shape.
Q4 What is the size of the bond angles in an octahedral complex?

Exam Questions

Q1 a) Using $[Ag(NH_3)_2]^+$ as an example, explain what is meant by the following terms:

   i) ligand [2 marks]

   ii) co-ordinate bond [2 marks]

   iii) co-ordination number [2 marks]

b) Predict the shape of the complex $[Ag(S_2O_3)_2]^{3-}$. [1 mark]

Q2 When concentrated hydrochloric acid is added to an aqueous solution of $Cu^{2+}_{(aq)}$ a yellow solution is formed.

a) State the co-ordination number and shape of the $Cu^{2+}_{(aq)}$ complex ion in the initial solution. [2 marks]

b) State the co-ordination number, shape and formula
of the complex ion responsible for the yellow solution. [3 marks]

c) What are the bond angles of the complex ion responsible for the yellow solution? [1 mark]

d) Explain why the co-ordination number of the Cu^{2+} complex ion in the yellow solution is different
to the co-ordination number of the Cu^{2+} complex ion in the starting aqueous solution of Cu^{2+}. [2 marks]

Put your hands up — we've got you surrounded...

You never get transition metal ions floating round by themselves in a solution — they'll always be surrounded by other molecules. It's kind of like what'd happen if you put a dish of sweets in a room of eight (or eighteen) year-olds. When you're drawing complex ions, don't forget to include the dashed and wedge-shaped bonds to show that it's 3D.

More on Complex Ions

The complex ions on this page are a bit more complicated than the ones you've seen before, but not much. There's some thinking in 3D coming up, so if it helps, grab some modelling clay and matchsticks and try making some models.

A Ligand Must Have at Least One Lone Pair of Electrons

A ligand must have **at least one lone pair of electrons**, or it won't have anything to use to form a **co-ordinate bond**.

1) Ligands that can only form **one co-ordinate bond** are called **monodentate** — e.g. $H_2\ddot{O}$, $\ddot{N}H_3$, $\ddot{C}l^-$.

2) Ligands that can form **more than one co-ordinate bond** are called **multidentate** — e.g. **EDTA⁴⁻** has six lone pairs (it's **hexadentate** to be precise) so it can form **six co-ordinate bonds** with a metal ion (see below).

3) **Bidentate** ligands are multidentate ligands that can form **two co-ordinate bonds** e.g. ethane-1,2-diamine, $\ddot{N}H_2CH_2CH_2\ddot{N}H_2$, or ethanedioate, $[\ddot{O}OCCO\ddot{O}]^{2-}$. These compounds both have two lone pairs, so can each form **two co-ordinate bonds** with a metal ion.

You'll normally see ethanedioate written as $C_2O_4{}^{2-}$.

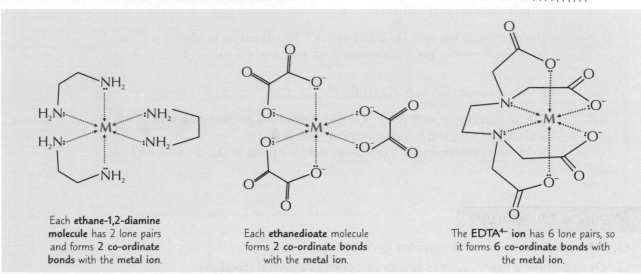

Each **ethane-1,2-diamine** molecule has 2 lone pairs and forms **2 co-ordinate bonds** with the metal ion.

Each **ethanedioate** molecule forms **2 co-ordinate bonds** with the **metal ion**.

The **EDTA⁴⁻ ion** has 6 lone pairs, so it forms **6 co-ordinate bonds** with the **metal ion**.

Haem in Haemoglobin Contains a Multidentate Ligand

1) **Haemoglobin** is a protein found in **blood** that helps to **transport oxygen** around the body.

2) **Haemoglobin** contains Fe^{2+} ions, which are **hexa-coordinated** — **six lone pairs** are donated to them to form **six co-ordinate bonds** in an **octahedral** structure.

3) Four of the co-ordinate bonds come from a single **multidentate ligand**. Four **nitrogen atoms** from the **same** molecule co-ordinate around Fe^{2+} to form a **circle**. This part of the molecule is called **haem**.

4) The other two co-ordinate bonds come from a protein called **globin**, and either an **oxygen** or a **water** molecule — so the complex can **transport oxygen** to where it's needed, and then swap it for a water molecule — here's **how it works**:

- In the lungs, where the oxygen concentration is high, an **oxygen molecule** substitutes the water ligand and bonds co-ordinately to the Fe(II) ion to form **oxyhaemoglobin**, which is carried **around the body** in the blood.

- When the **oxyhaemoglobin** gets to a place where oxygen is needed, the **oxygen molecule** is **exchanged** for a **water molecule**. The haemoglobin then **returns to the lungs** and the whole process starts again.

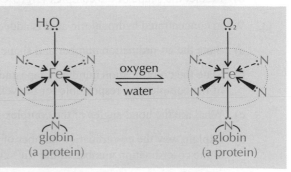

5) This process can be disrupted if **carbon monoxide** is inhaled. The **haemoglobin** swaps its **water** ligand for a **carbon monoxide** ligand, forming **carboxyhaemoglobin**. This is bad news because carbon monoxide is a **strong** ligand and **doesn't** readily exchange with oxygen or water ligands, meaning the haemoglobin **can't transport oxygen** any more. **Carbon monoxide poisoning** starves the organs of oxygen — it can cause **headaches**, **dizziness**, **unconsciousness** and even **death** if it's not treated.

More on Complex Ions

Complex Ions Can Show *Optical Isomerism*

1) **Optical isomerism** is a type of **stereoisomerism**.
   (Have a look back at your Year 1 notes if you need a reminder about stereoisomerism.)

2) Complex ions can show **optical isomerism** — where an ion can exist in two forms that are **non-superimposable mirror images**. This happens with octahedral complexes when **three bidentate ligands**, such as ethane-1,2-diamine, $NH_2CH_2CH_2NH_2$, co-ordinately bond with a central metal ion, like **nickel**.

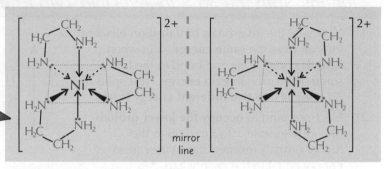

Cis-Trans Isomers Can Form in *Octahedral* and *Square Planar* Complexes

1) Cis-trans isomerism is another type of **stereoisomerism**. In fact, it's a special case of **E/Z isomerism**.

2) **Octahedral** complexes with four monodentate ligands of one type and two monodentate ligands of another type can show **cis-trans isomerism**. If the **two odd** ligands are **opposite** each other, you've got the **trans isomer**. If they're **next** to each other, you've got the **cis isomer**. For example, the complex $[NiCl_2(H_2O)_4]$ has a trans and a cis isomer.

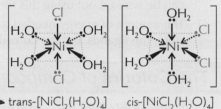
trans-$[NiCl_2(H_2O)_4]$ cis-$[NiCl_2(H_2O)_4]$

3) **Square planar** complex ions that have **two pairs** of ligands also show cis-trans isomerism. When two paired ligands are **opposite** each other it's the **trans isomer** and when they're **next** to each other it's the **cis isomer**.

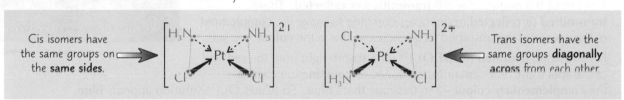
Cis isomers have the same groups on the **same sides**.
Trans isomers have the same groups **diagonally across** from each other.

4) The molecule in the example above, is a complex of platinum(II) with two chloride ions and two ammonia molecules in a square planar shape. The **cis isomer** (cisplatin) is used as an anti-cancer drug (see page 93).

Practice Questions

Q1 Give an example of a monodentate ligand.
Q2 How many co-ordinate bonds can the ion $EDTA^{4-}$ form with a metal ion?
Q3 Name two types of stereoisomerism that an octahedral complex could show.

Exam Questions

Q1 Iron(III) can form the complex ion $[Fe(C_2O_4)_3]^{3-}$ with three ethanedioate ions. The ethanedioate ion is a bidentate ligand. Its structure is shown on the right.

a) What is a bidentate ligand? [1 mark]
b) i) Draw the two stereoisomers of $[Fe(C_2O_4)_3]^{3-}$. [2 marks]
   ii) What type of stereoisomerism is this? [1 mark]

Q2 In the body, the chloride ion ligands of cisplatin are replaced by water ligands to form $[Pt(NH_3)_2(H_2O)_2]^{2+}$. Draw this compound, given that it is the cis isomer of a square planar complex. [1 mark]

Iron & EDTA^{4-} used to be together, but now their status is 'it's complicated'...

Phew, whoever called them 'complex' ions really wasn't joking. Make sure you can look at a complex ion and figure out whether or not it will have isomers. Octahedral complexes form optical isomers, and even then only if they're bonded to three bidentate ligands. But both octahedral and square planar complexes can form cis-trans isomers.

Formation of Coloured Ions

Transition metal complex ions have distinctive colours, which is handy when it comes to identifying them.
This page explains why they're so colourful.

Ligands **Split** the 3d Sub-level into **Two Energy Levels**

1) Normally the 3d orbitals of transition element ions **all** have the **same energy**. But when **ligands** come along and bond to the ions, some of the orbitals **gain energy**. This splits the 3d orbitals into **two different energy levels**.

2) Electrons tend to **occupy the lower orbitals** (the ground state). To jump up to the higher orbitals (excited states) they need **energy** equal to the energy gap, ΔE. They get this energy from **visible light**.

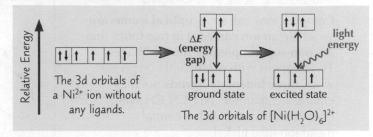

The 3d orbitals of a Ni^{2+} ion without any ligands.

ground state   excited state

The 3d orbitals of $[Ni(H_2O)_6]^{2+}$

3) The energy **absorbed** when electrons jump up from the ground state to an excited state can be worked out using this formula.

$$\Delta E = h\nu = \frac{hc}{\lambda}$$

ν = frequency of light absorbed (hertz/Hz)
h = Planck's constant (6.63×10^{-34} J s)
c = the speed of light (3.00×10^8 m s^{-1})
λ = wavelength of light absorbed (m)

4) The amount of energy needed to make electrons jump depends upon the **central metal ion** and its **oxidation state**, the **ligands** and the **co-ordination number**, as these affect the **size of the energy gap** (ΔE).

The **Colours** of Compounds are the **Complement** of Those That are **Absorbed**

1) When **visible light** hits a transition metal ion, some frequencies are **absorbed** when electrons jump up to the higher orbitals. The frequencies absorbed depend on the size of the **energy gap** (ΔE).

> The larger the energy gap, the higher the frequency of light that is absorbed.

2) The rest of the frequencies are **transmitted** or **reflected**. These **transmitted** or **reflected** frequencies combine to make the **complement** of the colour of the absorbed frequencies — this is the **colour** you see.

frequency increases ⟹

3) For example, **hydrated $[Cu(H_2O)_6]^{2+}$** ions absorb light from the **red** end of the spectrum. The remaining frequencies **combine** to produce the **complementary colour** — in this case that's blue. So $[Cu(H_2O)_6]^{2+}$ solution appears **blue**.

4) If there are **no** 3d electrons or the 3d sub-level is **full**, then no electrons will jump, so **no energy** will be absorbed. If there's no energy absorbed, the compound will look **white** or **colourless**.

Transition Metal Ions can be Identified by their Colour

It'd be nice if each transition metal formed ions or complexes with just one colour, but sadly it's not that simple. The **colour of a complex** can be altered by any of the factors that can affect the size of the **energy gap** (ΔE).

1) **Changes in oxidation state.**

Complex:	$[Fe(H_2O)_6]^{2+}_{(aq)}$	→	$[Fe(H_2O)_6]^{3+}_{(aq)}$		$[V(H_2O)_6]^{2+}_{(aq)}$	→	$[V(H_2O)_6]^{3+}_{(aq)}$
Oxidation state:	+2		+3	and	+2		+3
Colour:	pale green		yellow		violet		green

2) **Changes in co-ordination number** — this always involves a change of ligand too.

Complex:	$[Cu(H_2O)_6]^{2+} + 4Cl^-$	→	$[CuCl_4]^{2-} + 6H_2O$
Co-ordination number:	6		4
Colour:	blue		yellow

3) **Changes in ligand** — this can cause a colour change even if the oxidation state and co-ordination number remain the same.

Complex:	$[Co(H_2O)_6]^{2+} + 6NH_3$	→	$[Co(NH_3)_6]^{2+} + 6H_2O$
Oxidation state:	+2		+2
Colour:	pink		straw coloured

Formation of Coloured Ions

Spectroscopy can be used to Find Concentrations of Transition Metal Ions

Spectroscopy can be used to determine the **concentration of a solution** by measuring how much **light** it **absorbs**.

1) **White light** is shone through a **filter**, which is chosen to **only** let through the **colour of light** that is **absorbed** by the sample.

2) The light passes through the sample to a **colorimeter**, which calculates **how much light** was **absorbed** by the sample.

3) The more **concentrated** a coloured solution is, the more light it will absorb. So you can use this measurement to work out the **concentration** of a solution of transition metal ions.

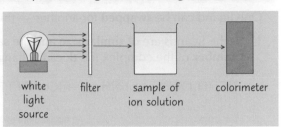

white light source · filter · sample of ion solution · colorimeter

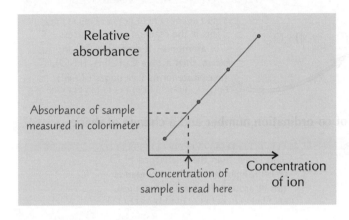

Relative absorbance

Absorbance of sample measured in colorimeter

Concentration of sample is read here

Concentration of ion

Before you can find the unknown concentration of a sample, you have to produce a **calibration curve** — like the lovely one on the left. This involves measuring the **absorbance** of **known concentrations** of solutions and plotting the results on a graph.

Once you've done this, you can measure the absorbance of your sample and read its **concentration** off the graph.

Stanley's concentration was strong — he'd show this cowboy who was boss.

Practice Questions

Q1 Which sub-level is split by the presence of ligands?

Q2 What two factors are changing in the following reaction that will cause a change in colour?

$$[Co(H_2O)_6]^{2+} + 4Cl^- \rightarrow [CoCl_4]^{2-} + 6H_2O$$

Q3 What is the purpose of the filter in spectroscopy?

Q4 What does a colorimeter measure?

Exam Questions

Q1 a) Explain why complex transition metal ions such as $[Fe(H_2O)_6]^{2+}$ are coloured. [1 mark]

    b) State three changes to a complex ion that would result in a change in colour. [3 marks]

Q2 Colorimetry can be used to determine the concentration of a coloured solution. Briefly describe how you would construct a calibration graph, given a coloured solution of known concentration. [3 marks]

Q3 The frequency of light absorbed by a transition metal complex ion can be determined from the equation $\Delta E = h\nu$.

    a) State what is meant by ΔE and what change this represents within the complex ion. [1 mark]

    b) Using a noble gas core, [Ar], complete the electron arrangements for the following ions:

        i) Cu^+ [1 mark]

        ii) Cu^{2+} [1 mark]

    c) Which one of the above ions has coloured compounds? State the feature of its electron arrangement that suggests this. [1 mark]

Blue's not my complementary colour — it clashes with my hair...

Transition metal ions are pretty colours, don't you think? The Romans did — they used iron, copper, cobalt and manganese compounds to add colour to glass objects. I'm not sure that they knew the colours were affected by variable oxidation states, ligands and co-ordination number, but it's pretty impressive even so.

Substitution Reactions

There are more equations on this page than the number of elephants you can fit in a Mini.

Ligands can Change Places with One Another

One ligand can be **swapped** for another — this is **ligand substitution** or **exchange**. It usually causes a **colour change**.

1) If the ligands are of **similar size** and the same **charge**, then the **co-ordination number** of the complex ion doesn't change, and neither does the **shape**.

$$[Co(H_2O)_6]^{2+}{}_{(aq)} + 6NH_{3(aq)} \rightarrow [Co(NH_3)_6]^{2+}{}_{(aq)} + 6H_2O_{(l)}$$

octahedral   octahedral
pink   straw coloured

Water and ammonia are a similar size and are both uncharged, so substitution between these ligands happens easily.

In some cases, the substitution is only partial:

$$[Cu(H_2O)_6]^{2+}{}_{(aq)} + 4NH_{3(aq)} \rightarrow [Cu(NH_3)_4(H_2O)_2]^{2+}{}_{(aq)} + 4H_2O_{(l)}$$

octahedral   octahedral
blue   deep blue

This is the reaction with an excess of ammonia. If ammonia isn't in excess, then a blue $Cu(OH)_2(H_2O)_4$ precipitate forms (see pages 60-61).

2) If the ligands are **different sizes**, there's a **change of co-ordination number** and a **change of shape**.

$$[Co(H_2O)_6]^{2+}{}_{(aq)} + 4Cl^-{}_{(aq)} \rightleftharpoons [CoCl_4]^{2-}{}_{(aq)} + 6H_2O_{(l)}$$

octahedral   tetrahedral
pink   blue

Cl^- is larger than the uncharged H_2O or NH_3 ligands, so only four ligands can fit around the central metal ion.

$$[Cu(H_2O)_6]^{2+}{}_{(aq)} + 4Cl^-{}_{(aq)} \rightleftharpoons [CuCl_4]^{2-}{}_{(aq)} + 6H_2O_{(l)}$$

octahedral   tetrahedral
pale blue   yellow

$$[Fe(H_2O)_6]^{3+}{}_{(aq)} + 4Cl^-{}_{(aq)} \rightleftharpoons [FeCl_4]^-{}_{(aq)} + 6H_2O_{(l)}$$

octahedral   tetrahedral
yellow   yellow

Climbing up was OK, but on the way down
Tess had a sudden loss of co-ordination.

Have a quick look at the reactions on page 61 — these are **ligand exchange reactions** too. In these, **hydroxide precipitates** are formed when a little bit of **sodium hydroxide** or **ammonia solution** is added to metal-aqua ions. The hydroxide precipitates sometimes **dissolves** when excess sodium hydroxide or ammonia solution is added.

Different Ligands Form Different Strength Bonds

Ligand substitution reactions can be easily **reversed**, **UNLESS** the new complex ion is much **more stable** than the old one.

1) If the new ligands form **stronger** bonds with the central metal ion than the old ligands did, the change is **less easy** to reverse. E.g. **CN⁻ ions** form stronger co-ordinate bonds with Fe^{3+} ions than H_2O molecules, so it's hard to reverse this reaction:

$$[Fe(H_2O)_6]^{3+}{}_{(aq)} + 6CN^-{}_{(aq)} \rightarrow [Fe(CN)_6]^{3-}{}_{(aq)} + 6H_2O_{(l)}$$

Another example is carbon monoxide bonding to Fe^{2+} in haemoglobin much more strongly than oxygen does — see page 48 for more on this.

2) **Multidentate** ligands form more stable complexes than monodentate ligands, so a change like the one below is hard to reverse:

$$[Cu(H_2O)_6]^{2+}{}_{(aq)} + 3NH_2CH_2CH_2NH_{2(aq)} \rightarrow [Cu(NH_2CH_2CH_2NH_2)_3]^{2+}{}_{(aq)} + 6H_2O_{(l)}$$

This is a bidentate ligand.

This is explained on the next page...

Substitution Reactions

A *Positive Entropy Change* Makes a *More Stable* Complex

1) When a **ligand exchange reaction** occurs, co-ordinate bonds are **broken** and **formed**. The **strength** of the bonds being broken is often very **similar** to the strength of the new bonds being made. So the **enthalpy change** for a ligand exchange reaction is usually very **small**. For example, the reaction substituting ammonia with ethane-1,2-diamine in a nickel complex has a very **small** enthalpy change of reaction:

$$[Ni(NH_3)_6]^{2+} + 3NH_2CH_2CH_2NH_2 \rightarrow [Ni(NH_2CH_2CH_2NH_2)_3]^{2+} + 6NH_3 \quad \Delta H = -13 \text{ kJ mol}^{-1}$$

    Break 6 co-ordinate bonds   Form 6 co-ordinate bonds
    between Ni and N.   between Ni and N.

2) This is actually a **reversible** reaction, but the equilibrium lies so **far to the right** that it is thought of as being irreversible — $[Ni(NH_2CH_2CH_2NH_2)_3]^{2+}$ is **much more stable** than $[Ni(NH_3)_6]^{2+}$. This isn't accounted for by an enthalpy change.

3) Instead, the **increase in stability**, known as the **chelate effect**, explains why multidentate ligands always form much more stable complexes than monodentate ligands:

> When monodentate ligands are substituted with bidentate or multidentate ligands, the number of particles in solution increases — the more particles, the greater the entropy. Reactions that result in an increase in entropy are more likely to occur.

4) When the **hexadentate ligand EDTA^{4-}** replaces monodentate or bidentate ligands, the complex formed is **a lot more stable**.

$$[Cr(NH_3)_6]^{3+} + EDTA^{4-} \rightarrow [Cr(EDTA)]^- + 6NH_3 \quad 2 \text{ particles} \rightarrow 7 \text{ particles}$$

The enthalpy change for this reaction is almost zero and the entropy change is big and positive. This makes the free energy change ($\Delta G = \Delta H - T\Delta S$) negative, so the reaction is feasible (see page 10).

5) It's difficult to reverse these reactions, because reversing them would cause a **decrease in entropy**.

Practice Questions

Q1 What colour is a solution of the complex ion $[Cu(NH_3)_4(H_2O)_2]^{2+}$?

Q2 When you add hydroxide ions to $[Cu(H_2O)_6]^{2+}$ you get a precipitate of $Cu(OH)_2(H_2O)_4$. Adding extra H_2O does not reverse the reaction. Which ligand bonds more strongly to Cu^{2+}, OH^- or H_2O?

Q3 What is the chelate effect?

Exam Questions

Q1 When a solution of EDTA^{4-} ions is added to an aqueous solution of $[Fe(H_2O)_6]^{3+}$ ions, a ligand substitution reaction occurs.

    a) Write an equation for the reaction that takes place.   **[1 mark]**

    b) The new complex that is formed is more stable than $[Fe(H_2O)_6]^{3+}$. Explain why.   **[1 mark]**

Q2 A scientist takes three samples of a solution that contains the complex ion $[Co(H_2O)_6]^{2+}$. She mixes the first sample with a solution of chloride ions, the second with an excess of ammonia solution, and the third with a solution containing ethane-1,2-diamine. She observes the reactions that occur. Write an equation for a reaction the scientist observed where:

    a) There was no change in the number of ligands surrounding the cobalt ion.   **[1 mark]**

    b) The number of ligands surrounding the cobalt ion changed, but the overall charge on the complex ion did not.   **[1 mark]**

    c) Both the number of ligands surrounding the cobalt ion and the overall charge on the complex ion changed.   **[1 mark]**

Ligand exchange — the musical chairs of the molecular world...

Ligands generally don't mind swapping with other ligands, so long as they're not too tightly attached to the central metal ion. They also won't fancy changing if it means forming fewer molecules and having less entropy. It's kind of like you wouldn't want to swap a cow for a handful of beans. Unless they're magic beans. But that almost never happens...

Variable Oxidation States

One of the reasons why transition metal complexes have such a big range of colours is their variable oxidation states.

Transition Metals Can Exist in **Variable Oxidation States**

You learnt on page 109 that one of the properties of transition metals is that they can exist in variable oxidation states.

When you switch between oxidation states, it's a **redox reaction** — the metal ions are either oxidised or reduced. For example, vanadium can exist in **four oxidation states** in solution — the +2, +3, +4 and +5 states. You can tell them apart by their colours:

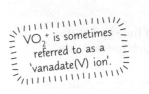

VO_2^+ is sometimes referred to as a 'vanadate(V) ion'.

Oxidation state of vanadium	Formula of ion	Colour of ion
+5	$VO_2^+{}_{(aq)}$	Yellow
+4	$VO^{2+}{}_{(aq)}$	Blue
+3	$V^{3+}{}_{(aq)}$	Green
+2	$V^{2+}{}_{(aq)}$	Violet

Vanadium(V) ions can be reduced by adding them to **zinc metal** in an **acidic solution**. Here are the equations for each of the reduction reactions:

1) To begin with, the solution turns from **yellow** to **blue** as vanadium(V) is reduced to vanadium(IV):

$$2VO_2^+{}_{(aq)} + Zn_{(s)} + 4H^+{}_{(aq)} \rightarrow 2VO^{2+}{}_{(aq)} + Zn^{2+}{}_{(aq)} + 2H_2O_{(l)}$$

2) The solution then changes colour from **blue** to **green** as vanadium(IV) is reduced to vanadium(III):

$$2VO^{2+}{}_{(aq)} + Zn_{(s)} + 4H^+{}_{(aq)} \rightarrow 2V^{3+}{}_{(aq)} + Zn^{2+}{}_{(aq)} + 2H_2O_{(l)}$$

3) Finally, vanadium(III) is reduced to vanadium(II), and so the solution changes from **green** to **violet**.

$$2V^{3+}{}_{(aq)} + Zn_{(s)} \rightarrow 2V^{2+}{}_{(aq)} + Zn^{2+}{}_{(aq)}$$

VO_2^+ VO^{2+} V^{3+} V^{2+}

*Redox Potentials Tell You How **Easy** it is to **Reduce** an Ion*

1) The **redox potential** of an ion or atom tells you how easily it is **reduced** to a lower oxidation state. They're the same as electrode potentials (see page 24).

2) The **larger** the redox potential, the **less stable** the ion will be, and so the **more likely** it is to be **reduced**. For example, in the table on the right, copper(II) has a redox potential of +0.15 V, so is less stable and more likely to be reduced than chromium(III) which has a redox potential of –0.41 V.

Half equation	Standard electrode potential (V)
$Cr^{3+}{}_{(aq)} + e^- \rightleftharpoons Cr^{2+}{}_{(aq)}$	–0.41
$Cu^{2+}{}_{(aq)} + e^- \rightleftharpoons Cu^+{}_{(aq)}$	+0.15

3) The redox potentials in the table are **standard electrode potentials** — they've been measured with the reactants at a concentration of 1 mol dm^3 against a standard hydrogen electrode under standard conditions (see page 25).

4) The redox potential of an ion won't always be the same as its standard electrode potential. It can **vary** depending on the environment that the ion is in. For example:

- **Ligands:** Standard electrode potentials are measured in **aqueous solution**, so any aqueous ions will be surrounded by **water ligands**. Different **ligands** may make the redox potential larger or smaller depending on how well they bind to the metal ion in a particular oxidation state.

- **pH:** Some ions need **H$^+$** ions to be present in order to be reduced, e.g. $2VO_2^+{}_{(aq)} + 4H^+{}_{(aq)} + 2e^- \rightleftharpoons 2VO^{2+}{}_{(aq)} + 2H_2O_{(l)}$
  Others **release OH$^-$** ions into solution when they are reduced, e.g. $CrO_4^{2-}{}_{(aq)} + 4H_2O_{(l)} + 3e^- \rightleftharpoons Cr(OH)_{3(s)} + 5OH^-{}_{(aq)}$

  For reactions such as these, the **pH** of the solution affects the size of the redox potential. In general, redox potentials will be **larger** in more **acidic** solutions, making the ion more easily reduced.

Variable Oxidation States

Tollens' Reagent Contains a Silver Complex

Silver is a transition metal that is most commonly found in the
+1 oxidation state (Ag^+). It is easily **reduced** to **silver metal**:

$$Ag^+_{(aq)} + e^- \rightarrow Ag_{(s)} \qquad \text{Standard electrode potential} = +0.80\,V$$

The standard electrode potential is large, so Ag^+ is easily reduced.

Tollens' reagent uses this reduction reaction to distinguish between **aldehydes** and **ketones**.
It's prepared by adding just enough ammonia solution to silver nitrate solution
to form a colourless solution containing the complex ion $[Ag(NH_3)_2]^+$.

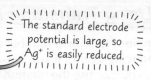

Steve had a serious silver complex.

When added to **aldehydes**, Tollens' reagent reacts to give a **silver mirror** on the inside of the
test tube. The aldehyde is **oxidised** to a **carboxylic acid**, and the Ag^+ ions are **reduced** to silver metal:

$$RCHO_{(aq)} + 2[Ag(NH_3)_2]^+_{(aq)} + 3OH^-_{(aq)} \rightarrow RCOO^-_{(aq)} + 2Ag_{(s)} + 4NH_{3(aq)} + 2H_2O_{(l)}$$

Tollens' reagent can't oxidise **ketones**, so it **won't react** with them, and no silver mirror will form.

Practice Questions

Q1 What colour changes are seen when zinc powder is added to an acidic solution of vanadium(V) ions?

Q2 What does the size of the redox potential tell you about a transition metal ion?

Q3 Name two things that can influence the size of the redox potential for a transition metal ion.

Q4 What would you observe if you were to react Tollens' reagent with an aldehyde?

Exam Questions

Q1 Tollens' reagent contains a transition metal complex ion.

   a) i)   What is the formula of the complex ion in Tollens' reagent?   **[1 mark]**

       ii)   What is the oxidation state of the transition metal ion in Tollens' reagent?   **[1 mark]**

   b) Explain, using an appropriate equation, how Tollens' reagent can be used
to distinguish between an aldehyde and a ketone.   **[3 marks]**

Q2 The vanadate(V) ion, VO_2^+, can be reduced to vanadium(II), V^{2+}.
The reduction occurs in three steps, which can be observed as the yellow vanadium(V)
solution first turns blue, then green and finally violet as a solution of V^{2+} ions is formed.

   a) What are the reagent(s) and conditions needed to carry out this reaction?   **[2 marks]**

   b) Identify the ions responsible for the blue and green solutions.   **[2 marks]**

   c) Write reactions to show the three steps in the reduction of vanadium(V) to vanadium(II).   **[3 marks]**

Q3 Which of the following statements about redox potentials is **not** correct?

   A The redox potential of a transition metal ion tells you how easily
it is transformed from a higher to a lower oxidation state.

   B The larger the redox potential of a transition metal ion, the more stable it is.

   C The ligands that co-ordinate to a transition metal ion can affect its redox potential.

   D Changing the pH will change the redox potential of the following half equation:
$$MnO_4^-{}_{(aq)} + 2H_2O_{(l)} + 3e^- \rightleftharpoons MnO_{2(s)} + 4OH^-_{(aq)}$$
    [1 mark]

My brother often puts me in the +6 or +8 aggravation state...

*This topic wasn't too bad — a few equations, some pretty colours and a nifty test to distinguish aldehydes from ketones.
Have another look at the reduction reactions of vanadium. Now write them down. And write them down again. Now
sing them to the tune of 'Dancing Queen'. And if you get bored of that, just sing 'Dancing Queen', or maybe 'Waterloo'.*

Titrations with Transition Metals

These titrations are redox titrations. They're similar to acid-base titrations, but they're not exactly the same.

Titrations Using **Transition Element Ions** are **Redox** Titrations

You can use titrations to let you find out how much **oxidising agent** is needed to **exactly** react with a quantity of **reducing agent**. If you know the **concentration** of either the oxidising agent or the reducing agent, you can use the titration results to work out the concentration of the other.

Transition metals have **variable oxidation states** which means they are often present in either the oxidising or the reducing agent. Their **colour changes** also make them useful in titrations as it's easy to spot the **end point**.

1) First you measure out a quantity of **reducing agent** (e.g. aqueous Fe^{2+} ions or aqueous $C_2O_4^{2-}$ ions) using a pipette, and put it in a conical flask.

2) Using a **measuring cylinder**, you add about **20 cm³** of **dilute sulfuric acid** to the flask — this is an excess, so you don't have to be too exact.

3) Now you add the **oxidising agent** to the reducing agent using a **burette**, **swirling** the conical flask as you do so.

4) The **oxidising agent** that you add reacts with the reducing agent. This reaction will continue until **all** of the reducing agent is used up. The **very next drop** you add to the flask will give the mixture the **colour of the oxidising agent**. (You could use a coloured reducing agent and a colourless oxidising agent instead — then you'd be watching for the moment that the colour in the flask disappears.)

5) Stop when the mixture in the flask **just** becomes tainted with the colour of the oxidising agent (the **end point**) and record the volume of the oxidising agent added. This is the **rough titration**.

6) Now you do some **accurate titrations**. You need to do a few until you get **two or more** readings that are **within 0.10 cm³** of each other.

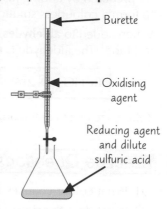

Burette

Oxidising agent

Reducing agent and dilute sulfuric acid

You can also do titrations the other way round — adding the reducing agent to the oxidising agent.

The main **oxidising agent** used is **aqueous potassium manganate(VII)**, which contains **purple** manganate(VII) ions. **Strong acidic** conditions are needed for the manganate(VII) ions to be reduced:

$$MnO_4^-{}_{(aq)} + 8H^+{}_{(aq)} + 5e^-{}_{(aq)} \rightarrow Mn^{2+}{}_{(aq)} + 4H_2O_{(l)}$$

Use the **Titration Results** to **Calculate** the **Concentration** of a Reagent...

Example: 27.5 cm³ of 0.0200 mol dm⁻³ aqueous potassium manganate(VII) reacted with 25.0 cm³ of acidified sodium ethanedioate solution. Calculate the concentration of $C_2O_4^{2-}$ ions in the solution.

$$2MnO_4^-{}_{(aq)} + 16H^+{}_{(aq)} + 5C_2O_4^{2-}{}_{(aq)} \rightarrow 2Mn^{2+}{}_{(aq)} + 8H_2O_{(l)} + 10CO_{2(g)}$$

$C_2O_4^{2-}$ ions are called ethanedioate or oxalate ions.

1) Work out the number of **moles of MnO_4^- ions** added to the flask.

Number of moles MnO_4^- added $= \dfrac{\text{concentration} \times \text{volume (cm}^3)}{1000} = \dfrac{0.0200 \times 27.5}{1000} = 5.50 \times 10^{-4}$ moles

2) Look at the balanced equation to find how many moles of $C_2O_4^{2-}$ react with **every mole** of MnO_4^-. Then you can work out the **number of moles of $C_2O_4^{2-}$** in the flask.

5 moles of $C_2O_4^{2-}$ react with 2 moles of MnO_4^-.

So moles of $C_2O_4^{2-} = (5.50 \times 10^{-4} \times 5) \div 2 = 1.38 \times 10^{-3}$ moles

3) Work out the **number of moles of $C_2O_4^{2-}$** that would be in 1000 cm³ (1 dm³) of solution — this is the **concentration**.

25.0 cm³ of solution contained 1.38×10^{-3} moles of $C_2O_4^{2-}$.

1000 cm³ of solution would contain $\dfrac{(1.38 \times 10^{-3}) \times 1000}{25.0} = 0.552$ moles of $C_2O_4^{2-}$

So the concentration of $C_2O_4^{2-}$ is **0.552 mol dm⁻³**.

Titrations with Transition Metals

...Or the Volume of a Reagent

Example: Aqueous potassium manganate(VII) with a concentration of 0.00800 mol dm^{-3} was used to completely oxidise 25.0 cm^3 of 0.0600 mol dm^{-3} acidified iron(II) sulfate solution. Calculate the volume of potassium manganate(VII) solution used.

$$MnO_4^{-}{}_{(aq)} + 8H^+{}_{(aq)} + 5Fe^{2+}{}_{(aq)} \rightarrow Mn^{2+}{}_{(aq)} + 4H_2O_{(l)} + 5Fe^{3+}{}_{(aq)}$$

1) Work out the number of **moles of Fe^{2+} ions** in the flask to begin with.

Number of moles Fe^{2+} = $\dfrac{\text{concentration} \times \text{volume (cm}^3)}{1000} = \dfrac{0.0600 \times 25.0}{1000} = 1.50 \times 10^{-3}$ moles

2) Look at the balanced equation to find how many moles of **Fe^{2+}** react with **every mole** of MnO$_4^{-}$. Then you can work out the **number of moles of MnO$_4^{-}$** needed.

5 moles of Fe^{2+} react with 1 mole of MnO$_4^{-}$.
So moles of MnO$_4^{-}$ = $1.50 \times 10^{-3} \div 5 = 3.00 \times 10^{-4}$ moles

3) Rearrange the formula above to find the **volume of 0.00800 mol dm^{-3} potassium manganate(VII) solution** that contains **3.00 × 10^{-4} moles of MnO$_4^{-}$**.

Volume of MnO$_4^{-}$ = $\dfrac{\text{number of moles} \times 1000}{\text{concentration}} = \dfrac{(3.00 \times 10^{-4}) \times 1000}{0.00800} =$ **37.5 cm^3**

Manganate 007, licensed to oxidise.

Practice Questions

Q1 Outline how you would carry out a titration of Fe^{2+} with MnO$_4^{-}$ in acid solution.

Q2 What colour marks the end point of a redox titration when potassium manganate(VII) is added from the burette?

Q3 Why is an excess of acid added to potassium manganate(VII) titrations?

Exam Questions

Q1 0.100 g of a sample of steel containing carbon and iron only was dissolved in sulfuric acid.
The resulting solution was titrated using 29.4 cm^3 of 0.0100 mol dm^{-3} potassium manganate(VII) solution.
The equation for the reaction is   MnO$_4^{-}$ + 5Fe^{2+} + 8H$^+$ → Mn^{2+} + 5Fe^{3+} + 4H$_2$O

    a) Calculate the number of moles of manganate ions present in the titre
       of potassium manganate(VII) solution.   [1 mark]

    b) Calculate the number of moles of Fe^{2+} that will have reacted with the manganate(VII) ions.   [1 mark]

    c) Calculate the mass of iron in the steel.   [1 mark]

    d) Calculate the percentage of iron in the steel.   [1 mark]

Q2 A sample of sodium ethanedioate is dissolved in dilute sulfuric acid.
The solution is titrated using 18.3 cm^3 of 0.0200 mol dm^{-3} potassium manganate(VII).
The equation for the reaction is: 2MnO$_4^{-}$ + 5C$_2$O$_4^{2-}$ + 16H$^+$ → 2Mn^{2+} + 10CO$_2$ + 8H$_2$O
Calculate the mass of Na$_2$C$_2$O$_4$ in the initial sample.   [4 marks]

Q3 A 0.100 mol dm^{-3} solution of iron(II) sulfate has been partly oxidised by the air to an iron(III) compound.
Explain how you could use a standard solution of potassium manganate(VII) to find the actual
concentration of Fe^{2+} remaining.   [4 marks]

And how many moles does it take to change a light bulb...

The example calculations on these two pages might look rather complicated, but if you break them down into a series of steps, they're really not that bad — especially as you've done titration calculations before. You know, the ones with acids and bases? Back on pages 38-39? What do you mean you don't remember? Go back and have another look.

Catalysts

Transition metals aren't just good — they're grrrreat.

Transition Metal Catalysts Work by Changing Oxidation States

Transition metals and their compounds make good catalysts because they can **change oxidation states** by gaining or losing electrons within their **d orbitals**. This means they can **transfer electrons** to **speed up** reactions.

For example, in the **Contact Process**, vanadium(V) oxide is able to **oxidise SO_2 to SO_3** because it can be **reduced** to vanadium(IV) oxide. It's then **oxidised** back to vanadium(V) oxide by oxygen ready to start all over again.

This example uses a heterogeneous catalyst (see below), but the principle also applies to homogeneous catalysts.

Vanadium oxidises SO_2 to SO_3 and is reduced itself.

$$V_2O_5 + SO_2 \rightarrow V_2O_4 + SO_3$$
vanadium(V) → vanadium(IV)

The reduced catalyst is then oxidised by oxygen gas back to its original state.

$$V_2O_4 + \tfrac{1}{2}O_2 \rightarrow V_2O_5$$
vanadium(IV) → vanadium(V)

Make sure you learn these equations showing how the V_2O_5 catalyst works.

Heterogeneous Catalysts are in a Different Phase From the Reactants

1) A heterogeneous catalyst is one that is in a **different phase** from the reactants — i.e. in a different **physical state**. For example, in the Haber Process (see below) **gases** are passed over a **solid iron catalyst**.

2) The **reaction** happens on active sites located on the **surface** of the **heterogeneous catalyst**. So, **increasing** the **surface area** of the catalyst increases the number of molecules that can **react** at the same time, **increasing the rate** of the reaction.

3) **Support mediums** are often used to make the **area** of a catalyst **as large as possible**. They help to **minimise** the **cost** of the reaction, because only a **small coating** of catalyst is needed to provide a large surface area.

You need to know these examples of **heterogeneous catalysts**:

1) **Iron** in the **Haber Process** for making **ammonia**: $N_{2(g)} + 3H_{2(g)} \xrightarrow{Fe_{(s)}} 2NH_{3(g)}$

2) **Vanadium(V) oxide** in the **Contact Process** for making **sulfuric acid**: $SO_{2(g)} + \tfrac{1}{2}O_{2(g)} \xrightarrow{V_2O_{5(s)}} SO_{3(g)}$

SO_3 is then reacted with water to produce sulfuric acid.

Impurities Can Poison Heterogeneous Catalysts

1) Heterogeneous catalysts often work by **adsorbing** reactants onto **active sites** located on their surfaces.

2) **Impurities** in the reaction mixture may also **bind** to the catalyst's surface and **block** **reactants** from being adsorbed. This process is called **catalyst poisoning**.

3) Catalyst poisoning **reduces the surface area** of the catalyst available to the reactants, **slowing down the reaction**.

4) Catalyst poisoning **increases the cost** of a chemical process because **less product** can be made in a certain **time** or with a certain amount of **energy**. The **catalyst** may even need **replacing or regenerating**, which costs money.

Sulfur poisons the iron catalyst in the Haber Process:
The **hydrogen** in the Haber process is produced from **methane**. The methane is obtained from natural gas, which contains impurities, including **sulfur** compounds. Any sulfur that is not removed is **adsorbed** onto the iron, forming iron sulfide, and stopping the iron from catalysing the reaction efficiently.

Homogeneous Catalysts are in the Same Phase as the Reactants

1) **Homogeneous catalysts** are in the **same physical state** as the reactants. Usually a **homogeneous** catalyst is an **aqueous catalyst** for a reaction between two **aqueous solutions**.

2) Homogeneous catalysts work by combining with the reactants to form an **intermediate species** which then reacts to form the **products** and **re-form the catalyst**.

3) The enthalpy profile for a **homogeneously catalysed** reaction has **two humps** in it, corresponding to the two steps in the reaction.

4) The activation energy needed to form the **intermediates** (and to form the products from the intermediates) is **lower** than that needed to make the products directly from the reactants.

5) The catalyst always **re-forms**, so it can carry on catalysing the reaction.

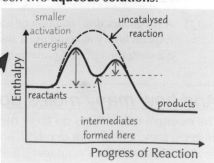

UNIT 2: SECTION 4 — TRANSITION METALS

Catalysts

Fe²⁺ Catalyses the Reaction Between $S_2O_8^{2-}$ and I^-

The **redox** reaction between iodide ions and peroxodisulfate ($S_2O_8^{2-}$) ions takes place **annoyingly slowly** because both ions are **negatively charged**. The ions **repel** each other, so it's unlikely they'll **collide** and **react**.

$$S_2O_8^{2-}{}_{(aq)} + 2I^-{}_{(aq)} \rightarrow I_{2(aq)} + 2SO_4^{2-}{}_{(aq)}$$

The negative charges of the two ions is one reason why this reaction has high activation energy.

But if **Fe²⁺ ions** are added, things really **speed up** because each stage of the reaction involves a **positive and a negative ion**, so there's **no repulsion**.

1) First, the Fe²⁺ ions are **oxidised** to Fe³⁺ ions by the $S_2O_8^{2-}$ ions.

$$S_2O_8^{2-}{}_{(aq)} + 2Fe^{2+}{}_{(aq)} \rightarrow 2Fe^{3+}{}_{(aq)} + 2SO_4^{2-}{}_{(aq)}$$

2) The newly formed intermediate Fe³⁺ ions now **easily oxidise** the I⁻ ions to iodine, and the **catalyst is regenerated**.

$$2Fe^{3+}{}_{(aq)} + 2I^-{}_{(aq)} \rightarrow I_{2(aq)} + 2Fe^{2+}{}_{(aq)}$$

The Fe²⁺ is a homogeneous catalyst — it's in the same phase as the reactants.

You can test for **iodine** by adding **starch solution** — it'll turn **blue-black** if iodine is present.

Autocatalysis is when a Product Catalyses the Reaction

Another example of a **homogeneous catalyst** is Mn²⁺ in the reaction between $C_2O_4^{2-}$ and MnO_4^-. It's an **autocatalysis reaction** because Mn²⁺ is a **product** of the reaction and **acts as a catalyst** for the reaction. This means that as the reaction progresses and the **amount** of the **product increases**, the reaction **speeds up**.

The reactant ions are both negatively charged so repel each other and cause the rate of the uncatalysed reaction to be very slow.

$$2MnO_4^-{}_{(aq)} + 16H^+{}_{(aq)} + 5C_2O_4^{2-}{}_{(aq)} \rightarrow 2Mn^{2+}{}_{(aq)} + 8H_2O_{(l)} + 10CO_{2(g)}$$

1) Mn²⁺ catalyses the reaction by first reacting with MnO_4^- to form **Mn³⁺** ions:

$$MnO_4^-{}_{(aq)} + 4Mn^{2+}{}_{(aq)} + 8H^+{}_{(aq)} \rightarrow 5Mn^{3+}{}_{(aq)} + 4H_2O_{(l)}$$

2) The newly formed **Mn³⁺** ions then react with $C_2O_4^{2-}$ ions to form carbon dioxide and **re-form** the Mn²⁺ catalyst ions:

$$2Mn^{3+}{}_{(aq)} + C_2O_4^{2-}{}_{(aq)} \rightarrow 2Mn^{2+}{}_{(aq)} + 2CO_{2(g)}$$

Practice Questions

Q1 What property of transition elements makes them good catalysts?

Q2 What's the difference between a homogeneous and a heterogeneous catalyst?

Q3 Why is the rate of the uncatalysed reaction between iodide and peroxodisulfate ions so slow?

Q4 What term describes the process when a product catalyses a reaction?

Exam Questions

Q1 a) Using equations, explain how vanadium(V) oxide acts as a catalyst in the Contact Process. [2 marks]

   b) i) Describe how heterogeneous catalysts can become poisoned and give an example. [2 marks]

     ii) Give two consequences of catalytic poisoning. [2 marks]

Q2 A student is measuring the rate of the reaction between MnO_4^- ions and $C_2O_4^{2-}$ over time. She predicts that the rate will decrease with time, but discovers instead that the rate of reaction over the first five minutes increases. Explain the student's results with use of appropriate equations. [5 marks]

What do you call an enthalpy profile diagram with no humps? Humphrey...

Hopefully you'll have realised from these two pages that transition metals are really useful. You should also know the difference between heterogeneous and homogeneous catalysts and some equations for how transition metals can catalyse certain reactions. If you do, then grab yourself a cup of tea— it speeds up the rate of revision, you know.

Metal-Aqua Ions

Metal-aqua ions are just complex ions where all of the ligands are water molecules. Pretty simple really.
Unlike their reactions, which are just a tiny bit complicated. Sorry about that...

Metal Ions Become **Hydrated** in Water

When **transition metal compounds** dissolve in water, the water molecules form **co-ordinate bonds** with the **metal ions**. This forms **metal-aqua complex ions**. In general, **six water molecules** form co-ordinate bonds with each metal ion.

The water molecules do this by donating a **non-bonding pair of electrons** from their oxygen.

The diagrams show the metal-aqua ions formed by **iron(II)**, $[Fe(H_2O)_6]^{2+}$, and by **aluminium(III)**, $[Al(H_2O)_6]^{3+}$.

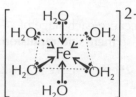
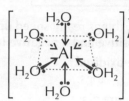

Water molecules are neutral so the overall charge of the complex is the same as the charge on the metal ion.

Solutions Containing **Metal-Aqua Ions** are **Acidic**

In a solution containing metal-aqua **2+** ions, there's a reaction between the metal-aqua ion and the water — this is a **hydrolysis** or **acidity reaction**.
E.g.

$$Cu(H_2O)_6{}^{2+}{}_{(aq)} + H_2O_{(l)} \rightleftharpoons [Cu(OH)(H_2O)_5]^+{}_{(aq)} + H_3O^+{}_{(aq)}$$

The metal-aqua **2+** ions release H^+ ions, so an **acidic** solution is formed. There's only **slight** dissociation though, so the solution is only **weakly acidic**.

Metal-aqua **3+** ions react in the same way. They dissociate **more** than 2+ ions, and so form **more acidic** solutions.
E.g.

$$Fe(H_2O)_6{}^{3+}{}_{(aq)} + H_2O_{(l)} \rightleftharpoons [Fe(OH)(H_2O)_5]^{2+}{}_{(aq)} + H_3O^+{}_{(aq)}$$

Aqua-ironing —
it keeps those
flat fish smooth.

Here's why 3+ metal-aqua ions form more acidic solutions than 2+ metal-aqua ions:

Metal 3+ ions are pretty **small** but have a **big charge** — so they've got a **high charge density** (otherwise known as **charge/size ratio**). The metal 2+ ions have a **much lower** charge density.

This makes the 3+ ions much more **polarising** than the 2+ ions. More polarising power means that they attract **electrons** from the oxygen atoms of the co-ordinated water molecules more strongly, weakening the O–H bond.

So it's more likely that a **hydrogen ion** will be released. And more hydrogen ions means a **more acidic** solution.

You Can **Hydrolyse** Metal-Aqua Ions **Further** to **Form Precipitates**

Adding **OH⁻ ions** to solutions of **metal-aqua ions** produces **insoluble metal hydroxides**. Here's why:

1) In water, **metal-aqua 3+ ions** such as Fe^{3+} or Al^{3+} form the equilibrium:

   $$M(H_2O)_6{}^{3+}{}_{(aq)} + H_2O_{(l)} \rightleftharpoons [M(OH)(H_2O)_5]^{2+}{}_{(aq)} + H_3O^+{}_{(aq)}$$

   If you add **OH⁻ ions** to the equilibrium, H_3O^+ ions are removed — this shifts the equilibrium to the **right**.

2) Now another equilibrium is set up in the solution:

   $$[M(OH)(H_2O)_5]^{2+}{}_{(aq)} + H_2O_{(l)} \rightleftharpoons [M(OH)_2(H_2O)_4]^+{}_{(aq)} + H_3O^+{}_{(aq)}$$

   Again the OH⁻ ions remove H_3O^+ ions from the solution, pulling the equilibrium to the right.

3) This happens one last time — now you're left with an **insoluble**, **uncharged metal hydroxide**:

   $$[M(OH)_2(H_2O)_4]^+{}_{(aq)} + H_2O_{(l)} \rightleftharpoons M(OH)_3(H_2O)_{3(s)} + H_3O^+{}_{(aq)}$$

4) The same thing happens with **metal-aqua 2+ ions** (e.g. Fe^{2+} or Cu^{2+}), except this time there are only **two** steps:

$$M(H_2O)_6{}^{2+}{}_{(aq)} + H_2O_{(l)} \rightleftharpoons [M(OH)(H_2O)_5]^+{}_{(aq)} + H_3O^+{}_{(aq)}$$

$$[M(OH)(H_2O)_5]^+{}_{(aq)} + H_2O_{(l)} \rightleftharpoons M(OH)_2(H_2O)_{4(s)} + H_3O^+{}_{(aq)}$$

There are only two steps this time because only two of the water ligands need to be deprotonated to make the +2 complex uncharged (and so insoluble).

Metal-Aqua Ions

Metal Hydroxides That Can Act as an *Acid OR* a *Base* are *Amphoteric*

1) You saw on the last page that if you hydrolyse a metal-aqua ion in a base then you form an insoluble **metal hydroxide precipitate**.

2) **All** these metal hydroxide precipitates **will dissolve in acid**. They act as Brønsted-Lowry bases and **accept H⁺ ions**. This **reverses** the hydrolysis reactions.

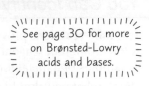
See page 30 for more on Brønsted-Lowry acids and bases.

3) Some metal hydroxides are **amphoteric** — they can act as both acids and bases. This means they'll **dissolve in an excess of base** as well as in **acids**.

4) **Aluminium hydroxide** is **amphoteric**. In the presence of a **base**, e.g. NaOH, it acts as a **Brønsted-Lowry acid** and **donates H⁺ ions** to the OH⁻ ions, forming a **soluble compound**. It also acts as a **Brønsted-Lowry base** in the presence of an **acid** and **accepts H⁺** ions from the H_3O^+ ions in solution.

$$[Al(H_2O)_6]^{3+}_{(aq)} + 3H_2O_{(aq)} \xleftarrow{\ +3H_3O^+_{(aq)}\ }_{\text{With acid}} Al(OH)_3(H_2O)_{3(s)} \xrightarrow{\ +OH^-_{(aq)}\ }_{\text{With base}} [Al(OH)_4(H_2O)_2]^-_{(aq)} + H_2O_{(l)}$$

Precipitates Form with *Ammonia Solution*...

1) The obvious way of adding hydroxide ions is to use a strong alkali, like **sodium hydroxide solution** — but you can use **ammonia solution** too. When ammonia dissolves in water this equilibrium occurs: $NH_{3(aq)} + H_2O_{(l)} \rightleftharpoons NH_4^+{}_{(aq)} + OH^-{}_{(aq)}$

2) Because hydroxide ions are formed, adding a **small** amount of ammonia solution gives the same results as sodium hydroxide.

3) In some cases, such as with $Cu(OH)_2(H_2O)_4$, a further reaction happens if you add **excess** ammonia solution — the H_2O and OH⁻ ligands are **displaced** by NH_3 ligands. This forms a **charged complex** which is **soluble** in water, so the precipitate dissolves.

$$Cu(OH)_2(H_2O)_{4(s)} + 4NH_{3(aq)} \rightleftharpoons [Cu(NH_3)_4(H_2O)_2]^{2+}_{(aq)} + 2OH^-_{(aq)} + 2H_2O_{(l)}$$

...and *Sodium Carbonate* Too

Metal 2+ ions react with **sodium carbonate** to form **insoluble metal carbonates**, like this:

$$[M(H_2O)_6]^{2+}_{(aq)} + CO_3^{2-}_{(aq)} \rightleftharpoons MCO_{3(s)} + 6H_2O_{(l)}$$

But metal 3+ ions are **stronger acids** so there is a **higher concentration** of H_3O^+ ions in solution. Rather than displacing water from the metal ions, the carbonate ions react with H_3O^+, removing them from the solution and shifting the equilibria of the reactions on the previous page to the right. So the precipitate that forms is $M(OH)_3(H_2O)_3$ rather than $M_2(CO_3)_3$.

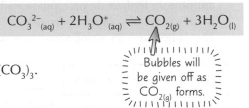
$$CO_3^{2-}_{(aq)} + 2H_3O^+_{(aq)} \rightleftharpoons CO_{2(g)} + 3H_2O_{(l)}$$

Bubbles will be given off as $CO_{2(g)}$ forms.

Practice Questions

Q1 Explain why 3+ metal-aqua ions form more acidic solutions than 2+ metal-aqua ions.

Q2 Write an equation to show what happens if you add an excess of ammonia to $Cu(OH)_2(H_2O)_{4(s)}$.

Q3 Show by equations how $Al(OH)_3$ can act as both a Brønsted-Lowry acid and a Brønsted-Lowry base.

Exam Questions

Q1 Why do separate solutions of iron(II) sulfate and iron(III) sulfate have different pH values? [2 marks]

Q2 a) Write an ionic equation to show the formation of the precipitate when sodium carbonate is added to aqueous iron(II) sulfate. [1 mark]

b) Explain how sodium carbonate reacts with aqueous iron(III) chloride to form a precipitate. Include equations in your answer. [2 marks]

I get grumpy when it rains — it's a precipitation reaction...

Quite a few more reactions to learn here, I'm afraid. Remember that the precipitates of these reactions will always be neutral compounds, and the soluble compounds will be charged. So if you know a precipitate forms but you can't remember the formula of the product, then it's a case of balancing out the charges until the compound is neutral.

More on Metal-Aqua Ions

It's true — learning about the reactions of metal-aqua ions is probably less exciting than reading the dictionary from cover to cover. Fortunately, you'll get to try them out for yourself in practical experiments. Oooo... pretty colours.

You Can Identify Metal Ions Using **Test Tube Reactions**

Test tube reactions provide a qualitative way of working out the identity of unknown metal ions in solution. Adding different reagents, such as sodium hydroxide solution, ammonia solution and sodium carbonate solution, to samples of a metal ion solution and recording what you see should help you identify what metal ion is present. Here's what you should do:

1) Measure out samples of the unknown metal ion solution into **three separate test tubes**.

2) To the first test tube, add **sodium hydroxide solution dropwise**, using a dropping pipette, and record any changes you see. Then add more NaOH dropwise so that it is in **excess**. Record any changes.

3) To the second test tube, add **ammonia solution** dropwise, using a dropping pipette, and record any changes you see. Keep adding ammonia so that it's in **excess**. Record any changes.

4) To the third test tube, add **sodium carbonate solution** dropwise. Record your observations.

   Some of the solutions may irritate your skin and eyes, so make sure you wear gloves, a lab coat and goggles. Ammonia is very smelly and can make you cough if you breathe it in, so it's best to use it in a fume hood.

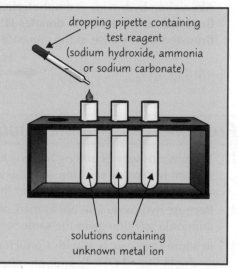

dropping pipette containing test reagent (sodium hydroxide, ammonia or sodium carbonate)

solutions containing unknown metal ion

On pages 60-61, you learnt about some of the reactions of copper(II), iron(II), iron(III) and aluminium(III) aqua ions. If you had four unknown solutions, each of which contained one of these metal aqua ions, you could use the method above and the **differences** in their reactivities to distinguish between them. Here's how:

Reactions with sodium hydroxide

All four metal aqua ions will form precipitates with sodium hydroxide, but only the **aluminium hydroxide** precipitate will **dissolve** in an **excess** of sodium hydroxide. This is because it's **amphoteric** (see page 61).

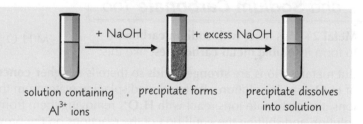

solution containing Al^{3+} ions — + NaOH → precipitate forms — + excess NaOH → precipitate dissolves into solution

Reactions with ammonia

All four metal aqua ions will form precipitates with ammonia, but only the **copper hydroxide** precipitate will **dissolve** in an **excess** of ammonia. This is because it undergoes a **ligand exchange** reaction with excess ammonia (see page 61).

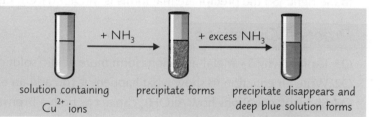

solution containing Cu^{2+} ions — + NH$_3$ → precipitate forms — + excess NH$_3$ → precipitate disappears and deep blue solution forms

Reactions with sodium carbonate

All four metal aqua ions will form precipitates with sodium carbonate. The solutions containing Al^{3+} or Fe^{3+} will also form **bubbles** as CO$_2$ formed (see page 61). So if you're not sure whether a sample contains Fe^{2+} or Fe^{3+} ions, (which behave identically in the other two tests), you can use this test to decide — a sample containing Fe^{3+} ions will give off a **gas**, but a sample containing Fe^{2+} ions **won't**.

The solutions should be freshly made — if Fe^{2+} ions are left too long in contact with air they will oxidise to Fe^{3+} ions.

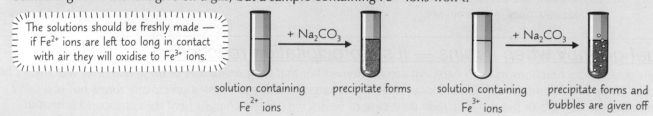

solution containing Fe^{2+} ions — + Na$_2$CO$_3$ → precipitate forms — solution containing Fe^{3+} ions — + Na$_2$CO$_3$ → precipitate forms and bubbles are given off

More on Metal-Aqua Ions

Learn the **Colours** of All the **Complex Ion Solutions** and **Precipitates**

This handy table summarises all the compounds that are formed in the reactions on these pages.
You need to know the **formulae** of all the complex ions, and their **colours**.

Metal-aqua ion	With $OH^-_{(aq)}$ or $NH_{3(aq)}$	With excess $OH^-_{(aq)}$	With excess $NH_{3(aq)}$	With $Na_2CO_{3(aq)}$
$[Cu(H_2O)_6]^{2+}$ blue solution	$Cu(OH)_2(H_2O)_4$ blue precipitate	no change	$[Cu(NH_3)_4(H_2O)_2]^{2+}$ deep blue solution	$CuCO_3$ green-blue precipitate
$[Fe(H_2O)_6]^{2+}$ green solution	$Fe(OH)_2(H_2O)_4$ green precipitate	no change	no change	$FeCO_3$ green precipitate
$[Al(H_2O)_6]^{3+}$ colourless solution	$Al(OH)_3(H_2O)_3$ white precipitate	$[Al(OH)_4(H_2O)_2]^-$ colourless solution	no change	$Al(OH)_3(H_2O)_3$ white precipitate
$[Fe(H_2O)_6]^{3+}$ yellow solution	$Fe(OH)_3(H_2O)_3$ brown precipitate	no change	no change	$Fe(OH)_3(H_2O)_3$ brown precipitate

Practice Questions

Q1 Outline an experiment you could carry out to distinguish between four unknown solutions which each contain either copper(II), iron(II), iron(III) or aluminium(III) ions.

Q2 Name any hazards associated with the experiment in Question 1. How would you minimise these hazards?

Q3 What differences would you observe if you were to add sodium carbonate solution to a solution containing iron(II) ions and to a solution containing iron(III) ions?

Q4 What colour solution is formed when you add excess ammonia to a solution containing $[Cu(H_2O)_6]^{2+}$ ions?

Exam Questions

Q1 Describe what you would see when ammonia solution is added slowly to a solution containing copper(II) sulfate until it is in excess. Write an equation for each reaction that occurs. [4 marks]

Q2 Aqueous sodium hydroxide was added to an aqueous solution of aluminium(III) chloride.

a) Identify the aluminium complex ion present in:

i) the aqueous aluminium(III) chloride. [1 mark]

ii) the white precipitate initially formed when aqueous sodium hydroxide is added. [1 mark]

iii) the colourless solution when an excess of aqueous sodium hydroxide is added. [1 mark]

b) Write an equation for the reaction in which the colourless solution is formed from the white precipitate. [1 mark]

Q3 a) Describe what you would observe when aqueous sodium carbonate is added to:

i) aqueous iron(III) chloride. [1 mark]

ii) freshly-prepared aqueous iron(II) sulfate. [1 mark]

b) Write an equation for the reaction of the iron(II)-aqua ion with the carbonate ion. [1 mark]

c) If iron(II) sulfate solution is left to stand overnight in an open beaker before the aqueous sodium carbonate is added, then a different reaction is observed.

i) Describe the new observation. [1 mark]

ii) Explain this change. [1 mark]

Test-tube reactions — proper Chemistry at last...

So many pretty colours. It's like walking into an exploded paint factory. Or my little sister's room when she's been doing arts and crafts. The only downside is that now you have to remember them all. You also need to know the reactions that make them. It's important that you learn them all, or come exam day you'll end up feeling blue. Or possibly green-blue...

Optical Isomerism

Optical isomerism isn't something your optician and a pair of glasses can sort — though you may well be cross-eyed after looking at these two pages of mirrors and molecules.

Optical Isomers are Mirror Images of Each Other

1) **Optical isomerism** is a type of stereoisomerism.
Stereoisomers have the **same structural formula**, but have their atoms arranged differently in **space**.

2) A **chiral** (or **asymmetric**) carbon atom is one that has **four different groups** attached to it.
It's possible to arrange the groups in two different ways around the carbon atom so that two different molecules are made — these molecules are called **enantiomers** or **optical isomers**.

3) The enantiomers are **mirror images** and no matter which way you turn them, they can't be **superimposed**.

4) You have to be able to **draw** optical isomers.
But first you have to identify the chiral centre...

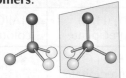

'Superimposed' means that you can put one thing on top of another and they will match up completely.

If molecules can be superimposed, they're achiral — and there's no optical isomerism.

1) **Locating the chiral centre:**
Look for the carbon atom with **four different groups** attached. Here it's the carbon with the four groups H, OH, COOH and CH₃ attached.

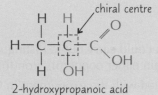

chiral centre

2-hydroxypropanoic acid

2) **Drawing isomers:**
Once you know the **chiral carbon**, draw one enantiomer in a **tetrahedral shape**. Don't try to draw the full structure of each group — it gets confusing. Then draw a **mirror image** beside it.

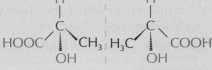

enantiomers of 2-hydroxypropanoic acid

Optical Isomers Rotate Plane-Polarised Light

1) Normal light vibrates in all directions. **Plane-polarised light** only vibrates in one direction.

2) Optical isomers are **optically active** — they **rotate plane-polarised light**.

3) One enantiomer rotates it in a **clockwise** direction, and the other rotates it in an **anticlockwise** direction.

Christmas is a time to embrace your choral centre.

A Racemate is a Mixture of Enantiomers

A **racemate** (or **racemic mixture**) contains **equal quantities** of each enantiomer of an optically active compound.

Racemates **don't** show any optical activity — the two enantiomers **cancel** each other's light-rotating effect.
Chemists often react two **achiral** things together and get a **racemic** mixture of a **chiral** product.
This is because when two molecules react there's an **equal chance** of forming each of the enantiomers.

Look at the reaction between butane and chlorine:

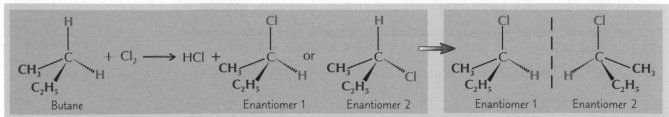

Butane + Cl₂ ⟶ HCl + Enantiomer 1 or Enantiomer 2 ⟶ Enantiomer 1 Enantiomer 2

A **chlorine atom** replaces one of the **H** atoms, to give **2-chlorobutane**.
Either of the H atoms can be replaced, so the reaction produces a **mixture** of the **two possible enantiomers**.
Each hydrogen has a **fifty-fifty chance** of being replaced, so the two optical isomers are formed in **equal amounts**.

You can modify a reaction to produce a **single enantiomer** using chemical methods, but it's **difficult** and **expensive**.

Optical Isomerism

Reactions Involving Planar Bonds often Produce Racemates

Double bonds, such as C=O and C=C bonds, are **planar** (flat). The products of reactions that happen at the carbonyl group of **aldehydes** and **unsymmetrical ketones** are often **enantiomers** present as a **racemic mixture**:

Example: The reaction of propanal (C_3H_6O) with acidified potassium cyanide (KCN).

1) The reaction of propanal with potassium cyanide involves a CN^- ion attacking the δ^+ carbon of propanal's planar C=O group.

2) The CN^- ion can attack from **two directions** — from **above** the plane of the molecule, or from **below** it.

3) Depending on which direction the nucleophilic attack happens from, one of two **enantiomers** is formed.

4) Because the C=O bond is **planar**, there is an **equal chance** that the nucleophile will attack from either of these directions. This means that an **equal amount** of each enantiomer will be formed.

5) So when propanal reacts with acidified potassium cyanide, you get a **racemic mixture** of products.

This reaction is covered in more detail on page 67.

If you start with a **symmetrical ketone** instead, you'll make a product that **doesn't** have a chiral centre, so it **won't** display optical isomerism.

Practice Questions

Q1 What's a chiral molecule?

Q2 The displayed formula of 2-methylbutan-1-al is shown on the right. Explain why the carbon atom marked with a * is a chiral centre.

Q3 What's a racemic mixture?

Exam Questions

Q1 There are sixteen possible structural isomers of the compound $C_3H_6O_2$, four of which show stereoisomerism.

   a) Explain the meaning of the term stereoisomerism. [2 marks]

   b) i) There are two chiral isomers of $C_3H_6O_2$. Draw the enantiomers of one of the chiral isomers. [2 marks]

   ii) State how you could distinguish between the enantiomers. [2 marks]

Q2 Parkinson's disease involves a deficiency of dopamine. It is treated by giving patients a single pure enantiomer of DOPA (dihydroxyphenylalanine), as shown on the right, a naturally occurring amino acid, which is converted to dopamine in the brain.

   a) DOPA is a chiral molecule. Mark the structure's chiral centre. [1 mark]

   b) DOPA was first synthesised as a racemate in 1911. Explain the meaning of the term racemate. [1 mark]

Q3 Pentanal reacts with potassium cyanide to produce an optically inactive product.

   a) Explain why the product of the reaction is optically inactive. [4 marks]

   b) Predict whether the reaction of pentan-3-one would produce an optically active product. Explain your answer. [2 marks]

Some quiet time for reflection...

This isomer stuff's not bad — well, not all bad... If you're having difficulty picturing them as 3D shapes, you could always make some models of them. It's easier to see the mirror image structure with a solid version in front of you.

Aldehydes and Ketones

You've already met aldehydes and ketones but it may have been a while ago, so here's a quick recap and then some more, meaty organic chemistry to learn. It's just the gift that never stops giving, isn't it?

Aldehydes and Ketones contain a Carbonyl Group

Aldehydes and ketones are both **carbonyl compounds** so they both contain the **carbonyl** functional group, **C=O**. The difference is, they've got their carbonyl groups in **different positions**.

Aldehydes have their carbonyl group at the **end** of the carbon chain. Their names end in **-al**.

R = carbon chain   methanal   propanal

Ketones have their carbonyl group in the middle of the carbon chain. Their names end in **-one**, and often have a number to show which **carbon** the carbonyl group is on.

propanone   pentan-2-one

Aldehydes can be Easily Oxidised but Ketones Can't

Oxidising agents will react with **aldehydes** to produce carboxylic acids, but not with **ketones**.

aldehyde   R—C + [O] ⟶ R—C   carboxylic acid   ketone   R—C + [O] ⟶ **✗**   nothing happens

As an aldehyde is oxidised, another compound is **reduced**. You can use compounds that change colour when they're reduced as a test for whether something could be an **aldehyde** or a **ketone**.

Tollens' reagent is a **colourless** solution of **silver nitrate** dissolved in **aqueous ammonia**.
- When heated in a test tube with an **aldehyde**, the Ag+ ions in Tollens' reagent are reduced to Ag atoms and a **silver mirror** forms after a few minutes.
- Ketones can't be oxidised by Tollens' reagent, so with ketones there's no reaction and no colour change.

Fehling's solution is a **blue** solution of **copper(II) ions** dissolved in **sodium hydroxide**.
- If it's heated with an **aldehyde** the copper(II) ions are reduced to a **brick-red precipitate** of **copper(I) oxide**.
- As with Tollens' reagent, ketones don't react with Fehling's solution, so no precipitate is formed.

You can Reduce Aldehydes and Ketones Back to Alcohols

You've already seen how **primary alcohols** can be **oxidised** to produce **aldehydes** and **carboxylic acids**, and how **secondary alcohols** can be **oxidised** to make **ketones**. Using a **reducing agent**, you can **reverse** these reactions. **NaBH$_4$** (sodium tetrahydridoborate(III) or sodium borohydride) dissolved in **water with methanol** is usually the reducing agent used. But in equations, **[H]** is often used to indicate a hydrogen from a reducing agent.

1) Reducing an **aldehyde** to a **primary alcohol**.

R—C + 2[H] ⟶ R—CH$_2$—OH

2) Reducing a **ketone** to a **secondary alcohol**.

R—C + 2[H] ⟶ R—C—OH

The reaction mechanism for ketones is the same as for aldehydes.

Here's the reaction mechanism: (It's shown with an aldehyde here, but the mechanism works just the same for a ketone.)

The H– ions come from the reducing agent.

The H+ ions usually come from water. Sometimes a weak acid is added as a source of H+.

These are **nucleophilic addition** reactions. The H– ion acts as a **nucleophile** and **adds** on to the δ+ carbon atom.

Aldehydes and Ketones

Potassium Cyanide will React with Carbonyls by Nucleophilic Addition

Potassium cyanide reacts with carbonyl compounds to produce **hydroxynitriles** (molecules with a CN and an OH group). It's a **nucleophilic addition reaction** — a **nucleophile** attacks the molecule, and **adds** itself as an extra group.

Potassium cyanide dissociates in water to form K^+ ions and CN^- ions: $KCN \rightarrow K^+ + CN^-$

1) The CN^- group **attacks** the partially positive carbon atom and **donates** a pair of electrons. Both electrons from the double bond transfer to the oxygen.

2) H^+ ions add to the oxygen to form the **hydroxyl group (OH)**. Acidified KCN is usually used so there's a source of H^+ ions.

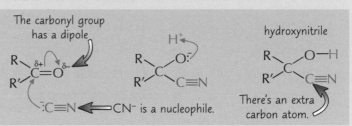

3) The overall reaction for an **aldehyde** is: $RCHO_{(aq)} + KCN_{(aq)} \xrightarrow{H^+_{(aq)}} RCH(OH)CN_{(aq)} + K^+_{(aq)}$

And for a **ketone**: $RCOR'_{(aq)} + KCN_{(aq)} \xrightarrow{H^+_{(aq)}} RCR'(OH)CN_{(aq)} + K^+_{(aq)}$

4) If you start with an **unsymmetrical ketone** or any **aldehyde** (except methanal), you will produce a mixture of **enantiomers** (see page 64).

Hydrogen cyanide (HCN) reacts with carbonyls in the same way, except you don't need the acid. Just swap KCN for HCN and drop the K^+ ion. E.g.: $RCHO + HCN \rightarrow RCH(OH)CN$

Potassium Cyanide is a Dangerous Chemical to Work With

Here's a risk assessment for reacting potassium cyanide with a carbonyl (as above): **Potassium cyanide** is an **irritant** and is also extremely dangerous if it's **ingested** (eaten) or **inhaled**. It can react with moisture to produce **hydrogen cyanide**, a highly **toxic gas**. To **reduce** any **risks**, any person carrying out this experiment should **wear gloves**, **safety goggles** and a **lab coat** and perform the experiment in a **fume cupboard**.

A risk assessment (see page 106) involves assessing the hazards that a reaction poses. You need to take all reasonable precautions to reduce the risk of an accident.

Practice Questions

Q1 What's the difference between the structures of aldehydes and ketones?

Q2 Explain why the reduction of an aldehyde or a ketone is a nucleophilic addition reaction.

Exam Questions

Q1 The compound C_3H_6O can exist as an aldehyde and a ketone.

a) Draw and name the carbonyl isomers of C_3H_6O. [4 marks]

b) Hydrogen cyanide, HCN, reacts with C_3H_6O carbonyl compounds to form a compound with the molecular formula C_4H_6ON.

 i) Name the type of mechanism that this reaction proceeds by. [1 mark]

 ii) Draw the mechanism for the reaction of hydrogen cyanide with the ketone with the molecular formula C_3H_6O. [5 marks]

c) The aldehyde C_3H_6O can be reduced to an alcohol, C_3H_7OH. Write an equation for the reaction, listing suitable reagents and conditions. [3 marks]

Q2 There are two straight-chain carbonyl compounds with the molecular formula C_4H_8O.

a) Name the two compounds. [2 marks]

b) Describe a test that could distinguish between the isomers and give the expected result for each. [3 marks]

Before I begin baking, I always carry out a whisk assessment...

Make sure you know how aldehydes differ from ketones and what you get when you oxidise or reduce them both. The mechanisms are a pain to learn, but you've just got to do it. Keep trying to write them out from memory till you can.

Carboxylic Acids and Esters

Carboxylic acids are much more interesting than cardboard boxes — as you're about to discover...

Carboxylic Acids contain –COOH

Carboxylic acids contain the **carboxyl** functional group **-COOH**.

> A carboxyl group contains a carbonyl group and a hydroxyl group.

To name them, you find and name the longest alkane chain, take off the 'e' and add **'–oic acid'**.

ethanoic acid   4-hydroxy-2-methylbutanoic acid   benzoic acid

> See page 77 for more about naming benzene compounds.

The carboxyl group is always at the **end** of the molecule and when naming, it's more important than other functional groups — so all the other functional groups in the molecule are numbered starting from this carbon.

Carboxylic Acids are **Weak Acids**

Carboxylic acids are **weak acids** — in water they partially dissociate into a **carboxylate ion** and an **H⁺ ion**:

> This equilibrium lies to the left because most of the molecules don't dissociate.

carboxylic acid   carboxylate ion

Pete was hoping for an A⁻ in his carboxylic acid practical, but he ended up with an H⁺.

Carboxylic Acids React with **Carbonates** to Form **Carbon Dioxide**

Carboxylic acids react with **carbonates** (which contain the CO_3^{2-} ion) to form a **salt**, **carbon dioxide** and **water**.

ethanoic acid   sodium ethanoate

$$2CH_3COOH_{(aq)} + Na_2CO_{3(s)} \rightarrow 2CH_3COONa_{(aq)} + H_2O_{(l)} + CO_{2(g)}$$

$$CH_3COOH_{(aq)} + NaHCO_{3(s)} \rightarrow CH_3COONa_{(aq)} + H_2O_{(l)} + CO_{2(g)}$$

> In these reactions, carbon dioxide fizzes out of the solution.

Carboxylic Acids React with **Alcohols** to form **Esters**

1) Esters are organic compounds that contain a -COO- group.

2) They're frequently made by heating a **carboxylic acid** with an **alcohol** in the presence of a **strong acid catalyst**.

3) It's called an **esterification** reaction. Concentrated sulfuric acid is usually used as the acid catalyst.

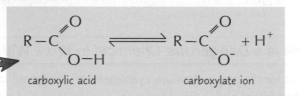

This oxygen comes from the alcohol.

carboxylic acid   alcohol   ester   water

> It's also a condensation reaction as it releases water.

Here's how ethanoic acid reacts with ethanol to make the ester, ethyl ethanoate:

ethanoic acid   ethanol   ethyl ethanoate   water

Carboxylic Acids and Esters

Esters have the Functional Group –COO–

You've just seen that an ester is formed by reacting an alcohol with a carboxylic acid. Well, the **name** of an **ester** is made up of **two parts** — the **first** bit comes from the **alcohol**, and the **second** bit from the **carboxylic acid**.

1) Look at the **alkyl group** that came from the **alcohol**. This is the first bit of the ester's name.

This is a **propyl** group.

2) Now look at the part that came from the carboxylic acid. Swap its '-oic acid' ending for 'oate' to get the second bit of the name.

This came from ethanoic acid, so it's an ethanoate.

3) Put the two parts together. It's **propyl** ethanoate $CH_3COOCH_2CH_2CH_3$

The name's written the opposite way round from the formula.

Naming esters where either the acid or alcohol chain is branched can be a bit trickier. For an ester, number the carbons from the C atoms in the C–O–C bond.

This is ethyl 2-methylbutanoate. $CH_3CH_2CH(CH_3)COOCH_2CH_3$

Esters are Used as Food Flavourings, Perfumes, Solvents and Plasticisers

1) Esters have a **sweet smell**, varying from glucy sweet for smaller esters to a fruity 'pear drop' smell for larger ones. This makes them useful in perfumes. The food industry uses esters to **flavour** things like drinks and sweets too.

2) Esters are **polar** liquids so lots of **polar organic compounds** will dissolve in them. They've also got quite **low boiling points**, so they **evaporate easily** from mixtures. This makes them good solvents in **glues** and **printing inks**.

3) Esters are used as **plasticisers** — they're added to plastics during polymerisation to make the plastic more **flexible**. Over time, the plasticiser molecules escape though, and the plastic becomes brittle and stiff.

Practice Questions

Q1 Name the catalyst used in an esterification reaction between an alcohol and a carboxylic acid.

Q2 Name the alcohol and carboxylic acid that can be used to make propyl butanoate.

Q3 What properties of esters make them good solvents?

Exam Questions

Q1 The structures of substances X and Y are shown on the right:

a) Write a balanced equation for the reaction between substance **X** and sodium carbonate, Na_2CO_3. [3 marks]

b) Substance **Y** can be synthesised from substance **X** in a single step process. Give the name of the other reagent necessary for this synthesis and name the type of reaction. [2 marks]

Q2 Ethyl butanoate is an ester that is made by reacting ethanol and butanoic acid.

a) Draw the structure of ethyl butanoate. [1 mark]

b) Ethyl butanoate is used as a solvent in some adhesives. Name another possible use for ethyl butanoate. [1 mark]

Q3 3-methylbutyl ethanoate is the ester responsible for the odour of pear essence.

a) Write an equation for the formation of this ester from an alcohol and a carboxylic acid. Include any reaction conditions. [3 mark]

b) Name the carboxylic acid used. [1 mark]

Ahh... the sweet smell of success...

You've met a pretty hefty number of organic molecules now, so make sure you don't start to get them muddled up. Esters and carboxylic acids look a little bit similar — they both contain a carbonyl group. But they're not the same — carboxylic acids have an -OH group stuck onto the carbonyl carbon too, whereas esters have an -OR group. Got it?

More on Esters

OK, brace yourself. There's some pure unadulterated lard coming up.

Esters are **Hydrolysed** to Form **Alcohols**

Hydrolysis is when a substance is split up by water — but using just water is often really slow, so an **acid** or an **alkali** is often used to speed it up. There are two types of hydrolysis of esters — **acid hydrolysis** and **base hydrolysis**. With both types you get an **alcohol**, but the second product in each case is different.

ACID HYDROLYSIS Splits the ester into an **acid** and an **alcohol** — it's the reverse of the reaction on page 68. You have to **reflux** the ester with a **dilute acid**, such as hydrochloric or sulfuric.

For example:

ethyl ethanoate $+ H_2O \underset{reflux}{\overset{H^+}{\rightleftharpoons}}$ ethanoic acid $+$ ethanol

As it's a reversible reaction, you add lots of water to push the equilibrium to the right.

BASE HYDROLYSIS Involves **refluxing** the ester with a **dilute alkali**, such as sodium hydroxide. You get a **carboxylate ion** and an **alcohol**.

For example:

ethyl ethanoate $+ OH^- \underset{reflux}{\rightleftharpoons}$ ethanoate $+$ ethanol

Fats and **Oils** are Esters of **Glycerol** and **Fatty Acids**

Fatty acids are long chain **carboxylic acids**.

They combine with glycerol (propane-1,2,3-triol) to make esters. These esters of glycerol are fats and oils. The fatty acids can be **saturated** (no double bonds) or **unsaturated** (have C=C double bonds).

Most of a fat or oil is made from fatty acid chains — so it's these that give them many of their properties.

- **Animal fats** have mainly **saturated** hydrocarbon chains — they fit neatly together, increasing the van der Waals forces between them. This means you need higher temperatures to melt them, so they're **solid** at room temperature.

- **Vegetable oils** have **unsaturated** hydrocarbon chains — the double bonds mean the chains are bent and don't pack together well, decreasing the van der Waals forces. So they're easier to melt and are **liquids** at room temperature.

Oils and Fats can be **Hydrolysed** to Make **Glycerol**, **Soap** and **Fatty Acids**

Like any ester, you can **hydrolyse** vegetable oils and animal fats by heating them with **sodium hydroxide**. And you'll never guess what the sodium salt produced is — **a soap**.

A soap is the salt of a long-chain carboxylic acid.

fat $+ 3NaOH \rightarrow$ glycerol $+ 3CH_3(CH_2)_{16}COO^-Na^+$

sodium salt (soap)

More on Esters

Biodiesel is a Mixture of Methyl Esters of Fatty Acids

1) Vegetable oils, e.g. rapeseed oil, make good vehicle fuels, but you can't burn them directly in engines.
2) The oils must be converted into **biodiesel** first.
   This involves reacting them with **methanol**, using **potassium hydroxide** as a **catalyst**.
3) You get a mixture of **methyl esters** of fatty acids — this is biodiesel.

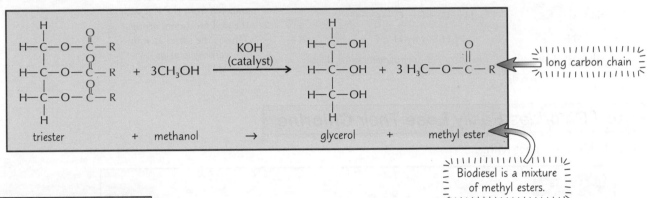

Practice Questions

Q1 Describe two different ways of hydrolysing an ester to make an alcohol.

Q2 Draw the structure of a fat.

Q3 What two products do you get when you hydrolyse an oil or fat with sodium hydroxide?

Q4 What does biodiesel consist of?

Exam Questions

Q1 Compound C, shown below, is found in raspberries.

a) Name compound C. [1 mark]

b) Draw and name the structures of the products formed when compound C
   is refluxed with dilute sulfuric acid. What kind of reaction is this? [5 marks]

c) If compound C is refluxed with excess sodium hydroxide, a similar reaction occurs.
   What is the difference between the products formed in this reaction and the products
   of the reaction described in b)? [1 mark]

Q2 When a vegetable oil was refluxed with concentrated aqueous sodium hydroxide,
   the products were propane-1,2,3-triol and a salt.

a) Draw the structure of propane-1,2,3-triol. [1 mark]

b) The salt was treated with excess hydrochloric acid and oleic acid, $CH_3(CH_2)_7CH=CH(CH_2)_7COOH$,
   was produced. Write an equation for the formation of this acid from its salt. [1 mark]

c) Describe a simple chemical test that you could use to distinguish oleic acid
   from stearic acid, $CH_3(CH_2)_{16}COOH$. [2 marks]

Sodium salts — it's all good, clean fun...

I bet you never knew that you could get from something you fry your chips in to something you wash your hands with in one small leap. There are lots of yukky, complicated structures to learn on these pages — you might find it easier if you think through where the ester breaks in each case and where the atoms of the other reactant add on. Keep at it...

Acyl Chlorides

Acyl chlorides are easy to make and are good starting points for making other types of molecule.

Acyl Chlorides have the Functional Group –COCl

Acyl (or acid) chlorides have the functional group **COCl**. All their names end in **–oyl chloride**.

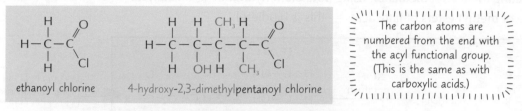

ethanoyl chlorine   4-hydroxy-2,3-dimethylpentanoyl chlorine

The carbon atoms are numbered from the end with the acyl functional group. (This is the same as with carboxylic acids.)

Acyl Chlorides Easily Lose Their Chlorine

Acyl chlorides react with...

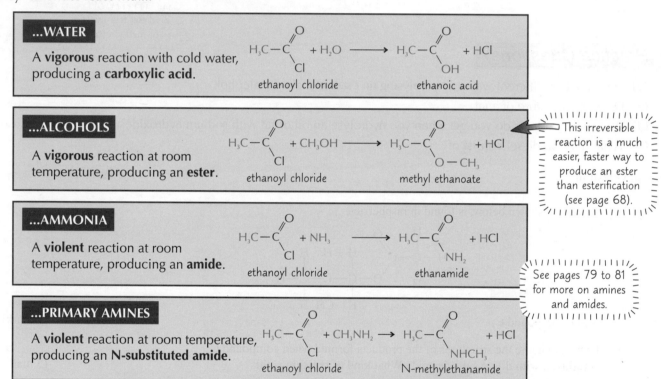

...WATER

A **vigorous** reaction with cold water, producing a **carboxylic acid**.

ethanoyl chloride   ethanoic acid

...ALCOHOLS

A **vigorous** reaction at room temperature, producing an **ester**.

ethanoyl chloride   methyl ethanoate

This irreversible reaction is a much easier, faster way to produce an ester than esterification (see page 68).

...AMMONIA

A **violent** reaction at room temperature, producing an **amide**.

ethanoyl chloride   ethanamide

See pages 79 to 81 for more on amines and amides.

...PRIMARY AMINES

A **violent** reaction at room temperature, producing an **N-substituted amide**.

ethanoyl chloride   N-methylethanamide

Each time, **Cl** is **substituted** by an oxygen or nitrogen group and misty fumes of **hydrogen chloride** are given off.

Acyl Chlorides and Acid Anhydrides React in the Same Way

An **acid anhydride** is made from two identical carboxylic acid molecules. If you know the name of the carboxylic acid, they're easy to name — just take away 'acid' and add 'anhydride'.

You need to know the reactions of **water**, **alcohol**, **ammonia** and **amines** with acid anhydrides. Luckily, they're almost the same as those of acyl chlorides — the reactions are just **less vigorous** and you get a **carboxylic acid** formed instead of HCl.

ethanoic acid   ethanoic anhydride

e.g. $(CH_3CO)_2O_{(l)}$ + $CH_3OH_{(aq)}$ → $CH_3COOCH_{3 (aq)}$ + $CH_3COOH_{(aq)}$

ethanoic anhydride + methanol → methyl ethanoate + ethanoic acid

Acyl Chlorides

Acyl Chloride Reactions are **Nucleophilic Addition-Elimination**

In acyl chlorides, both the chlorine and the oxygen atoms draw electrons **towards** themselves, so the carbon has a slight **positive** charge — meaning it's easily attacked by **nucleophiles**.
Here's the mechanism for a **nucleophilic addition-elimination** reaction between ethanoyl chloride and methanol:

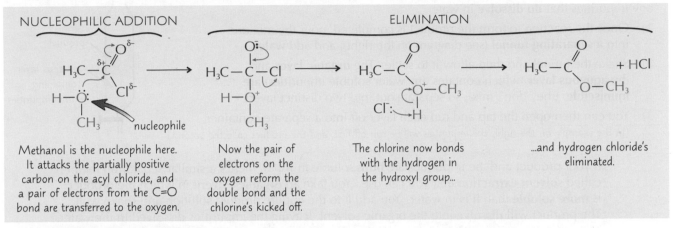

NUCLEOPHILIC ADDITION / ELIMINATION

Methanol is the nucleophile here. It attacks the partially positive carbon on the acyl chloride, and a pair of electrons from the C=O bond are transferred to the oxygen.

Now the pair of electrons on the oxygen reform the double bond and the chlorine's kicked off.

The chlorine now bonds with the hydrogen in the hydroxyl group...

...and hydrogen chloride's eliminated.

The other reactions of acyl chlorides that you need to know all work in exactly the same way.
You just need to change the nucleophile to water (H_2O:), ammonia ($\dot{N}H_3$) or an amine (e.g. $CH_3\dot{N}H_2$).

Ethanoic Anhydride is Used for the **Manufacture** of **Aspirin**

Aspirin is an **ester** — it's made by reacting **salicylic acid** with **ethanoic anhydride** or **ethanoyl chloride**.

Ethanoic anhydride is used in industry because:

* it's **cheaper** than ethanoyl chloride.
* it's **safer** to use than ethanoyl chloride as it's **less corrosive**, reacts **more slowly** with water, and **doesn't produce dangerous hydrogen chloride** fumes.

Reacting **salicylic acid** with **ethanoic anhydride** to make **aspirin**:

salicylic acid + ethanoic anhydride → aspirin + ethanoic acid

Practice Questions

Q1 Write the equation for the reaction between ethanoyl chloride and ammonia.

Q2 What part of an acyl chloride is attacked by nucleophiles?

Q3 Give TWO reasons why ethanoic anhydride is preferred to ethanoyl chloride when producing aspirin.

Exam Questions

Q1 Ethanoyl chloride and ethanoic anhydride both react with methanol.

a) Write equations for both reactions and name the organic product that is formed in both reactions. [3 marks]

b) Give an observation that could be made for the reaction with ethanoyl chloride that would not occur with ethanoic anhydride. [1 mark]

c) Ethanoic acid can also be used with methanol to prepare the organic product named in (a). Give one advantage of using ethanoyl chloride. [1 mark]

Q2 Ethanoyl chloride and ethylamine react together at room temperature.

a) Write an equation for this reaction and name the organic product. [2 marks]

b) Draw a mechanism for this reaction. [4 marks]

I'll take the low road, you take the hydride...

As if all those acyl chlorides reactions weren't enough, you've got to know about acid anhydrides reactions too. It may sound like a bit of a bore, but acid anhydrides and acyl chlorides do react in the same way — that makes things easier.

Purifying Organic Compounds

Synthesising organic compounds is hardly ever as simple as it sounds. The products of organic reactions are almost always riddled with impurities. It's a good thing there are many magical ways of purifying them, outlined on these pages.

Separation Removes *Water Soluble Impurities* From a Product

If a product is **insoluble** in water then you can use **separation** to remove any impurities that **do dissolve** in water.

1) Once the reaction to form the product is completed, pour the mixture into a **separating funnel** (see diagram on the right), and add **water**.

2) Shake the funnel and then allow it to settle. The **organic layer** and the **aqueous layer** (which contains any water soluble impurities) are **immiscible**, (they don't mix), so separate out into two distinct layers.

3) You can then open the tap and run each layer off into a separate container.
   (In the example on the right, the impurities will be run off first, and the product collected second.)

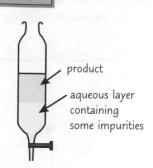

product

aqueous layer
containing
some impurities

> If your product and the impurities are **both** soluble in water, there's a similar separation method called **solvent extraction** that you can use. You take an **organic solvent** in which the product is **more soluble** than it is in water. You add it to the impure product solution and shake well. The product will **dissolve** into the organic solvent, leaving the impurities dissolved in the water. The solvent containing the product can then be run off using a **separating funnel**, as above.

Remove *Water* from a Purified Product by *Drying* it

1) If you use separation to purify a product, the organic layer will end up containing **trace amounts** of water — so it has to be **dried**.

2) To do this, you add an **anhydrous salt** such as **magnesium sulfate** ($MgSO_4$) or **calcium chloride** ($CaCl_2$). The salt is used as a **drying agent** — it **binds** to any water present to become **hydrated**.

3) When you first add the salt to the organic layer it will **clump** together. You keep adding drying agent until it disperses **evenly** when you swirl the flask.

4) Finally, you **filter** the mixture to remove the solid drying agent — pop a piece of filter paper into a funnel that feeds into a flask and pour the mixture into the filter paper.

The filter paper can be fluted (concertina folded) to increase its surface area.

Remove *Other Impurities* by *Washing*

The product of a reaction can be **contaminated** with leftover reagents or unwanted side products. You can **remove** some of these by **washing** the product (which in this case means adding another liquid and shaking).

For example, aqueous **sodium hydrogencarbonate** can be added to an impure product in solution to remove **acid** from it. The acid reacts with the sodium hydrogencarbonate to give CO_2 gas, and the organic product can be removed using a separating funnel (as above).

Volatile Liquids Can be Purified by *Distillation*

Distillation separates out liquids with different boiling points. It works by gently **heating** a mixture in **distillation apparatus**. The substances will evaporate out of the mixture in order of increasing boiling point.

1) Connect a **condenser** to a **round bottomed flask** containing your impure product in solution.

2) Place a **thermometer** in the neck of the flask so that the bulb sits next to the entrance to the condenser. The temperature on the thermometer will show the boiling point of the substance that's evaporating at any given time.

3) **Heat** the impure product.
   (Many organic chemicals are flammable, so you should use an electric heater.)

4) When the product that you want to collect **boils** (i.e. when the thermometer is showing its boiling point), place a flask at the open end of the condenser to collect your **pure product**.

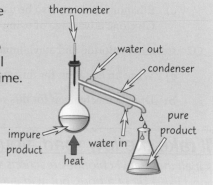

thermometer

water out

condenser

impure product

pure product

water in

heat

Purifying Organic Compounds

Organic Solids can be Purified by Recrystallisation

If the product of an organic reaction is a solid, then the simplest way of purifying it is **recrystallisation**.

First, you dissolve your solid in a hot solvent to make a **saturated** solution (that's a solution in which the **maximum possible** amount of solid is dissolved in the solvent). Then you let it cool. As the solution cools, the **solubility** of the product falls. When it reaches the point where it can't stay in solution, it forms pure **crystals**. Here's how it's done:

1) Add **very hot solvent** to the **impure** solid until it **just** dissolves. It's really important not to add too much solvent — this should give a **saturated solution** of the **impure product**.

2) Filter the hot solution through a **heated funnel** to remove any **insoluble impurities**.

3) Leave the solution to **cool** down **slowly**. **Crystals** of the **product** will form as it cools.

4) Remove the liquid containing the **soluble impurities** from the crystals by **filtering** the mixture under **reduced pressure**. (To do this, you pour the mixture into a filter paper lined **Büchner funnel** – a flat-bottomed funnel with holes in the base – that's sitting in a **side-arm flask** attached to a **vacuum line**.)

5) Finally, **wash** the crystals with ice-cold solvent to remove any soluble impurities from their surface. Leave your purified crystals to **dry**.

Melting and Boiling Points are Good Indicators of Purity

Pure substances have a **specific melting** and **boiling point**. If they're **impure**, the **melting point's lowered** and the **boiling point is raised**. If they're **very impure**, melting and boiling will occur across a wide range of temperatures.

1) You can use **melting point apparatus** to accurately determine the melting point of an **organic solid**.

2) Pack a small sample of the solid into a **glass capillary tube** and place it inside the **heating element**

3) **Increase the temperature** until the sample turns from solid to **liquid**.

4) You usually measure a **melting range**, which is the range of temperatures from where the solid **begins to melt** to where it has **melted completely**.

5) You can look up the melting point of a substance in **data books** and compare it to your measurements.

6) **Impurities** in the sample will **lower** the **melting point** and **broaden** the **melting range**.

Practice Questions

Q1 Describe the procedure for drying an organic product using a drying agent.

Q2 Describe how you would purify a product using distillation.

Exam Questions

Q1 A student carries out an organic synthesis. The product that he makes is insoluble in water and contains water soluble impurities. Which of the following techniques would be the most appropriate for extracting the product?

A Distillation   B Separation   C Recrystallisation   D Drying   [1 mark]

Q2 A scientist has produced some impure solid sodium ethanoate, which she wants to purify using recrystallisation. She begins by dissolving the impure sodium ethanoate in the minimum possible amount of hot solvent.

a) Explain why the scientist used the minimum possible amount of hot solvent.   [1 mark]

b) Outline the rest of the procedure that the scientist would need to follow to recrystallise the solid.   [5 marks]

c) Describe the melting point range of the impure sodium ethanoate compared to the pure product.   [1 mark]

My organic compound isn't volatile — it's just highly strung...

Nobody wants loads of impurities in their reaction products. But now you're well kitted out to get rid of them using these purification techniques. Once you think you've got your product pure, you can check its melting point to make sure.

Aromatic Compounds

We start this section with a fantastical tale about the magical Ring of Benzene. Our story opens in a far away land where our hero is throwing a party for some dwarves... Actually no, that's something else.

Benzene has a **Ring** Of Carbon Atoms

1) Benzene has the formula C_6H_6. It has a **planar cyclic** structure (which is just a complicated way of saying that its six carbon atoms are joined together in a **flat ring**).

A plane ring

2) Each carbon atom forms single covalent bonds to the carbons on either side of it and to one hydrogen atom. The final unpaired electron on each carbon atom is located in a p-orbital that sticks out above and below the plane of the ring. The p-orbitals on each carbon atom combine to form a **ring** of **delocalised electrons**.

('Delocalised' just means that the electrons don't belong to a specific carbon atom, but are shared between them all.)

3) All the carbon-carbon bonds in the ring are the same, so they are the **same length** — 140 pm. This lies in between the length of a single C–C bond (154 pm) and a double C=C bond (135 pm).

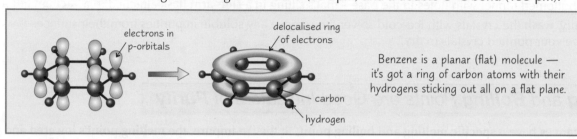

electrons in p-orbitals

delocalised ring of electrons

carbon

hydrogen

Benzene is a planar (flat) molecule — it's got a ring of carbon atoms with their hydrogens sticking out all on a flat plane.

You usually draw benzene like this:

delocalised ring of electrons

Remember, though — there's a hydrogen attached to each of the carbons in the ring, like this

delocalised ring of electrons

You may also see benzene drawn like this:

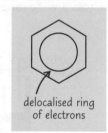

Don't get confused — there aren't really alternating single and double bonds between the carbon atoms. Scientists used to think this was the structure, and their way of drawing it has just stuck around.

The **Delocalised Ring** of Electrons Makes Benzene Very **Stable**

Benzene is far more **stable** than the theoretical compound cyclohexa-1,3,5-triene would be (where the ring would be made up of alternating single and double bonds). You can see this by comparing the enthalpy change of hydrogenation for benzene with the enthalpy change of hydrogenation for cyclohexene:

1) Cyclohexene has **one** double bond. When it's hydrogenated, the enthalpy change is **–120 kJ mol⁻¹**. If benzene had three double bonds, you'd expect it to have an enthalpy of hydrogenation of –360 kJ mol⁻¹.

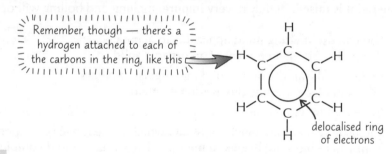

cyclohexene

$\Delta H^{\ominus}_{hydrogenation}$ = –120 kJ mol⁻¹

2) But the **experimental** enthalpy of hydrogenation of benzene is **–208 kJ mol⁻¹** — far **less exothermic** than expected.

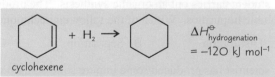

cyclohexa-1,3,5-triene

predicted $\Delta H^{\ominus}_{hydrogenation}$ = –360 kJ mol⁻¹

actual $\Delta H^{\ominus}_{hydrogenation}$ = –208 kJ mol⁻¹

3) Energy is put in to break bonds and released when bonds are made. So **more energy** must have been put in to break the bonds in benzene than would be needed to break the bonds in a theoretical cyclohexa-1,3,5-triene molecule.

4) This difference indicates that benzene is **more stable** than cyclohexa-1,3,5-triene would be. This is thought to be due to the **delocalised ring of electrons**.

Aromatic Compounds

Aromatic Compounds are Derived from Benzene

Compounds containing a **benzene ring** are called **arenes** or 'aromatic compounds'.
There are **two** ways of **naming** arenes — here are some examples:

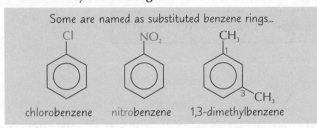

Some are named as substituted benzene rings...

chlorobenzene   nitrobenzene   1,3-dimethylbenzene

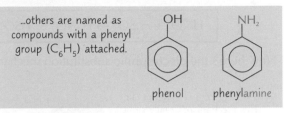

...others are named as compounds with a phenyl group (C_6H_5) attached.

phenol   phenylamine

Arenes Undergo Electrophilic Substitution Reactions

The benzene ring is a region of **high electron density**, so it attracts **electrophiles**. As the benzene ring's so stable, it **doesn't** undergo **electrophilic addition** reactions, which would destroy the delocalised ring of electrons. Instead, it undergoes **electrophilic substitution reactions** where one of the hydrogen atoms (or another functional group on the ring) is substituted for the electrophile.

You need to know two **electrophilic substitution mechanisms** for benzene — **Friedel-Crafts acylation** (shown below) and the **nitration reaction** on the next page.

Friedel-Crafts Acylation Reactions Produce Phenylketones

1) Many **useful** chemicals such as **dyes** and **pharmaceuticals** contain benzene rings. But because benzene is so **stable**, it's fairly **unreactive** — so it can be tricky to make chemicals that contain benzene.

2) **Friedel-Crafts acylation** reactions are used to add an **acyl group** (**RCO–**) to the benzene ring. Once an acyl group has been added, the side chains can be **modified** using further reactions to make **useful products**.

3) An electrophile has to have a strong **positive charge** to be able to attack the stable benzene ring — most aren't **polarised** enough. But some can be made into **stronger electrophiles** using a catalyst called a **halogen carrier**.

4) Friedel-Crafts acylation uses an **acyl chloride** (see page 72) as an electrophile and a **halogen carrier**, e.g. $AlCl_3$.

Here's how the $AlCl_3$ makes the acyl chloride electrophile stronger:
$AlCl_3$ accepts a **lone pair of electrons** from the acyl chloride. As the lone pair of electrons is pulled away, the **polarisation** in the acyl chloride **increases** and it forms a **carbocation**. This makes it a much **stronger electrophile**, and gives it a strong enough charge to **react** with the **benzene ring**.

5) Here's how the electrophile is substituted into the benzene ring. The mechanism has **two steps**:

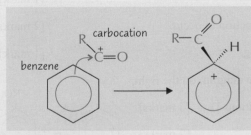

1) **Electrons** in the benzene ring are **attracted** to the positively charged **carbocation**. Two electrons from the benzene **bond** with the carbocation. This **partially breaks the delocalised ring** and gives it a **positive charge**.

2) The **negatively charged $AlCl_4^-$** ion is attracted to the **positively charged ring**. One **chloride ion** breaks away from the aluminium chloride ion and **bonds** with the **hydrogen ion**. This **removes the hydrogen** from the ring forming **HCl**. It also allows the catalyst to reform.

6) The reactants need to be **heated under reflux** in a **non-aqueous solvent** (like dry ether) for the reaction to occur.

Aromatic Compounds

Nitration is Used in the Manufacture of Explosives and Dyes

When you warm **benzene** with **concentrated nitric** and **sulfuric acids**, you get **nitrobenzene**.
Sulfuric acid acts as a **catalyst** — it helps to make the nitronium ion, NO_2^+, which is the electrophile.

$$HNO_3 + H_2SO_4 \rightarrow H_2NO_3^+ + HSO_4^- \quad \Longrightarrow \quad H_2NO_3^+ \rightarrow NO_2^+ + H_2O$$

Now here's the electrophilic substitution mechanism:

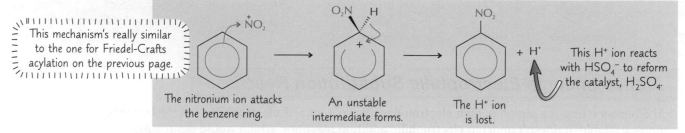

This mechanism's really similar to the one for Friedel-Crafts acylation on the previous page.

The nitronium ion attacks the benzene ring.

An unstable intermediate forms.

The H$^+$ ion is lost.

This H$^+$ ion reacts with HSO_4^- to reform the catalyst, H_2SO_4.

If you only want one NO_2 group added (**mononitration**), you need to keep the temperature **below 55 °C**.
Above this temperature you'll get lots of substitutions.

Nitration reactions are really useful

1) Nitro compounds can be **reduced** to form **aromatic amines** (see page 81). These are used to manufacture **dyes** and **pharmaceuticals**.

2) Some nitro compounds can be used as **explosives**, such as 2,4,6-trinitromethylbenzene (trinitrotoluene — TNT).

Practice Questions

Q1 Explain why electrophiles are attracted to benzene.

Q2 Which halogen carrier is used in the Friedel-Crafts acylation reaction?

Q3 What is used as a catalyst in the nitration of benzene?

Q4 What type of compound is this?

Exam Questions

Q1 A halogen carrier, such as $AlCl_3$, is used as a catalyst in the reaction between benzene and ethanoyl chloride.

a) Describe the conditions needed for this reaction. [1 mark]

b) Explain why the halogen carrier is needed as a catalyst for this reaction to occur. [2 marks]

c) Draw the structure of the electrophile that attacks the benzene ring. [1 mark]

Q2 An electrophilic substitution reaction of benzene is summarised in the diagram on the right.

a) Name the product A, and the reagents B and C, and give the conditions D. [3 marks]

b) Write equations to show the formation of the electrophile. [2 marks]

c) Outline a mechanism for this reaction. [2 marks]

benzene   A

Everyone needs a bit of stability in their life...

The structure of benzene is really odd — even top scientists struggled to find out what its molecular structure was.
If you're asked why benzene reacts the way it does, it's bound to be something to do with the ring of delocalised
electrons. Remember there's a hydrogen at every point on the benzene ring — it's easy to forget they're there.

Amines and Amides

Two more types of organic compound coming up — amines and amides. Both these families contain nitrogen atoms.

Amines are Organic Derivatives of **Ammonia**

If one or more of the **hydrogens** in **ammonia** (NH_3) is replaced with an organic group, you get an **amine**.
If **one** hydrogen is **replaced** with an organic group, you get a **primary amine**. If **two** are replaced, it's a **secondary amine**, and **three** means it's a **tertiary amine**. The lone pair of electrons on the nitrogen atom in a tertiary amine can also bond with a fourth organic group — that gives you a **quaternary ammonium ion**.

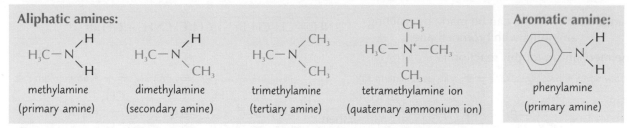

Aliphatic amines:

methylamine
(primary amine)

dimethylamine
(secondary amine)

trimethylamine
(tertiary amine)

tetramethylamine ion
(quaternary ammonium ion)

Aromatic amine:

phenylamine
(primary amine)

Quaternary Ammonium Salts are Used as Cationic Surfactants

Because quaternary ammonium ions are **positively charged**, they will hang around with any negative ions that are near. The complexes formed are called **quaternary ammonium salts** — like **tetramethylammonium chloride**, $(CH_3)_4N^+Cl^-$.

Quaternary ammonium salts with at least one long hydrocarbon chain are used as **cationic surfactants**. The hydrocarbon tail will bind to nonpolar substances such as **grease**, whilst the **cationic** head will dissolve in water, so they are useful in things like **fabric cleaners** and **hair products**.

In addition, the **positively charged** part (ammonium ion) will bind to negatively charged surfaces such as hair and fibre. This gets rid of **static**, so they are often used in **fabric conditioners**.

Amines Have A Lone Pair of Electrons

1) Amines act as **weak bases** because they **accept protons**. There's a **lone pair of electrons** on the **nitrogen** atom that can form a **dative covalent (coordinate) bond** with an H^+ ion.

2) The **strength** of the **base** depends on how **available** the nitrogen's lone pair of electrons is. The more **available** the **lone pair** is, the more likely the amine is to **accept a proton**, and the **stronger** a base it will be. A **lone pair** of electrons will be **more available** if its **electron density** is **higher**.

3) **Primary aliphatic amines** are **stronger** bases than **ammonia**, which is a **stronger** base than **aromatic amines**. Here's why:

The more **available** the lone pair of electrons, the **stronger** the base...

Greater availability of lone pair of electrons

Stronger bases

primary aromatic
amine (phenylamine)

ammonia

primary aliphatic
amine

= distribution of
negative charge

The benzene ring draws electrons towards itself and the nitrogen lone pair gets partially delocalised onto the ring. So the electron density on the nitrogen decreases, making the lone pair much less available.

Alkyl groups push electrons onto attached groups. So the electron density on the nitrogen atom increases. This makes the lone pair more available.

4) The lone pair of electrons also means that amines are **nucleophiles**. They react with **halogenoalkanes** in a **nucleophilic substitution reaction** (see next page), or with **acyl chlorides** and **acid anhydrides** in **nucleophilic addition-elimination** reactions (see pages 72-73).

Amines and Amides

Aliphatic Amines are made from Halogenoalkanes or Nitriles

There are **two** ways to produce aliphatic amines — either from **halogenoalkanes** or by **reducing nitriles**. (The method for producing **aromatic amines** is different again — as you'll see on the next page.)

You Can Heat a Halogenoalkane with Ammonia...

Amines can be made by heating a **halogenoalkane** with **excess ammonia**.

Example: Ethylamine can be made by reacting ammonia with bromoethane:

$$2NH_3 + CH_3CH_2Br \rightarrow CH_3CH_2NH_2 + NH_4Br$$

The mechanism for this reaction is:

ammonia + halogenoalkane ⟶ alkylammonium salt

Ammonia attacks the carbon in the halogenoalkane

The halogen is released

...then...

alkylammonium salt ⇌ primary amine + ammonium salt

A second ammonia molecule donates its lone pair of electrons to a hydrogen, which breaks off from the alkylammonium salt.

If you make amines using this method, you end up with a **mixture** of primary, secondary and tertiary amines and quaternary ammonium salts. This is because the primary amine that you produce first has a **lone pair of electrons** — it's a **nucleophile**. This means that it can react with any remaining halogenoalkane in a **nucleophilic substitution reaction**. As long as there's some of the halogenoalkane around, further substitutions can take place. They keep happening until you get a **quaternary ammonium salt**, which can't react any further as it has no lone pair:

primary amine → (halogenoalkane) → secondary amine → (halogenoalkane) → tertiary amine → (halogenoalkane) → quaternary ammonium ion

The **mechanism** is similar to the reaction of ammonia with a halogenoalkane — two **amine molecules** react with the halogenoalkane in succession to form a **more substituted amine** (e.g. a primary amine forms a secondary amine) and an **ammonium salt** with a similar structure to the original amine. For example:

$$2\ H_3C-N\underset{H}{\overset{H}{<}} + CH_3CH_2Br \rightarrow H_3C-N\underset{CH_2CH_3}{\overset{H}{<}} + CH_3NH_3{}^+Br^-$$

...Or You Can Reduce a Nitrile

You can **reduce** a nitrile to a **primary amine** by a number of different methods:

1) You can use **lithium aluminium hydride** (**LiAlH$_4$** — a strong reducing agent) in a non-aqueous solvent (such as dry ether), followed by some **dilute acid**. For example:

$$R-CH_2-C\equiv N + 4[H] \xrightarrow[\text{(2) dilute acid}]{\text{(1) LiAlH}_4} R-CH_2-CH_2N\underset{H}{\overset{H}{<}}$$

nitrile → primary amine

[H] is just the reducing agent (here it's LiAlH$_4$).

I can't afford LiAlH$_4$...

Becky was reduced to tears by lithium aluminium hydride.

2) This method is fine in the lab, but LiAlH$_4$ is too **expensive** for industrial use. In industry, nitriles are reduced using **hydrogen gas** with a **metal catalyst** such as platinum or nickel at high temperature and pressure. This is called **catalytic hydrogenation**. For example:

$$R-CH_2-C\equiv N + 2H_2 \xrightarrow[\text{high temperature and pressure}]{\text{nickel catalyst}} R-CH_2-CH_2N\underset{H}{\overset{H}{<}}$$

nitrile → primary amine

Amines and Amides

Aromatic Amines are made by Reducing a Nitro Compound

Aromatic amines are produced by **reducing** a nitro compound, such as **nitrobenzene**.
There are **two steps** to the method:

1) First you need to heat a mixture of a **nitro compound**, **tin metal** and **concentrated hydrochloric acid** under **reflux** — this makes a salt. For example, if you use nitrobenzene, the salt formed is $C_6H_5NH_3^+Cl^-$.

2) Then to turn the salt into an **aromatic amine**, you need to add an alkali, such as **sodium hydroxide** solution.

3) Aromatic amines are useful compounds in organic synthesis — they're used as the starting molecules for lots of **dyes** and **pharmaceuticals**.

And now for a weeny bit about amides...

Amides are Carboxylic Acid Derivatives

Amides contain the functional group **–CONH$_2$**.

The **carbonyl group** pulls electrons away from the NH$_2$ group, so amides behave differently from amines.

one of the hydrogens is replaced with an alkyl group

Practice Questions

Q1 Predict, with reasoning, whether ammonia or ethylamine will be a stronger base.

Q2 Explain why amines and ammonia can act as nucleophiles.

Q3 What conditions are needed to reduce nitrobenzene to phenylamine?

Exam Questions

Q1 a) Explain how methylamine, CH_3NH_2, can act as a base. [1 mark]

b) Methylamine is a stronger base than ammonia, NH_3. However, phenylamine, $C_6H_5NH_2$, is a weaker base than ammonia. Explain these differences in base strength. [2 marks]

Q2 a) Propylamine can be synthesised from bromopropane.
Suggest a disadvantage of this synthesis route. [1 mark]

b) Propylamine can also be synthesised from propanenitrile.

i) Suggest suitable reagents for its preparation in a laboratory. [1 mark]

ii) Why is this method not suitable for industrial use? [1 mark]

iii) What reagents and conditions are used in industry? [2 marks]

Q3 Ethylamine can react with bromoethane to form a compound of molecular formula $C_4H_{11}N$.
Write an equation and outline a mechanism for the reaction [3 marks]

You've got to learn it — amine it might come up in your exam...

Did you know that rotting fish smells so bad because the flesh releases diamines as it decomposes? But the real question is: is it fish that smells of amines or amines that smell of fish — it's one of those chicken or egg things that no one can answer. Well, enough philosophical pondering — we all know the answer to the meaning of life. It's 42.

Condensation Polymers

You met addition polymers in Year 1. Now it's time to meet their big brothers — condensation polymers...

Condensation Polymers Include **Polyamides**, **Polyesters** and **Polypeptides**

1) **Condensation polymerisation** usually involves two different types of monomer, each with at least **two functional groups**. Each functional group reacts with a group on another monomer to form a link, creating polymer chains.
2) Each time a link is formed, a small molecule is lost (water) — that's why it's called **condensation** polymerisation.
3) Examples of condensation polymers include **polyamides**, **polyesters** and **polypeptides** (or proteins, see page 88).

Reactions Between **Dicarboxylic Acids** and **Diamines** Make **Polyamides**

The **carboxyl** groups of **dicarboxylic acids** react with the **amino** groups of **diamines** to form **amide links**. Dicarboxylic acids and diamines have functional groups at each end of the molecule, so **long chains** can form.

Example: Nylon 6,6 is a polyamide made from **1,6-diaminohexane** and **hexanedioic acid**. It's used to make clothing, carpet, rope, airbags and parachutes.

This is the formula of the polymer. The bit inside the brackets is called the repeating unit of the polymer.

Example: Kevlar® is a polyamide made from **1,4-diaminobenzene** and **benzene-1,4-dicarboxylic acid**. It's used in bulletproof vests, boat construction, car tyres and lightweight sports equipment.

Reactions Between **Dicarboxylic Acids** and **Diols** Make **Polyesters**

The **carboxyl** groups of dicarboxylic acids can also react with the **hydroxyl** groups of **diols** to form **ester links**. Polymers joined by **ester links** are called **polyesters**.

Example: Terylene™ (PET) — formed from **benzene-1,4-dicarboxylic acid** and **ethane-1,2-diol**. It's used in plastic bottles, clothing, sheets and sails.

Condensation Polymers

Hydrolysis Produces the Original Monomers

1) Condensation polymerisation can be reversed by **hydrolysis** — water molecules are added back in and the links are broken. For example, this equation shows a polyamide being hydrolysed:

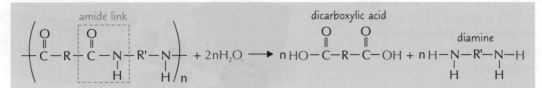

This is just the reverse of the reaction shown on the previous page.

2) To draw the **monomers** from the repeating unit of a condensation polymer, break the chain through the **middle bond** of the amide or ester link. Then just add an **OH** or an **H** to each end of both new molecules.

If you're starting from a diagram showing a section of the polymer chain and you need to draw the repeating unit first, you just need to find and draw out the longest chunk of the chain that repeats.

3) To work out what you need to add where, just remember — for a **polyamide** you want the monomers to be a **dicarboxylic acid** and a **diamine**, and for a **polyester** you need to end up with a **dicarboxylic acid** and a **diol**.

Condensation Polymers Contain Polar Bonds

1) Condensation polymers are generally **stronger** and **more rigid** than addition polymers.

2) This is because condensation polymers are made up of chains containing **polar bonds**, e.g. C–N and C–O. So, as well as Van der Waals forces, there are **permanent dipole-dipole forces** and **hydrogen bonds** between the polymer chains.

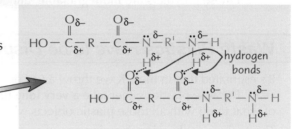

Practice Questions

Q1 What molecule is eliminated when a polyester is made?

Q2 Why are condensation polymers usually stronger than addition polymers?

Exam Questions

Q1 Kevlar® is a polymer used in bulletproof vests. Its repeating unit is shown on the right.

a) What type of polymer is Kevlar®? [1 mark]

b) Kevlar® is made by reacting two different monomers together. What type of compounds are each of these monomers? [1 mark]

c) Which reaction could you use to break up Kevlar® into its constituent monomers? [1 mark]

Q2 Nylon 6,6 is the most commonly produced nylon. A section of the polymer chain is shown on the right.

Draw the structural formulas of the monomers from which nylon 6,6 is formed. It is not necessary to draw the carbon chains out in full. [2 marks]

Q3 A polyester is formed by the reaction between the monomers hexanedioic acid and 1,6-hexanediol.

a) Draw the repeating unit for the polyester. [1 mark]

b) Explain why this is an example of condensation polymerisation. [1 mark]

Conversation polymerisation — when someone just goes on and on and on...

Condensation polymers are like people who are in an on-off relationship. They get together, then they hydrolyse apart, only to get back together again. And you have to keep up with it — monomers, polymers, amides, esters and all. You'll also need to know the structures and links involved in nylon 6,6, Kevlar® and Terylene™ for your exams. So get swotting...

Disposing of Polymers

Polymers are amazingly useful. But they have one big drawback...

Polymers — *Useful* but Difficult to *Get Rid Of*

1) Synthetic polymers have loads of **advantages**, so they're incredibly widespread these days — we take them pretty much for granted.

   Just imagine what you'd have to live without ⇨ if there were no polymers...

   (Okay... I could live without the polystyrene head, but the rest of this stuff is pretty useful.)

2) **Polyalkenes** such as poly(ethene) and polystyrene are addition polymers. They are made up of **non-polar** carbon chains, which makes them unreactive and chemically inert.

3) This is an advantage when they are being used — e.g. a polystyrene cup won't react with your coffee, but has the disadvantage of making them **non-biodegradable**.

4) **Condensation polymers** such as polyesters and polyamides do have **polar bonds** in their chains, which makes them open to attack by **nucleophiles**.

5) This means that condensation polymers can be broken down by **hydrolysis** (see page 83). So these polymers are **biodegradable**, although the process is **very slow**.

Waste Plastics Have to be Disposed Of

It's estimated that in the UK we throw away over **3 million tons** of plastic (i.e. synthetic polymers) every year. Because plastics either take a **very long time** to biodegrade or are **non-biodegradable**, the question of what to do with all those plastic objects when we've finished using them is an important one.

The options are **burying**, **burning** or sorting for **reusing** or **recycling**. None of these methods is an ideal solution — they all have **advantages** and **disadvantages** associated with them.

```
                    Waste
burying      ⇦      plastics      ⇨      burning
in landfill                               as fuel
                      ⇩
                   sorting
                  ⇙      ⇘
           remoulding      cracking
                ⇩             ⇩
             new          processing
            objects        ⇙      ⇘
                        other      new
                       chemicals  plastics
```

Waste Plastics can be *Buried*

1) **Landfill** is one option for dealing with waste plastics. It is generally used when the plastic is:
   - difficult to separate from other waste,
   - not in sufficient quantities to make separation financially worthwhile,
   - too difficult technically to recycle.

2) Landfill is a relatively **cheap** and **easy** method of waste disposal, but it requires **areas of land**.

3) As the waste decomposes it can release **methane** — a **greenhouse gas**. **Leaks** from landfill sites can also **contaminate water supplies**.

4) The **amount of waste** we generate is becoming more and more of a problem, so there's a need to **reduce** landfill as much as possible.

Waste Plastics can be *Burned*

1) Waste plastics can be **burned** and the heat used to generate **electricity**.

2) This process needs to be carefully **controlled** to reduce the release of **toxic** gases. For example, polymers that contain **chlorine** (such as **PVC**) produce **HCl** when they're burned — this has to be removed.

3) So, waste gases from the combustion are passed through **scrubbers** which can **neutralise** gases such as HCl by allowing them to react with a **base**.

4) But the waste gases, e.g. carbon dioxide, will still contribute to the **greenhouse effect**.

Rex and Dirk enjoy some waist plastic.

Disposing of Polymers

Waste Plastics can be Recycled

Because many plastics are made from non-renewable **oil-fractions**, it makes sense to recycle plastics as much as possible. There's more than one way to recycle plastics. After **sorting** into different types:

- some plastics (poly(propene), for example) can be **melted** and **remoulded**,

- some plastics can be **cracked** into **monomers**, and these can be used to make more plastics or other chemicals.

Plastic products are usually marked to make sorting easier. The different numbers show different polymers, e.g.

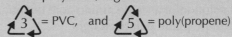

$\triangle$ 3 = PVC, and $\triangle$ 5 = poly(propene)

Like other disposal methods, there are advantages and disadvantages to recycling plastics:

Advantages	Disadvantages
It reduces the amount of waste going into landfill.	It is technically difficult to recycle plastics.
It saves raw materials — which is important because oil is non-renewable.	Collecting, sorting and processing the plastic is more expensive than burning/landfill.
The cost of recycling plastics is lower than making the plastics from scratch.	You often can't remake the plastic you started with — you have to make something else.
It produces less CO_2 emissions than burning the plastic.	The plastic can be easily contaminated during the recycling process.

Practice Questions

Q1 Why aren't polyalkenes biodegradable?

Q2 Name a type of polymer that is biodegradable.

Q3 Explain why burning PVC produces HCl gas, but burning poly(ethene) doesn't.

Q4 Give two advantages and two disadvantages of recycling waste plastics.

Exam Questions

Q1 Waste plastics can be disposed of by burning.

    a) Describe one advantage of disposing of waste plastics by burning. [1 mark]

    b) Describe a disadvantage of burning waste plastic that contains chlorine, and explain how the negative impact of this disadvantage could be reduced. [2 marks]

Q2 Give one advantage and one disadvantage of landfill as a disposal method for waste plastic. [2 marks]

Q3 The diagram below shows sections of two polymers.

A

$$-\underset{\underset{H}{|}}{\overset{\overset{O}{\|}}{C}}-N-(CH_2)_5-\underset{\underset{H}{|}}{\overset{\overset{O}{\|}}{C}}-N-(CH_2)_5-$$

B

$$-\underset{\underset{H}{|}}{\overset{\overset{CH_3}{|}}{C}}-\underset{\underset{H}{|}}{\overset{\overset{H}{|}}{C}}-\underset{\underset{H}{|}}{\overset{\overset{CH_3}{|}}{C}}-\underset{\underset{H}{|}}{\overset{\overset{H}{|}}{C}}-$$

    a) State which of these polymers is biodegradable. Explain why the polymer you have selected is more reactive and can be broken down. [2 marks]

    b) Name the type of chemical reaction that occurs when a polymer biodegrades. [1 mark]

Phil's my recycled plastic plane — but I don't know where to land Phil...

You might have noticed that all this recycling business is a hot topic these days. And not just in the usual places, such as chemistry books. No, no, no... recycling even makes it regularly onto the news as well. This suits examiners just fine — they like you to know how useful chemistry is. So learn this stuff, pass your exam, and do some recycling.

Amino Acids

Wouldn't it be nice if you could go to sleep with this book under your pillow and when you woke up you'd know it all.

Amino Acids have an **Amino Group** and a **Carboxyl** Group

An amino acid has a **basic amino group** (NH₂) and an **acidic carboxyl group** (COOH). This makes them **amphoteric** — they've got both acidic and basic properties.

They're **chiral molecules** (see page 64) because the carbon has **four** different groups attached. So a solution of a single amino acid enantiomer will **rotate plane polarised light**.

Glycine's the exception to this as its R group is just a hydrogen.

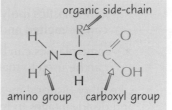

organic side-chain

amino group   carboxyl group

Amino Acids Have **Common** and **Systematic** Names

Most amino acids have a **common name** (like glycine or valine), but each one has a **systematic name** too. You should be given the common names if you need them, but you could be asked to work out their systematic names, using the **IUPAC naming system**. (Look back at your Year 1 notes for more on how the IUPAC naming system works.)

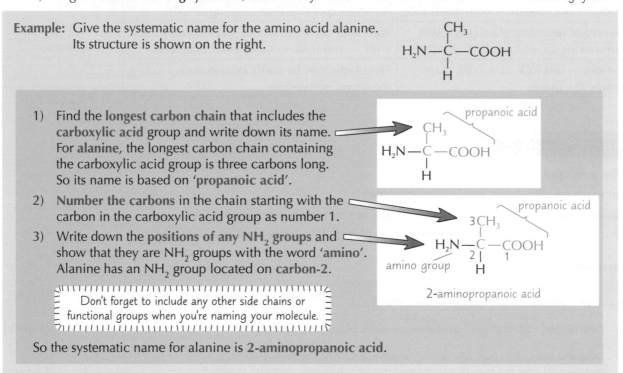

Example: Give the systematic name for the amino acid alanine. Its structure is shown on the right.

1) Find the **longest carbon chain** that includes the **carboxylic acid** group and write down its name. For **alanine**, the longest carbon chain containing the carboxylic acid group is three carbons long. So its name is based on 'propanoic acid'.

2) **Number the carbons** in the chain starting with the carbon in the carboxylic acid group as number 1.

3) Write down the **positions of any NH₂ groups** and show that they are NH₂ groups with the word 'amino'. Alanine has an NH₂ group located on **carbon-2**.

Don't forget to include any other side chains or functional groups when you're naming your molecule.

propanoic acid

propanoic acid

amino group   2-aminopropanoic acid

So the systematic name for alanine is **2-aminopropanoic acid**.

Amino Acids Can Exist As **Zwitterions**

A zwitterion is a **dipolar ion** — it has both a **positive** and a **negative charge** in different parts of the molecule. Zwitterions only exist near an amino acid's **isoelectric point**. This is the **pH** where the **average overall charge** on the amino acid is zero. It's different for different amino acids — it depends on their R-group.

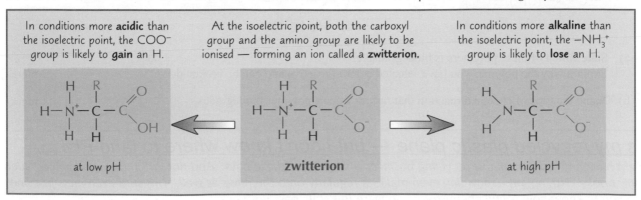

In conditions more **acidic** than the isoelectric point, the COO⁻ group is likely to **gain** an H.

At the isoelectric point, both the carboxyl group and the amino group are likely to be ionised — forming an ion called a **zwitterion**.

In conditions more **alkaline** than the isoelectric point, the −NH₃⁺ group is likely to **lose** an H.

at low pH

zwitterion

at high pH

Amino Acids

Thin-Layer Chromatography is used to *Identify Unknown* Amino Acids

Since different amino acids have different 'R' groups, they will all have different **solubilities** in the same solvent. This means you can easily separate and identify the different amino acids in a mixture using **thin-layer chromatography**. Each amino acid will move up the thin-layer chromatography plate at a different rate depending on how soluble it is in the solvent you've used. Here's what you do:

This is a piece of plastic or glass covered with a thin layer of silica gel or alumina powder.

1) Draw a **pencil line** near the bottom of a thin-layer chromatography plate and put a **concentrated spot** of the mixture of amino acids on it.

2) Dip the bottom of the plate (not the spot) into a solvent.

3) As the solvent spreads up the plate, the different amino acids move with it, but at **different rates**, so they separate out.

4) When the solvent's **nearly** reached the top, take the plate out and **mark** the **solvent front** with pencil. Then leave the plate to dry.

5) Amino acids aren't coloured so you will need to make the spots **visible**.

- You can do this by spraying **ninhydrin solution** on the plate, which will turn the spots purple.

- Alternatively, you can use a special plate that has a **fluorescent dye** added to it. The dye glows when **UV light** shines on it. Where there are spots of chemical on the plate, they cover the fluorescent dye — so the spots appear dark. You can put the plate under a **UV lamp** and draw around the dark patches to show where the spots are.

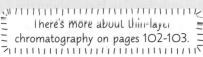

6) You can work out the R_f **value** of each amino acid spot using this formula:

$$R_f \text{ value of amino acid} = \frac{x}{y} = \frac{\text{distance travelled by spot}}{\text{distance travelled by solvent}}$$

Measure the distance from the point of origin to the middle of the spot when you're working out R_f values.

7) Then you can use a **table of known amino acid R_f values** to identify the amino acids in the mixture.

There's more about thin-layer chromatography on pages 102-103.

Practice Questions

Q1 Draw the structure of a typical amino acid.

Q2 Draw the zwitterion that would be formed from this typical amino acid.

Q3 Describe how you could use thin-layer chromatography to identify the amino acids present in a mixture.

Exam Questions

Q1 Valine is an amino acid with the molecular formula $C_5H_{11}NO_2$.
The longest carbon chain in valine is four carbons long.

a) Draw the displayed formula of valine. Label any chiral carbons with an asterisk*. [2 marks]

b) Give the systematic name for valine. [1 mark]

Q2 Leucine is an amino acid with the systematic name 2-amino-4-methylpentanoic acid.

a) Draw the displayed formula of leucine. [1 mark]

b) Draw the displayed formula of the zwitterion formed by leucine when it is at its isoelectric point. [1 mark]

c) Draw the displayed formula of the species formed by leucine when it is dissolved in an alkaline solution. [1 mark]

Everybody run — the Zwitterions are coming...

'The Zwitterions' do sound a bit like a bunch of aliens from a sci-fi show. Or a band. Zwitterion is a lovely word though — it flutters off your tongue like a butterfly. Well, these pages aren't too bad. A few structures, a bit on how to name them and an experiment. Make sure you know how to do thin-layer chromatography and how to work out R_f values.

Proteins and Enzymes

Amino acids are often called the building blocks of life. They're like little plastic building bricks, but for chemistry. Instead of putting them together to make houses and rockets though, they're used to make all the proteins in your body.

Proteins are Condensation Polymers of Amino Acids

1) Proteins are made up of **lots** of amino acids joined together by **peptide links**. The chain is put together by **condensation** reactions and broken apart by **hydrolysis** reactions.

2) Here's how two amino acids join together to make a **dipeptide**:

Proteins are really polyamides — the monomers are joined by amide groups. In proteins these are called peptide links.

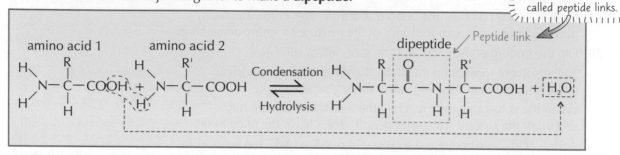

3) The dipeptide still has an NH_2 group at one end and a COOH group at the other. So if you want to **add** more amino acids to the chain, you can just keep repeating the **condensation reaction**.

4) A protein can be broken back down into its individual amino acids (**hydrolysed**), but pretty harsh conditions are needed. You add hot aqueous 6 M hydrochloric acid and heat the mixture under reflux for 24 hours.

5) Proteins are condensation polymers, so to work out which **amino acids** a protein chain was made from, you can use the same method as on page 83 — just **break** each of the peptide links down the middle, then add either an **H atom** or an **OH group** to each of the broken ends to get the amino acids back.

Proteins have Different Levels of Structure

Proteins are **big**, **complicated** molecules. They're easier to explain if you describe their structure in four 'levels'. These levels are called the **primary**, **secondary**, **tertiary** and **quaternary** structures. You only need to know about the first three though.

1) PRIMARY STRUCTURE

The **primary structure** is the **sequence of amino acids** in the long chain that makes up the protein (the **polypeptide chain**).

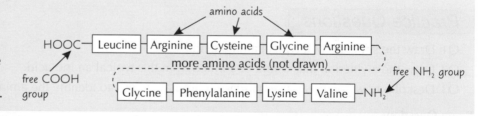

2) SECONDARY STRUCTURE

The **peptide links** can form **hydrogen bonds** with each other (see next page), meaning the chain isn't a straight line. The shape of the chain is called its **secondary structure**. The most common secondary structure is a **spiral** called an **alpha (α) helix**. Another common type of secondary structure is a β–**pleated sheet**. This is a layer of protein folded like a concertina.

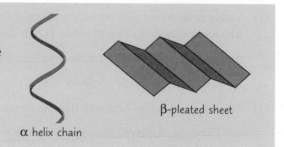

α helix chain

β-pleated sheet

3) TERTIARY STRUCTURE

The chain of amino acids is itself often coiled and folded in a characteristic way that identifies the protein. **Extra bonds** can form between different parts of the polypeptide chain, which gives the protein a kind of **three-dimensional shape**. This is its **tertiary structure**.

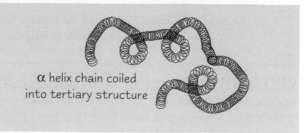

α helix chain coiled into tertiary structure

Proteins and Enzymes

Hydrogen Bonds and Disulfide Bonds Help Keep Proteins in Shape

The secondary and tertiary structures of proteins are formed by **intermolecular forces** causing the amino acid chains to **fold** or **twist**. These intermolecular forces are really important, because the three-dimensional shape of a protein is **vital** to how it **functions**. For example, changing the shape of an **enzyme** (see below) can stop it working.

There are two main types of bond that hold proteins in shape:

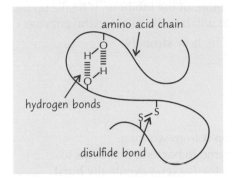

1) **Hydrogen bonding** is one type of force that holds proteins in shape. Hydrogen bonds exist between polar groups — e.g. –OH and –NH$_2$. They stabilise both the secondary and the tertiary structure of the protein.

2) The amino acid **cysteine** contains a **thiol group** (-SH). Thiol groups on different cysteine residues can lose their H atoms and **join together** by forming a **disulfide** (or **sulfur-sulfur**) bond (-S–S-). These disulfide bonds link together different parts of the protein chain, and help to stabilise the tertiary structure.

Factors such as **temperature** and **pH** can affect hydrogen bonding and the formation of disulfide bonds and so can **change the shape** of proteins.

Enzymes are Proteins that Act as Biological Catalysts

Enzymes speed up chemical reactions by acting as biological catalysts.

1) They catalyse every **metabolic reaction** in the bodies of living organisms.
2) Enzymes are **proteins**. Some also have **non-protein components**.
3) Every enzyme has an area called its **active site**. This is the part that the **substrate** fits into so that it can interact with the enzyme.
4) The active site is three-dimensional — it's part of the **tertiary structure** of the enzyme protein (see page 88).

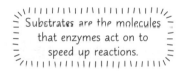
Substrates are the molecules that enzymes act on to speed up reactions.

Enzymes have High Specificity

1) Enzymes are a bit picky. They only work with **specific substrates** — usually only one.
2) This is because, for the enzyme to work, the substrate has to **fit** into the **active site**. If the substrate's shape doesn't match the active site's shape, the reaction won't be catalysed. This is called the '**lock and key**' model.

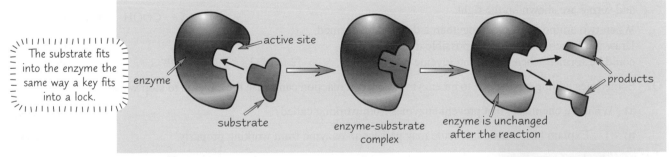

The substrate fits into the enzyme the same way a key fits into a lock.

3) Enzymes are made up of **amino acids**, so they contain **chiral centres**.
4) This makes their active sites **stereospecific** — they'll only work on **one enantiomer** of a substrate. The other enantiomer won't **fit properly** in the active site, so the enzyme can't work on it — it's a bit like how your left shoe doesn't fit on your right foot properly.

Dougal had found the perfect loch, but he was in completely the wrong key.

Proteins and Enzymes

Inhibitors Slow Down the Rate of Reaction

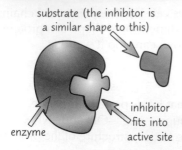

substrate (the inhibitor is a similar shape to this)

inhibitor fits into active site

enzyme

1) Molecules that have a **similar shape** to the **substrate** act as enzyme **inhibitors**.
2) They compete with the substrate to bond to the active site, but no reaction follows. Instead they **block** the active site, so **no substrate** can **fit** in it.
3) How much inhibition happens depends on the **relative concentrations** of inhibitor and substrate — if there's a lot more of the inhibitor, it'll take up most of the active sites and very little substrate will be able to get to the enzyme.
4) The amount of inhibition is also affected by how **strongly** the inhibitor bonds to the active site.

Some Drugs Work as Inhibitors

1) Some **drugs** are **inhibitors** that block the active site of an enzyme and **stop it** from working. For example, some **antibiotics** work by blocking the active site of an enzyme in bacteria that helps to make their cell walls. This causes their cell walls to **weaken** over time, so the bacteria eventually **burst**.

2) The active site of an enzyme is very **specific**, so it takes a lot of effort to find a drug molecule that will **fit** into the active site. It's even trickier if the drug molecule is **chiral** — then only one **enantiomer** will fit into the active site, because the active sites of enzymes are **stereospecific** (see page 89).

3) Often, new drug molecules are found by **trial and error**. Scientists will carry out experiments using lots of compounds to see if they work as inhibitors for a particular enzyme. They'll then **adapt** any that work to try and improve them. This process takes a long time.

4) One way that scientists are speeding this process up is by using **computers** to **model** the shape of an enzyme's active site and **predict** how well potential drug molecules will interact with it. They can **quickly** examine hundreds of molecules to look for ones that might be the right shape **before** they start synthesising and testing things in the laboratory.

Practice Questions

Q1 What type of link joins the two amino acids in a dipeptide?

Q2 Name two types of secondary structure that proteins can form.

Q3 Name two types of bond that can help to hold together the tertiary structure of a protein.

Q4 What is an enzyme?

Q5 Explain the advantage of using computer-aided drug design instead of trial and error.

Exam Questions

Q1 The structures of the amino acids glycine and serine are shown on the right.

When two amino acids react together, a dipeptide is formed. Draw the structures of the two possible dipeptides that could be formed when serine and glycine react together. [2 marks]

$$NH_2-\overset{\overset{\displaystyle H}{|}}{\underset{\underset{\displaystyle H}{|}}{C}}-COOH$$
glycine

$$NH_2-\overset{\overset{\displaystyle HO-CH_2}{|}}{\underset{\underset{\displaystyle H}{|}}{C}}-COOH$$
serine

Q2 Sometimes adding a chemical to an enzyme-catalysed reaction can cause the enzyme to stop working properly.

a) What are chemicals that prevent enzymes from working called? [1 mark]

b) i) Explain how a drug molecule may prevent an enzyme from working properly. [2 marks]

ii) A scientist has developed a drug that stops a bacterial enzyme from working. The drug molecule is chiral. Explain why only one enantiomer of the drug will be effective against the enzyme. [2 marks]

Procrastination — the ultimate revision inhibitor...

There's almost as many proteins on these pages as in a big steak topped with cheese and a peanut sauce. Have another look at the reaction that links amino acids together — it's the same as the condensation polymerisation reactions on page 82, just using amino acids rather than diamines and dicarboxylic acids — so you're already halfway to knowing it.

DNA

DNA — the molecule of life. And unfortunately, just like life, it's complicated.

DNA is a Polymer of Nucleotides

DNA (**d**eoxyribo**n**ucleic **a**cid) contains all the genetic information of an organism.
DNA is made up from lots of **monomers** called **nucleotides**.
Nucleotides are made from the following:

1) **A phosphate group:**

$$^-O{-}P{=}O$$
(with OH above and OH below)

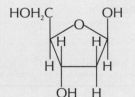

phosphate

sugar

base

Chris and Rita had forgotten about the rising nucleotide

2) **A pentose sugar** — a five-carbon sugar.
In DNA, the sugar is **2-deoxyribose**.

> You don't need to learn the structures of phosphate and 2-deoxyribose, or of the bases — they'll all be in your data booklet.

3) **A base** — one of four different bases. In DNA they are **adenine (A)**, **cytosine (C)**, **guanine (G)** and **thymine (T)**.

adenine   guanine   cytosine   thymine

The circled nitrogens are the atoms that bond with the deoxyribose molecule (see below).

Here are the **structures** of all four DNA **nucleotides**:

adenine nucleotide

guanine nucleotide

cytosine nucleotide

thymine nucleotide

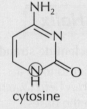

> You should be able to work out these structures from the info in the exam data booklet if you need to, so you don't need to learn them. But you do need to know where the phosphate group and the bases join to the sugar.

The nucleotides join together to form a **polynucleotide chain**. Covalent bonds form between the phosphate group of one nucleotide and the sugar of another — this makes what's called the **sugar-phosphate backbone** of the chain.

cytosine   thymine   adenine   guanine

sugar-phosphate backbone

DNA

DNA Forms by Condensation Polymerisation

The **sugar-phosphate backbone** of DNA is formed by condensation polymerisation, like this:

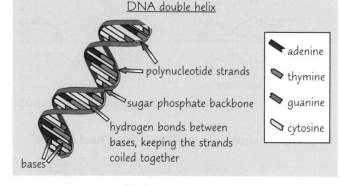

A molecule of H₂O is lost

The sugar group of another nucleotide can attach here

Phosphodiester bond

The phosphate group of another nucleotide can attach here

$+ \ H_2O$

1) A molecule of water is lost and a covalent **phosphodiester bond** is formed.

2) There are still OH groups at the top and bottom of the chain, so further links can be made. This allows the nucleotides to form a **polymer** made up of an alternating sugar-phosphate-sugar-phosphate chain.

DNA Forms a **Double Helix**

1) **DNA** is made of **two polynucleotide strands**.

2) The two strands spiral together to form a **double helix** structure, which is held together by **hydrogen bonds** between the bases.

3) Each base can only join with one particular partner — **adenine** always pairs with **thymine** (A – T) and **guanine** always pairs with **cytosine** (G – C).

4) This causes the two strands of DNA to be **complementary** — this means that they match up so that whenever there is an **adenine** base on one strand, there will be a **thymine** base on the other, and whenever there is a **guanine** base on one strand, there will be a **cytosine** base on the other, and vice versa.

DNA double helix

polynucleotide strands

sugar phosphate backbone

hydrogen bonds between bases, keeping the strands coiled together

bases

- adenine
- thymine
- guanine
- cytosine

Hydrogen Bonding Causes the Bases to Form **Specific Pairs**

As you saw above, **complementary base pairing** exists in the DNA helix, where **adenine (A)** always pairs to **thymine (T)** and **guanine (G)** always pairs to **cytosine (C)**. It happens because of the arrangement and number of atoms in the base molecules that are capable of forming **hydrogen bonds**.

A **hydrogen bond** forms between a polar positive **H atom** (an H attached to anything highly electronegative like N) and a lone pair of electrons on a nearby **O** or **N atom**. To bond, the two atoms have to be the **right distance apart**.

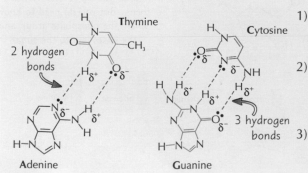

Thymine

2 hydrogen bonds

Adenine

Cytosine

Guanine

3 hydrogen bonds

1) A and T have the right atoms in the right places to each form **2 hydrogen bonds**, so they can pair up. G and C can each form **3 hydrogen bonds**, so they can pair up too.

2) These are the **only** possible base combinations. Other base pairings would put the partially charged atoms too close together (they'd repel each other), or too far apart, or the bonding atoms just wouldn't line up properly.

3) The DNA helix has to twist so that the bases are in the **right alignment** and at the **right distance** apart for the complementary base pairs to form.

DNA

Cisplatin Can Bind to DNA in Cancer Cells

1) **Cisplatin** is a complex of platinum(II) with two chloride ion ligands and two ammonia ligands in a **square planar shape** (see page 46). It is used as an **anti-cancer drug**.

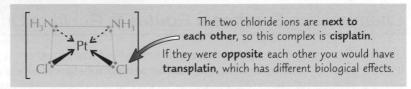

The two chloride ions are **next to each other**, so this complex is **cisplatin**. If they were **opposite** each other you would have **transplatin**, which has different biological effects.

2) **Cancer** is caused by cells in the body **dividing uncontrollably** and forming **tumours**.

3) In order for a cell to divide it has to **replicate** its DNA.

4) Cisplatin binds to DNA, causing **kinks** in the DNA helix which **stop** the proteins that replicate the DNA from copying it properly. This **stops** tumour cells reproducing. Here's how it works:

- A nitrogen atom on a **guanine base** in DNA forms a **co-ordinate bond** with cisplatin's platinum ion, replacing one of the chloride ion ligands. (This is a **ligand substitution** reaction, see page 52).

- A **second** nitrogen atom from a nearby guanine (either on the same strand of the DNA or the opposite strand) can bond to the platinum and replace the **second** chloride ion.

- The presence of the cisplatin complex bound to the DNA strands causes the strands to **kink**. This means that the DNA strands **can't unwind** and be **copied** properly — so the cell can't **replicate**.

This damage to the DNA also triggers mechanisms that lead to the death of the cell.

5) Unfortunately, cisplatin can bind to DNA in **normal cells** as well as cancer cells. This is a particular problem for any healthy cells that **replicate frequently**, such as **hair cells** and **blood cells**, because cisplatin stops them from replicating in the same way as it does the cancer cells. This means that cisplatin can cause **hair loss** and suppress the **immune system** (which is controlled by white blood cells). It can also cause kidney damage.

6) These side effects can be lessened by giving patients very **low dosages** of cisplatin.

7) Another way to reduce the side effects of cisplatin is to **target** it to the tumour — this means using a method that delivers the drug only to the cancer cells, so it doesn't get the chance to attack healthy cells.

8) Despite the side effects of cisplatin, it is still used as a chemotherapy drug. This is because the **balance** of the long-term positive effects (curing cancer) **outweigh** the negative short-term effects.

Practice Questions

Q1 What are the three components of a DNA nucleotide?
Q2 Briefly describe how the sugar-phosphate backbone of the DNA polymer is formed.
Q3 What is the complementary base of adenine?
Q4 Draw the structure of cisplatin. Explain how it stops DNA from replicating.

Exam Question

Q1 The structures of a phosphate group, the base guanine and the sugar 2-deoxyribose are shown below.

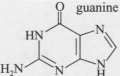
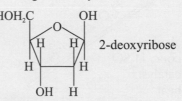

a) Use these structures to draw a diagram showing a DNA nucleotide containing the base guanine. [2 marks]

b) The complementary base of guanine is cytosine, shown on the right. Draw a diagram to show how guanine bonds to cytosine in a DNA double helix. What type of bonds are formed between the bases? [4 marks]

Sissy-platin: scared of spiders, loud noises and sandwiches...

Let's face it, I'm a science geek, but this DNA stuff never ceases to amaze me. It's just so flippin' clever. Sadly, even if you don't share my enthusiasm for genetics, you do have to know it. If you happen to be skipping the extremely useful exam questions (naughty, naughty), then have a go at this one. Seriously, try it. You can have a biscuit afterwards.

Organic Synthesis

In your exam you may be asked to suggest a pathway for the synthesis of a particular molecule. These pages contain a summary of some of the reactions you should know.

Chemists use **Synthesis Routes** to Get from One Compound to Another

Chemists have got to be able to make one compound from another. It's vital for things like **designing medicines**. It's also good for making imitations of **useful natural substances** when the real things are hard to extract.

These reactions are all covered either elsewhere in this book or in your Year 1 notes, so check back for extra details.

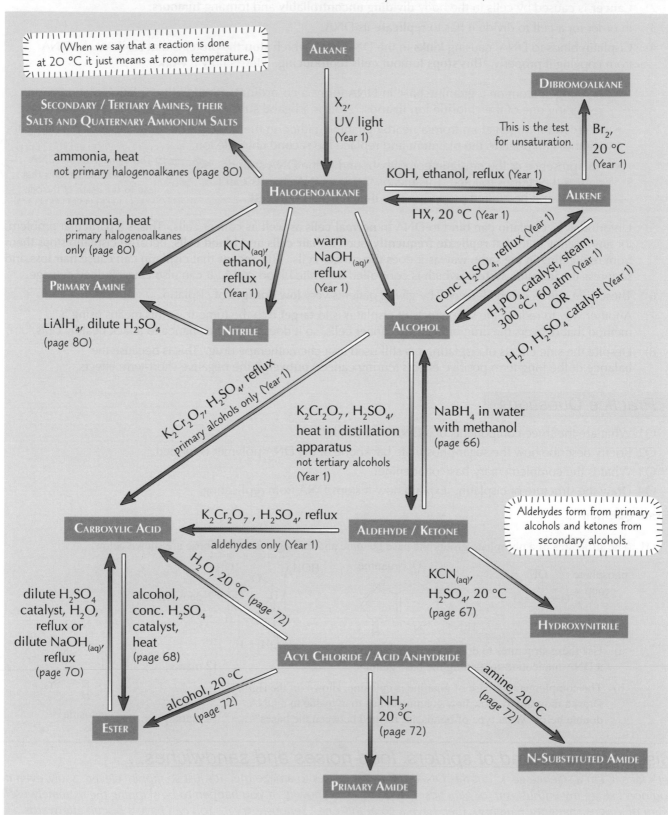

(When we say that a reaction is done at 20 °C it just means at room temperature.)

ALKANE

X_2, UV light (Year 1)

Aldehydes form from primary alcohols and ketones from secondary alcohols.

SECONDARY / TERTIARY AMINES, THEIR SALTS AND QUATERNARY AMMONIUM SALTS

ammonia, heat
not primary halogenoalkanes (page 80)

HALOGENOALKANE

KOH, ethanol, reflux (Year 1)

HX, 20 °C (Year 1)

ALKENE

This is the test for unsaturation.

Br_2, 20 °C (Year 1)

DIBROMOALKANE

ammonia, heat
primary halogenoalkanes only (page 80)

$KCN_{(aq)}$, ethanol, reflux (Year 1)

warm $NaOH_{(aq)}$, reflux (Year 1)

conc H_2SO_4, reflux (Year 1)

H_3PO_4 catalyst, steam, 300 °C, 60 atm (Year 1) OR H_2O, H_2SO_4 catalyst (Year 1)

PRIMARY AMINE

$LiAlH_4$, dilute H_2SO_4 (page 80)

NITRILE

ALCOHOL

$K_2Cr_2O_7$, H_2SO_4, reflux
primary alcohols only (Year 1)

$K_2Cr_2O_7$, H_2SO_4, heat in distillation apparatus
not tertiary alcohols (Year 1)

$NaBH_4$ in water with methanol (page 66)

CARBOXYLIC ACID

$K_2Cr_2O_7$, H_2SO_4, reflux
aldehydes only (Year 1)

ALDEHYDE / KETONE

H_2O, 20 °C (page 72)

$KCN_{(aq)}$, H_2SO_4, 20 °C (page 67)

HYDROXYNITRILE

dilute H_2SO_4 catalyst, H_2O, reflux or dilute $NaOH_{(aq)}$, reflux (page 70)

alcohol, conc. H_2SO_4 catalyst, heat (page 68)

ACYL CHLORIDE / ACID ANHYDRIDE

amine, 20 °C (page 72)

N-SUBSTITUTED AMIDE

alcohol, 20 °C (page 72)

ESTER

NH_3, 20 °C (page 72)

PRIMARY AMIDE

Organic Synthesis

Synthesis Routes for Making **Aromatic Compounds**

There are not so many of these reactions to learn — but make sure you still know all the itty-bitty details.

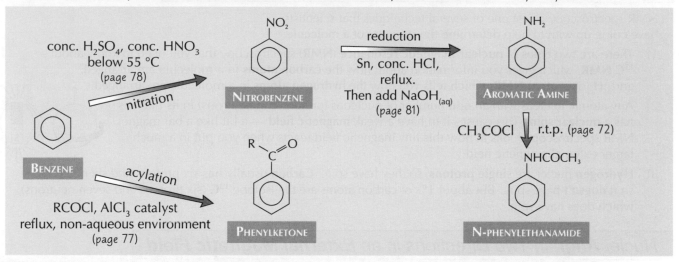

Chemists Aim to Design Synthesis Routes Which are **Safe** and **Efficient**

1) Chemists try to design synthesis routes that use **non-hazardous starting materials** to limit the potential for accidents and environmental damage.

2) Chemists are also concerned with designing processes that are **not too wasteful**. Processes with **high atom economies** and **high percentage yields** are preferred, because they convert more of the starting materials into useful products. Waste can also be reduced by designing synthesis routes that have as **few steps** as possible.

> Avoiding using **solvents** wherever possible is one way of **reducing** both the **hazards** associated with a process and the amount of **waste** created by a synthesis route. Solvents are often **flammable** and **toxic** so can pose safety risks. If the solvent has to be disposed of after the reaction is complete that can create a lot of **waste** too.

Practice Questions

Q1 What type of organic product is formed by the reaction between a primary halogenoalkane and ammonia?

Q2 Give two reagents that when combined with an alcohol will give an ester.

Q3 What reagents and conditions are needed to synthesise nitrobenzene from phenylamine?

Exam Questions

Q1 The diagram on the right shows a possible reaction pathway for the two-step synthesis of a ketone from a halogenoalkane.

$$H-\overset{\overset{\displaystyle H}{|}}{\underset{\underset{\displaystyle H}{|}}{C}}-\overset{\overset{\displaystyle X}{|}}{\underset{\underset{\displaystyle H}{|}}{C}}-\overset{\overset{\displaystyle H}{|}}{\underset{\underset{\displaystyle H}{|}}{C}}-H \xrightarrow[\text{NaOH}]{\text{Step 1}} H-\overset{\overset{\displaystyle H}{|}}{\underset{\underset{\displaystyle H}{|}}{C}}-\overset{\overset{\displaystyle OH}{|}}{\underset{\underset{\displaystyle H}{|}}{C}}-\overset{\overset{\displaystyle H}{|}}{\underset{\underset{\displaystyle H}{|}}{C}}-H \xrightarrow{\text{Step 2}} H-\overset{\overset{\displaystyle H}{|}}{\underset{\underset{\displaystyle H}{|}}{C}}-\overset{\overset{\displaystyle O}{\overset{||}{C}}}{}-\overset{\overset{\displaystyle H}{|}}{\underset{\underset{\displaystyle H}{|}}{C}}-H$$

Halogenoalkane P   Alcohol Q   Ketone R

a) Give the conditions needed to carry out Step 1. [1 mark]

b) Give the reagents and the conditions needed to carry out Step 2. [2 marks]

Q2 Ethyl methanoate is one of the compounds responsible for the smell of raspberries.
Outline, with reaction conditions, how it could be synthesised in the laboratory from methanol. [7 marks]

Q3 How would you synthesise propanol starting with propane? State the reaction conditions and reagents needed for each step and any particular safety considerations. [8 marks]

I saw a farmer turn a tractor into a field once — now that's impressive...

There's loads of information here, but you need to know it all. If you're asked in an exam how you would make one compound from another, make sure you include any procedures needed (e.g. refluxing), any reaction conditions and any safety precautions that should be taken. Why? Because that's the only way you can be sure you'll get all the marks.

NMR Spectroscopy

NMR isn't the easiest of things, so ingest this information one piece at a time — a bit like eating a bar of chocolate...

NMR *Gives You Information About a Molecule's* Structure

NMR spectroscopy is just one of several techniques that scientists have come up with to help determine the structure of a molecule.

1) There are two types of **nuclear magnetic resonance** (**NMR**) spectroscopy that you need to know about — ^{13}**C NMR**, which gives you information about how the **carbon atoms** in a molecule are arranged, and ^{1}**H** (or **proton**) **NMR**, which tells you how the **hydrogen atoms** in a molecule are arranged.

2) Any atomic nucleus with an **odd** number of nucleons (protons and neutrons) in its nucleus has a **nuclear spin**. This causes it to have a weak **magnetic field** — a bit like a bar magnet. NMR spectroscopy looks at how this tiny magnetic field reacts when you put in a much larger external magnetic field.

3) **Hydrogen** nuclei are **single protons**, so they have spin. **Carbon** usually has six protons and six neutrons, so it **doesn't** have spin. But about 1% of carbon atoms are the isotope ^{13}**C** (six protons and seven neutrons), which does have spin.

Nuclei **Align** *in Two Directions in an* **External Magnetic Field**

1) Normally the nuclei are spinning in **random directions** — so their magnetic fields **cancel out**.

2) But when a strong **external** magnetic field is applied the nuclei will all align either **with the field** or **opposed to it**.

3) The nuclei aligned with the external field are at a **slightly lower energy level** than the opposed nuclei.

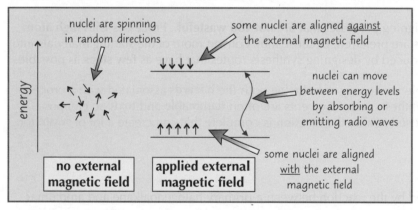

4) **Radio waves** of the right frequency can give the nuclei that are aligned with the external magnetic field enough energy to flip up to the higher energy level. The nuclei opposed to the external field can **emit** radio waves and flip down to the lower energy level.

5) To start with, there are more nuclei **aligned** with the external field, so there will be an **overall absorption** of energy. NMR spectroscopy **measures** this **absorption**.

Nuclei in **Different Environments** *Absorb* **Different Amounts of Energy**

1) A nucleus is partly **shielded** from the effects of external magnetic fields by its **surrounding electrons**.

2) Any **other atoms** and **groups of atoms** that are around a nucleus will also affect its amount of electron shielding. E.g. If a carbon atom bonds to a more electronegative atom (like oxygen) the amount of electron shielding around its nucleus will decrease.

3) This means that the nuclei in a molecule feel different magnetic fields depending on their **environments**. Nuclei in different environments will absorb **different amounts** of energy at **different frequencies**.

4) It's these **differences in energy absorption** between environments that you're looking for in **NMR spectroscopy**.

5) An atom's **environment** depends on **all** the groups that it's connected to, going **right along the molecule** — not just the atoms it's actually bonded to. To be in the **same environment**, two atoms must be joined to **exactly the same things**.

Chloroethane has 2 hydrogen environments — 3Hs in a CH_3 group bonded to CH_2Cl and **2Hs** in a CH_2Cl group bonded to CH_3.

2-chloropropane has 2 carbon environments:
• 1 C in a CHCl group, bonded to $(CH_3)_2$
• 2 Cs in CH_3 groups, bonded to $CHCl(CH_3)$

1-chlorobutane has 4 carbon environments. (The two carbons in CH_2 groups are **different** distances from the electronegative Cl atom — so their **environments** are **different**.)

NMR Spectroscopy

Chemical Shift is Measured Relative to Tetramethylsilane

1) Nuclei in different environments absorb energy of **different frequencies**. NMR spectroscopy measures these differences relative to a **standard substance** — the difference is called the **chemical shift (δ)**.

2) The standard substance is **tetramethylsilane (TMS)**, $Si(CH_3)_4$. This molecule has 12 hydrogen atoms all in **identical environments**, so it produces a **single** absorption peak, well away from most other absorption peaks.

Tetramethylsilane is also inert (so it doesn't react with the sample), non-toxic, and volatile (so it's easy to remove from the sample).

3) Chemical shift is measured in **parts per million** (or **ppm**) relative to TMS. So the single peak produced by TMS is given a **chemical shift value of 0**.

4) You'll often see a peak at δ = 0 on spectra because TMS is added to the test compound for calibration purposes.

^{13}C NMR Tells You How Many Different Carbon Environments a Molecule Has

The number of peaks on a ^{13}C NMR spectrum tells you how many different carbon environments are present in a particular molecule. The spectrum will have **one peak** on it for each **carbon environment** in the molecule.

There are **two carbon atoms** in a molecule of **ethanol**:

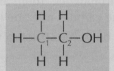

Because they are bonded to **different** atoms, each has a **different** amount of **electron shielding** — so there are **two carbon environments** in the ethanol molecule and **two peaks** on its ^{13}C NMR **spectrum**.

C_2 peak ⟶ (less shielded due to bond with O atom)

C_1 peak

TMS Peak ↓

chemical shift, δ (ppm)   0

Molecules containing an **aromatic ring** look a bit more complicated, but you can still **predict** what their spectra will look like by looking at the number of different carbon environments. Just keep a keen eye out for **lines of symmetry**.

In cyclohexane-1,3-diol there are **four different carbon environments**. If you think about the symmetry of the molecule you can see why this is. So cyclohexane-1,3-diol's ^{13}C NMR spectrum will have **4 peaks**.

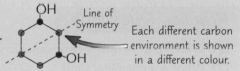

Line of Symmetry

Each different carbon environment is shown in a different colour.

You Can Look Up Chemical Shifts in a Data Table

In your exam you'll get a **data sheet** that will include a **table** like this one. The table shows the **chemical shifts** experienced by **carbon–13 nuclei** in **different environments**.

You need to **match up** the **peaks** in the spectrum with the **chemical shifts** in the table to work out which **carbon environments** they could represent.

Matching peaks to the groups that cause them isn't always straightforward, because the chemical shifts can **overlap**. For example, a peak at δ ≈ **30** might be caused by **C–C, C–Cl** or **C–Br**. A peak at δ ≈ **210**, is due to a **C=O** group in an **aldehyde** or a **ketone** — but you **don't** know which.

Ralph was trying to get a better look at his table.

^{13}C NMR Chemical Shifts Relative to TMS	
Chemical Shift, δ (ppm)	**Type of Carbon**
5 – 40	C – C
10 – 70	R – C – Cl or Br
20 – 50	O ‖ R – C – C
25 – 60	R – C – N (amines)
50 – 90	C – O (alcohols, ethers or esters)
90 – 150	C = C (alkenes)
110 – 125	R – C ≡ N
110 – 160	aromatic
160 – 185	O ‖ R – C – carbonyl (ester or carboxylic acid)
190 – 220	O ‖ R – C – carbonyl (ketone or aldehyde)

NMR Spectroscopy

Interpreting NMR Spectra Gets Easier with Practice

^{13}C NMR spectra are usually much **simpler** than ^1H NMR spectra (see pages 99-101) — they have fewer, sharper peaks. So, interpreting ^{13}C spectra really isn't all that bad — it's just a case of using your data sheet to work out what **carbon environment** is responsible for **each peak**.

Example: The diagram shows the carbon-13 NMR spectrum of an alcohol with the molecular formula $C_4H_{10}O$. Analyse and interpret the spectrum to identify the structure of the alcohol.

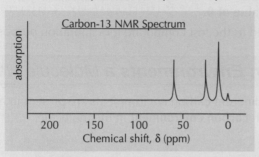

Carbon-13 NMR Spectrum

absorption

Chemical shift, δ (ppm)

200   150   100   50   0

1) Looking at the **table** on the **previous page**, the peak with a **chemical shift** of δ ≈ 65 is likely to be due to a **C–O** bond.

2) The two peaks around δ ≈ **20** probably both represent carbons in **C–C** bonds, but with slightly different environments. Remember the alcohol doesn't contain any **chlorine**, **bromine** or **nitrogen** so you can **ignore** those entries in the table.

3) The spectrum has **three peaks**, so the alcohol must have three **carbon environments**. There are **four carbons** in the alcohol, so two of the carbons must be in the **same environment**.

4) Put together all the **information** you've got so far, and try out some **structures**:

H H H H
H–C–C–C–C–OH
H H H H

This has a C–O bond, and some C–C bonds, which is right. But all four carbons are in different environments.

H H H H
H–C–C–C–C–H
H H OH H

Again, this has a C–O bond, and some C–C bonds. But the carbons are still all in different environments.

OH
H–C–H
H | H
H–C–C–C–H
H H H

This molecule has a C–O bond and C–C bonds and two of the carbons are in the same environment. So this must be the correct structure.

Practice Questions

Q1 Which part of the electromagnetic spectrum is absorbed in NMR spectroscopy?

Q2 What is a chemical shift?

Q3 Explain what the number of peaks in a ^{13}C NMR shows.

Exam Questions

Q1 Draw the molecular structures of each of the following compounds and predict the number of peaks in the ^{13}C NMR spectrum of each compound.

a) ethyl ethanoate [2 marks]

b) 1-chloro-2-methylpropane [2 marks]

c) 1,3,5-trichlorocyclohexane [2 marks]

Q2 The molecule shown on the right is methoxyethane. It has the molecular formula C_3H_8O.

H H   H
H–C–C–O–C–H
H H   H

a) Draw the displayed formulas of the two other possible isomers of C_3H_8O. [2 marks]

b) The ^{13}C NMR spectrum of one of the three isomers is on the right. Deduce which of the three isomers it represents. Explain your answer. [2 marks]

c) What is responsible for the peak at 0? [1 mark]

chemical shift, δ (ppm)   0

NMR, TMS — IMO this page goes a bit OTT on the TLAs...

The ideas behind NMR are difficult, so don't worry if you have to read these pages quite a few times before they make sense. You've got to make sure you really understand the stuff on these three pages as there's loads more about NMR on the next few pages — and it isn't any easier. Keep bashing away at it though — you'll eventually go "aaah... I get it."

¹H NMR

And now that you know the basics, here's the really crunchy bit for you to get your teeth stuck in.

¹H NMR — How Many **Environments** and How Many **Hydrogens** Are In Each

1) ¹H NMR is all about how **hydrogen nuclei** react to a magnetic field. The nucleus of a hydrogen atom is a **single proton**. So ¹H NMR is also known as '**proton NMR**' — and you might see the hydrogen atoms involved being called 'protons'.

2) **Each peak** on a ¹H NMR spectrum is due to one or more hydrogen nuclei (protons) in a **particular environment** — this is similar to a ¹³C NMR spectrum (which tells you the number of different carbon environments).

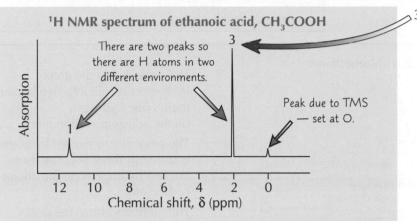

1) There are **two peaks** — so there are **two environments**.

2) The area ratio is **1:3** — so there's 1 H atom in the environment at δ ≈ 11.5 ppm to every 3 H atoms in the other environment.

3) If you look at the structure of ethanoic acid, this makes sense:

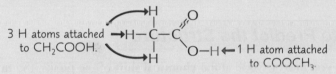

3 H atoms attached to CH₂COOH. 1 H atom attached to COOCH₃.

3) The **numbers above the peaks** on a ¹H NMR spectrum tell you the **ratio** of the areas under the peaks. This **relative area** under each peak also tells you the **relative number** of H atoms in each environment. Don't worry if they're not always whole numbers — they are ratios and not exact numbers.

Sometimes an integration trace is drawn on ¹H NMR spectrums, to show more clearly the ratio of the areas under the peaks (see page 101 for more).

Doug took great pride in his peak counting ability.

Use a **Table** to Identify the **Hydrogen Atom** Causing the **Chemical Shift**

You use a table like this to **identify** which functional group each peak is due to.

Don't worry — **you don't need to learn it**. You'll be given one in your exam, so you just need to learn how to use it. The copy you get in your exam may look a little different, and have different values — they depend on the solvent, temperature and concentration.

The hydrogen atoms that cause the shift are highlighted in red. R stands for any alkyl group.

According to the table, ethanoic acid (CH₃COOH) should have a peak at **10.0 – 12.0** ppm due to R-COOH, and a peak at **2.1 – 2.6 ppm** due to R-COCH₃.

You can see these peaks on ethanoic acid's spectrum above.

¹H NMR Chemical Shifts Relative to TMS	
Chemical Shift, δ (ppm)	**Type of H atom**
0.5 – 5.0	ROH
0.7 – 1.2	RCH₃
1.0 – 4.5	RNH₂
1.2 – 1.4	R₂CH₂
1.4 – 1.6	R₃CH
2.1 – 2.6	R–C–C– / O H
3.1 – 3.9	R–O–C– / H
3.1 – 4.2	RCH₂Br or Cl
3.7 – 4.1	R–C–O–C– / O H
4.5 – 6.0	R₂C=CH
9.0 – 10.0	R–C(=O)H
10.0 – 12.0	R–C(=O)O–H

¹H NMR

Splitting Patterns *Provide More Detail About Structure*

The peaks may be **split** into smaller peaks.
Peaks always split into the number of hydrogens
on the neighbouring carbon, **plus one**.
It's called the **n+1 rule**.

Type of Peak	Number of Hydrogens on Adjacent Carbon
Singlet (not split)	0
Doublet (split into two)	1
Triplet (split into three)	2
Quartet (split into four)	3

Here's the ¹H NMR spectrum for **1,1,2-trichloroethane**:

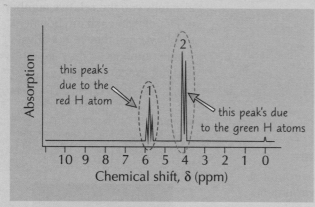

this peak's due to the red H atom

this peak's due to the green H atoms

The peak due to the green hydrogens is split into **two** because there's **one hydrogen** on the adjacent carbon atom.

The peak due to the red hydrogen is split into **three** because there are **two hydrogens** on the adjacent carbon atom.

The numbers above the peaks confirm that the **ratio** of **hydrogens** in the red environment to those in the green environment is **1 : 2**.

Put All the **Information Together** *to* **Predict the Structure**

To successfully interpret a proton NMR spectrum, you need to look at the **chemical shift** of the peaks, the **ratio of the areas under the peaks** and the **splitting patterns**. It sounds like an awful lot to think about, but if you go through each step carefully, you can predict the structure of an entire molecule just from the ¹H NMR spectra.

Example: Using the spectrum below, and the table of chemical shift data on page 99, predict the structure of the compound.

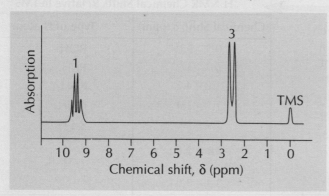

1) The peak at δ = 2.5 ppm is likely to be due to an **R–COCH₃** group, and the peak at δ = 9.5 ppm is likely to be due to an **R–CHO** group.

2) From the areas, there's one proton in the peak at δ = 9.5 ppm, for every three in the peak at δ = 2.5 ppm. This fits nicely with the first bit — so far so good.

3) The quartet's got **three** neighbouring hydrogens, and the doublet's got **one** — so it's likely these two groups are next to each other.

Now you know the molecule has to contain: and

All you have to do is fit them together:

¹H NMR

Integration Traces *Show Areas More Clearly*

When the peaks are split, it's not as easy to see the ratio of the **areas** under the peaks. So, sometimes an **integration trace** is shown instead of peak ratios. The increases in height are proportional to the areas under each peak.

You can use a ruler to measure the height of each vertical bit of the trace and then use the heights to work out the ratio of the peak areas.

The **integration ratio** for this spectrum is **1:2** — this means that there's 1 H atom in the first environment for every 2 H atoms in the second environment.

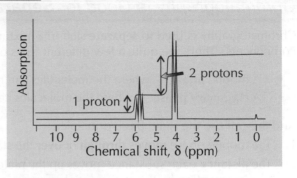

Samples are Dissolved in **Hydrogen-Free Solvents**

1) If a sample has to be dissolved, then a solvent is needed that doesn't contain any **¹H atoms** — because these would show up on the spectrum and confuse things.

2) **Deuterated solvents** are often used — their hydrogen atoms have been replaced by **deuterium** (D or ²H). Deuterium's an isotope of hydrogen that's got two nucleons (a proton and a neutron).

3) Because deuterium has an **even number** of nucleons, it doesn't have a spin (so it doesn't create a magnetic field).

4) **CCl₄** can also be used as a solvent — it doesn't contain any ¹H atoms either.

Practice Questions

Q1 What causes peaks to split in proton NMR?

Q2 What causes a triplet of peaks?

Q3 Why are deuterated solvents used when carrying out ¹H NMR spectroscopy?

Exam Questions

Q1 The ¹H NMR spectrum on the right is that of an haloalkane. Use the table of chemical shifts on page 99 to do the following:

a) Predict the environment of the two H atoms with a shift of 3.6 ppm. [1 mark]

b) Predict the environment of the three H atoms with a shift of 1.0 ppm. [1 mark]

c) The relative molecular mass of the molecule is 64.5. Suggest a possible structure and explain your suggestion. [2 marks]

d) Explain the shapes of the two peaks. [2 marks]

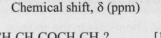

Q2 How many hydrogen environments are present in the molecule pentan-3-one, $CH_3CH_2COCH_2CH_3$? [1 mark]

Q3 The molecule ethyl ethanoate has three hydrogen environments, as shown in the diagram on the right. For the ¹H NMR spectrum of ethyl ethanoate, state:

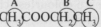

a) the integration ratio of the peaks, in the form A : B : C. [1 mark]

b) the type of peak that will be caused by each of the hydrogen environments. [3 marks]

Never mind splitting peaks — this stuff's likely to cause splitting headaches...

Is your head spinning yet? I know mine is. Round and round like a merry-go-round. It's a hard life when you're tied to a desk trying to get NMR spectroscopy firmly fixed in your head. You must be looking quite peaky yourself by now... so go on, learn this stuff, take the dog around the block, then come back and see if you can still remember it all.

Chromatography

You've probably tried chromatography with a spot of ink on a piece of filter paper — it's a classic experiment.

Chromatography is Good for **Separating** and **Identifying** Things

Chromatography is used to **separate** stuff in a mixture — once it's separated out, you can often **identify** the components. There are quite a few different types of chromatography — but they all have the same basic set-up:

- A **mobile phase** — where the molecules can move. This is always a liquid or a gas.
- A **stationary phase** — where the molecules can't move. This must be a solid, or a liquid on a solid support.

And they all use the same basic principle:

1) The mobile phase **moves through** or **over** the stationary phase.
2) The **distance** each substance moves up the plate depends on its **solubility** in the mobile phase and its **retention** by the stationary phase.
3) Components that are **more soluble** in the mobile phase will **travel further** up the plate.
4) It's these **differences** in solubility and retention by the stationary phase that **separate** out the different substances.

Thin-Layer Chromatography is a Simple Way of **Separating Mixtures**

1) In thin-layer chromatography (TLC), the **stationary phase** is a thin layer of **silica** (**silicon dioxide**) or **alumina** (**aluminium oxide**) fixed to a glass or metal plate.

2) Draw a line **in pencil** near the bottom of the TLC plate (the baseline) and put a very small drop of each mixture to be separated on the line.

3) Allow the spots on the plate to **dry**.

4) Place the plate in a beaker with a small volume of solvent (this is the **mobile phase**). The solvent level must be **below** the baseline, so it doesn't dissolve your samples away.

5) The solvent will start to move up the plate. As it moves, the solvent carries the substances in the mixture with it — some chemicals will be carried **faster** than others and so travel further up the plate.

> It's a good idea to wear gloves when handling the plate, to avoid any contamination by substances on your hands.

Labels on diagram: Watch glass lid (to stop solvent evaporating) · TLC plate · Beaker · Spot of mixture · Solvent · Baseline

6) Leave the beaker until the solvent has moved almost to the top of the plate. Then remove the plate from the beaker. Before it evaporates, use a pencil to mark how far the solvent travelled up the plate (this line is called the **solvent front**).

7) Place the plate in a fume cupboard and leave it to **dry**. The fume cupboard will prevent any **toxic** or **flammable fumes** from escaping into the room.

8) The result is called a **chromatogram**. You can use the **positions of the spots** on the chromatogram to identify the chemicals.

Colourless Chemicals are Revealed Using **UV Light** or **Iodine**

1) If the chemicals in the mixture are **coloured** (such as the dyes that make up an ink) then you'll see them as a **set of coloured dots** at different heights on the TLC plate...

2) But if there are **colourless chemicals**, such as amino acids, in the mixture, you need to find a way of making them **visible**. Here are two ways:

> Many TLC plates have a special **fluorescent dye** added to the silica or alumina layer that glows when **UV light** shines on it. You can put the plate under a **UV lamp** and draw around the dark patches to show where the spots of chemical are.

> Expose the chromatogram to **iodine vapour** (leaving the plate in a sealed jar with a couple of iodine crystals does the trick). Iodine vapour is a **locating agent** — it sticks to the chemicals on the plate and they'll show up as **brown/purple spots**.

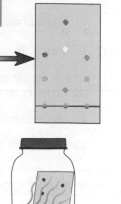

Chromatography

The **Position** of the Spots on a Plate Can Help to **Identify Substances**

1) If you just want to know **how many** chemicals are present in a mixture, all you have to do is **count the number of spots** that form on the plate.

2) But if you want to find out what each chemical **is**, you can calculate something called an R_f value. The formula for this is:

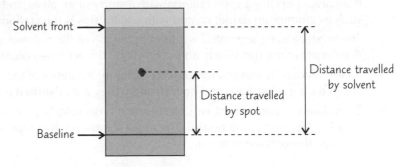

$$R_f = \frac{\text{distance travelled by spot}}{\text{distance travelled by solvent}}$$

Solvent front →

Distance travelled by solvent

Distance travelled by spot

Baseline →

3) R_f values aren't dependent on how big the plate is or how far the solvent travels — they're properties of the chemicals in the mixture and so can be used to identify those chemicals.

4) This means you can look your R_f value up in a table of **standard R_f values** to identify what that substance is.

5) BUT — if the composition of the TLC plate, the solvent, or the temperature change even slightly, you'll get **different R_f values**.

6) It's hard to keep the conditions identical. So, if you suspect that a mixture contains, say, chlorophyll, it's best to put a spot of chlorophyll on the baseline of the **same plate** as the mixture and run them both at the **same time**.

Practice Questions

Q1 Explain the terms 'stationary phase' and 'mobile phase' in the context of chromatography.

Q2 What is the stationary phase in TLC?

Q3 Describe how you would calculate the R_f value of a substance on a TLC plate.

Exam Questions

Q1 A student is carrying out a thin-layer chromatography experiment.

a) The student uses a pair of gloves to hold the TLC plate. Give one reason for taking this precaution. [1 mark]

b) Once the plate has been placed inside the beaker of solvent, a lid is placed on top. Why is it necessary to seal the plate inside the beaker? [1 mark]

c) Once the solvent is nearing the top of the plate, the student removes it from the beaker and marks how far the solvent has travelled. What is the next step that the student needs to do? [1 mark]

Q2 The diagram below shows a chromatogram of four known substances (1 to 4) and two unknowns, labelled X and Y. One of the unknowns is pure and the other is a mixture.

a) Which of the unknowns, X or Y is a pure substance? [1 mark]

b) Suggest which of the known substances (1 to 4) are present in the unknown that is a mixture. Explain your answer. [2 marks]

c) The solvent front on the chromatogram was measured at 8 cm from the baseline, and Substance 1 travelled 5.6 cm. Calculate the R_f value of Substance 1. [1 mark]

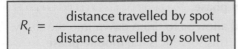

A little bit of TLC is what you need...

There's nothing better than watching small dots racing up a plate. Hours of fun. Working out R_f values comes close though and it's easy marks if you remember that it's the distance travelled by the spot divided by distance travelled by the solvent, and not the other way around — it might help to think of it as a fraction (and it'll always be less than 1).

More on Chromatography

As well as the thin-layer chromatography on the previous pages, there are also some weirder, wackier versions. The good thing is the principle is still the same — you've still got a mobile phase and a stationary phase. Phew.

Column Chromatography is Used To Separate Out Solutions

Column chromatography is mostly used for **purifying an organic product**.

This is done to separate the product from unreacted chemicals and by-products.

1) It involves packing a glass column with a slurry of an absorbent material such as aluminium oxide, coated with water. This is the **stationary phase**.

2) The mixture to be separated is added to the top of the column and allowed to drain down into the slurry. A **solvent** is then run slowly and continually through the column. This solvent is the **mobile phase**.

3) As the mixture is washed through the column, its components **separate out** according to **how soluble** they are in the mobile phase and **how strongly they are adsorbed** onto the stationary phase (**retention**).

4) Each different component will spend some time adsorbed onto the stationary phase and some time dissolved in the mobile phase. The **more** soluble each component is in the mobile phase, the **quicker** it'll pass through the column.

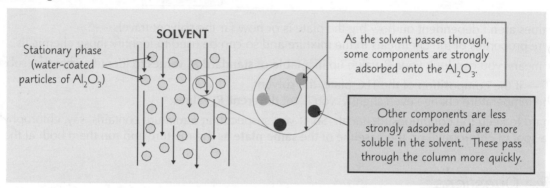

SOLVENT

Stationary phase (water-coated particles of Al₂O₃)

As the solvent passes through, some components are strongly adsorbed onto the Al₂O₃.

Other components are less strongly adsorbed and are more soluble in the solvent. These pass through the column more quickly.

Gas Chromatography is Used To Separate Mixtures of Volatile Liquids

1) If you've got a mixture of **volatile liquids** (ones that turn into gases easily), then **gas chromatography** (GC) is the way to separate them out so that you can **identify** them.

2) The stationary phase is a **solid** or a solid coated by a **viscous liquid**, such as an oil, packed into a long tube. The tube is coiled to save space and built into an oven. The mobile phase is an **unreactive carrier gas** such as nitrogen.

3) Each component takes a different amount of time from being **injected** into the tube to being **recorded** at the other end. This is the **retention time**.

The retention time depends on how much time the component spends moving along with the carrier gas, and how much time it spends stuck to the viscous liquid.

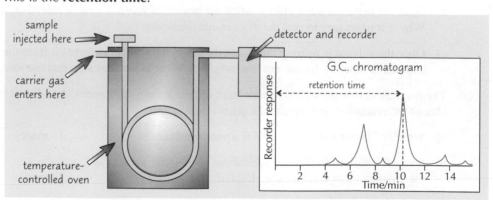

sample injected here

detector and recorder

carrier gas enters here

temperature-controlled oven

G.C. chromatogram

retention time

Recorder response

Time/min

4) Each separate substance will have a unique retention time — so you can use the retention time to **identify** the components of the mixture. (You have to run a known sample under the same conditions for comparison.) For example, if you wanted to know if a mixture contained **octane**, you could run a sample of the **mixture** through the system, then run a sample of **pure octane** through, and see if there's a peak at the **same retention time** on both spectra.

5) The **area** under each peak tells you the relative **amount** of each component that's present in the mixture.

6) GC can be used to find the **level of alcohol** in **blood** or **urine** — the results are **accurate** enough to be used as evidence in court. It's also used to find the **proportions** of various **esters in oils** used in **paints** — this lets picture restorers know exactly what paint was originally used.

More on Chromatography

Mass Spectrometry can be Combined with Gas Chromatography

1) **Mass spectrometry** is a technique used to identify substances from their mass/charge ratio. It is very good at **identifying** unknown compounds, but would give confusing results from a mixture of substances.

2) **Gas chromatography** (see previous page), on the other hand, is very good at **separating** a mixture into its individual components, but not so good at identifying those components.

3) If you put these **two techniques together**, you get an **extremely useful** analytical tool.

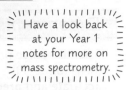
Have a look back at your Year 1 notes for more on mass spectrometry.

> **Gas chromatography-mass spectrometry** (or GC-MS for short) **combines the benefits** of gas chromatography and mass spectrometry to make a super analysis tool.
>
> The sample is **separated** using **gas chromatography**, but instead of going to a detector, the separated components are fed into a **mass spectrometer**.
>
> The spectrometer produces a **mass spectrum** for each **component**, which can be used to **identify** each one and show what the original **sample** consisted of.

4) The **advantage** of this method over normal GC is that the components separated out by the chromatography can be **positively identified**, which can be impossible from a chromatogram alone.

5) **Computers** can be used to match up the **mass spectrum** for each component of the mixture against a **database**, so the whole process can be **automated**.

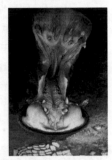
Oh, excuse me — chemistry always sends me to sleep, I'm afraid.

Practice Questions

Q1 In column chromatography, explain why the components pass through the column at different rates.

Q2 What is the mobile phase in GC?

Q3 GC can identify which substances are present and their relative amounts. How is the relative amount determined?

Exam Questions

Q1 A mixture of 25% ethanol and 75% benzene is run through gas chromatography apparatus.

   a) Describe what happens to the mixture in the apparatus. [4 marks]

   b) Explain why the substances separate. [2 marks]

   c) How will the resulting chromatogram show the proportions of ethanol and benzene present in the mixture? [1 mark]

Q2 GC can be used to detect the presence and quantity of alcohol in the blood or urine samples of suspected drink-drivers.

   a) What do the letters GC stand for? [1 mark]

   b) Explain how 'retention time' is used to identify ethanol in a sample of blood or urine. [2 marks]

   c) Why is nitrogen used as the carrier gas? [1 mark]

Q3 Which of these statements about column chromatography are correct?

   1. It can be used as a purification technique.
   2. The stationary phase is a slurry of an adsorbent material coated in water.
   3. The more soluble each component is in the mobile phase, the slower it will pass through the column.

   A Only 1   B 1 and 2   C 2 and 3   D 1, 2 and 3   [1 mark]

Cromer-tography — pictures from my holiday in Norfolk...

The fun need not stop with thin-layer chromatography. Column chromatography and gas chromatography are potentially even more exciting. It may seem like a lot of techniques to learn, but the theory behind all these different types of chromatography is the same. You've got a mobile phase, a stationary phase and a mixture that wants separating.

Planning Experiments

As well as doing practical work in class, you can get asked about it in your exams too. Harsh I know, but I'm afraid that's how it goes. You need to be able to plan experiments and to spot the good and bad points of plans that you're shown.

Experiments Need to be **Carefully Planned**

Scientists solve problems by **suggesting answers** and then doing **experiments** that **test** their ideas to see if the evidence supports them. Being able to plan experiments that will give you **accurate** and **precise results** is an important part of this process. Here's how you go about it:

There's more about what accurate and precise results are on page 112.

1) State the **aim** of your experiment — what question are you trying to answer?
2) Make a **prediction** — a specific testable statement about what will happen in the experiment, based on observation, experience or a **hypothesis** (a suggested explanation for a fact or observation).
3) Identify the **independent**, **dependent** and other **variables** (see below) in your experiment.
4) Decide what **data** you need to collect.
5) Select **appropriate equipment** for your experiment.
6) Do a **risk assessment** and plan any safety precautions that you will need to take.
7) Write out a **detailed method** for your experiment.

After step 7), you can actually go ahead and do your experiment. Lucky you...

Make it a **Fair Test** — Control your **Variables**

You probably already know what the different kinds of **variable** are, but they're easy to mix up, so here's a recap:

Variable — A variable is a **quantity** that has the **potential to change**, e.g. temperature, mass, or volume. There are two types of variable commonly referred to in experiments:
- **Independent variable** — the thing that you **change** in an experiment.
- **Dependent variable** — the thing that you **measure** in an experiment.

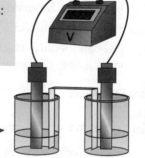

As well as the independent and dependent variables, you need to think of all the **other variables** (sometimes called **control variables**) that could affect the result of the experiment and plan ways to keep each of them **the same**.

So, if you're investigating the effect of changing the temperature on the EMF of a zinc/copper cell using this equipment, then the variables will be:

Independent variable	Temperature.
Dependent variable	The voltage (EMF) of the cell.
Other variables — you MUST keep these the same	The concentration and volume of the zinc and copper solutions. The pressure. The equipment used to carry out the experiment (i.e. you should use the same wires, voltmeter and thermometer each time).

Work **Safely** and **Ethically** — Don't Blow Up the Lab or Harm Small Animals

1) When you plan an experiment, you need to think about how you're going to make sure that you work **safely**.
2) The first step is to identify all the **hazards** that might be involved in your experiment (e.g. dangerous chemicals or naked flames). Then you need to come up with ways to reduce the **risks** that these hazards pose.

This means things like wearing **goggles** and a **lab coat** when handling any **hazardous chemicals** (e.g. those that are **irritants**, **toxic** or **corrosive**), using a **fume cupboard** to do any reactions that produce nasty gases, or heating anything flammable with a **water bath**, **sand bath** or **electric heater** (rather than over a flame).

3) Doing this procedure is sometimes referred to as doing a '**risk assessment**'.
4) You need to make sure you're working **ethically** too. This is most important if there are other people or animals involved. You have to put their welfare first.

Planning Experiments

Choose *Appropriate* Equipment — *Think about* **Size** *and* **Sensitivity**

Selecting the right equipment may sound easy but it's something you need to think carefully about.

1) The equipment has to be **appropriate** for the experiment.

> E.g. if you want to measure the amount of gas produced in a reaction, you need to make sure you use apparatus which will collect the gas, without letting any escape.

2) The equipment needs to be the right **size**.

> E.g. if you're using a gas syringe to measure the volume of gas produced by a reaction, it needs to be big enough to collect all the gas, or the plunger will be pushed out of the end. You might need to do some rough calculations to work out what size of equipment to use.

3) The equipment needs to have the right level of **sensitivity**.

> E.g. if you want to measure out 2 cm^3 of a solution, you need to use a measuring cylinder that has a scale marked off in steps of at least 1 cm^3, not one that only has markings every 10 cm^3. If you want to measure small changes in pH, then you need to use a pH meter, which can measure pH to several decimal places, rather than indicator paper.

Since his nursery school didn't have any retort stands, Zak bravely attempted to build his own.

> If you want to measure out a solution really accurately (e.g. 20.0 cm^3 of solution) you'll need to use a burette or a pipette.

Know Your Different Sorts of **Data**

Experiments always involve some sort of measurement to provide **data** and you need to decide what data to collect. There are different types of data — so it helps to know what they are.

> **Discrete** — a discrete variable can only have **certain values** on a scale. For example the number of bubbles formed in a reaction is discrete (you can't have 1.77 bubbles). You usually get discrete data by **counting** things.

> **Continuous** — a continuous variable can have **any value** on a scale. For example, the volume of gas produced or the voltage of an electrochemical cell. You can never measure the exact value of a continuous variable.

> **Categoric** — a categoric variable has values that can be sorted into **categories**. For example, the colours of solutions might be blue, red and green, or types of material might be wood, steel and glass.

> **Ordered (ordinal)** — ordered data is similar to categoric, but the categories can be **put in order**. For example, if you classified reactions as 'slow', 'fairly fast' and 'very fast' you'd have ordered data.

Methods Must be **Clear** and **Detailed**

When **writing** or **evaluating** a method, you need to think about all of the things on these two pages. The method must be **clear** and **detailed** enough for **anyone** to follow — it's important that other people can recreate your experiment and get the **same** results. Make sure your method includes:

1) All the **substances** needed and what **quantity** of each to use.
2) How to **control** variables.
3) The exact **apparatus** needed (a **diagram** is often helpful to show the set-up).
4) Any **safety precautions** that should be taken.
5) What **data** to collect and **how** to collect it.

Presenting Results

Once you've collected the data from your experiment, it's not time to stop, put your feet up and have a cup of tea —
you've got to present your results too. That might well mean putting them in a table or turning them into a graph.

Organise Your Results in a **Table**

It's a good idea to set up a table to **record** the **results** of your experiment. Make sure that you **include** enough
rows and **columns** to **record all of the data** you need. You might also need to include a column for **processing**
your data (e.g. working out an average).

Make sure each **column** has a **heading** so you
know what's going to be recorded where.

The **units** should be in the
column heading, not the table itself.

Concentration of KI / mol dm⁻³	Duration of clock reaction / s			Mean duration of clock reaction / s
	Run 1	Run 2	Run 3	
0.045	32	34	33	(32 + 34 + 33) ÷ 3 = 33
0.033	50	50	47	(50 + 50 + 48) ÷ 3 = 49
0.021	72	70	71	(72 + 70 + 71) ÷ 3 = 71

You can find the **mean result** by **adding up** the data
from each repeat and **dividing** by the number of repeats.

Graphs: *Line, Bar or Scatter* — Use the *Best Type*

When drawing graphs, the
dependent variable should
go on the y-axis, and the
independent on the x-axis.

You'll often need to make a **graph** of your results. Not only are graphs **pretty**,
they make your data **easier to understand** — so long as you choose the right type.

Scatter plots are great for showing how two sets of continuous data are related (or **correlated** — see page 110).
Don't try to join all the points on a scatter plot — draw a straight or curved **line of best fit** to show the **trend**.

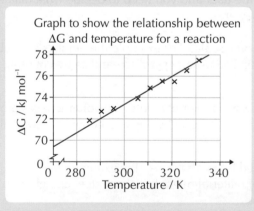

Graph to show the relationship between
ΔG and temperature for a reaction

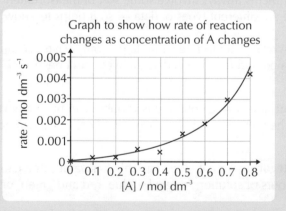

Graph to show how rate of reaction
changes as concentration of A changes

You should use a bar chart when one of your data
sets is **categoric or ordered data**. For example:

Graph to show
the pH of
rainwater samples

Pie charts can also
be used to display
categoric data.

Whatever type of graph you draw,
you'll ONLY get full marks if you:

- Choose a sensible scale —
  don't draw a tiny graph in the
  corner of the paper.

- Label both axes — including units.

- Plot your points accurately —
  using a sharp pencil.

Presenting Results

Don't Forget About *Units*

Units are really important — 10 g is very different from 10 kg — so make sure you don't forget to add them to your **tables** and **graphs**. They're also important in **calculations**, particularly if you need to **convert** between two different units.

Here are some useful examples:

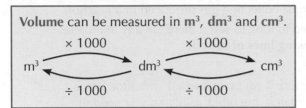

Volume can be measured in m^3, dm^3 and cm^3.

$$m^3 \xrightarrow{\times 1000} dm^3 \xrightarrow{\times 1000} cm^3$$
$$\xleftarrow{\div 1000} \qquad \xleftarrow{\div 1000}$$

Example: Write 1.1 dm^3 in m^3 and cm^3.

First, to convert 1.1 dm^3 into m^3 you divide by 1000.
$$1.1 \text{ dm}^3 \div 1000 = 0.0011 \text{ m}^3 = \mathbf{1.1 \times 10^{-3} \text{ m}^3}$$
Then, to convert 1.1 dm^3 into cm^3 you multiply by 1000.
$$1.1 \text{ dm}^3 \times 1000 = 1100 \text{ cm}^3 = \mathbf{1.1 \times 10^3 \text{ cm}^3}$$

This is written in standard form. Standard form is a useful way to write very big or very small numbers neatly.

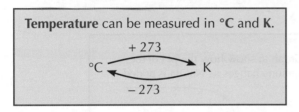

Temperature can be measured in **°C** and **K**.

$$°C \xrightarrow{+ 273} K$$
$$\xleftarrow{- 273}$$

Example: Write 267 K in °C .

To convert 267 K into °C you subtract 273.
$$267 \text{ K} - 273 = \mathbf{-6 \text{ °C}}$$

Round to the *Lowest Number* of *Significant Figures*

The first **significant figure** (or **s.f.**) of a number is the **first digit that isn't a zero**. The second, third and fourth significant figures follow on immediately after the first (even if they're zeros). For example, the number **0.02094** is **0.02** to 1 s.f., **0.021** to 2 s.f., and **0.0209** to 3 s.f.

1) When you're doing a calculation, use the number of significant figures given in the data as a guide for how many you need to give in your answer.

2) Whether you're doing calculations with the results from an experiment or doing calculations in an exam, the rule is the same — round your answer to the **lowest number of significant figures** that's in your data.

Example: 13.5 cm^3 of a 0.51 mol dm^{-3} solution of sodium hydroxide reacts with 1.5 mol dm^{-3} hydrochloric acid. Calculate the volume of hydrochloric acid, in cm^3, required to neutralise the sodium hydroxide.

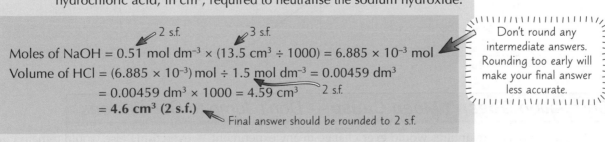

Moles of NaOH = 0.51 mol dm^{-3} (2 s.f.) × (13.5 cm^3 ÷ 1000) (3 s.f.) = 6.885 × 10^{-3} mol

Volume of HCl = (6.885 × 10^{-3}) mol ÷ 1.5 mol dm^{-3} = 0.00459 dm^3

= 0.00459 dm^3 × 1000 = 4.59 cm^3 (2 s.f.)

= **4.6 cm^3 (2 s.f.)** ← Final answer should be rounded to 2 s.f.

Don't round any intermediate answers. Rounding too early will make your final answer less accurate.

3) You should always **write down** the number of significant figures you've rounded to after your answer (as in the example above), so that other people can see what rounding you've done.

4) If you get told in an exam question **how many** significant figures you should give your answer to, make sure you follow those instructions — you'll **lose marks** if you don't.

5) If you're converting an answer into **standard form**, keep the same number of significant figures, e.g. 0.0041 mol dm^{-3} has the same number of significant figures as 4.1 × 10^{-3} mol dm^{-3}.

If you're ever asked to give an answer to "an appropriate degree of precision", this just means "to a sensible number of significant figures".

PRACTICAL SKILLS

Analysing Results

You're not quite finished yet... there's still time to look at your results and try and make sense of them. Graphs are really useful for helping you to spot patterns in your data. There are lots of examples on these pages. Ooh, pretty...

Watch Out For **Anomalous** Results

1) **Anomalous results** are ones that **don't fit** in with the other values — this means they are likely to be wrong.

2) They're often caused by mistakes or problems with apparatus, e.g. if a drop in a titration is too big and puts you past the end point, or if a syringe plunger gets stuck whilst collecting gas produced in a reaction.

3) When looking at results in tables or graphs, you always need to look to see if there are any anomalies — you **ignore** these results when **calculating means** or **drawing lines of best fit**.

Example: Calculate the mean titre volume from the results in the table below.

Titration Number	1	2	3	4
Titre Volume (cm³)	15.20	15.30	15.25	(15.70)

Titre **4** isn't **concordant** with (doesn't match) the other results so you need to ignore that one and just use the other three:

$$\frac{15.20 + 15.30 + 15.25}{3} = \textbf{15.25 cm}^3$$

Look at the pH curve on the right.

The result at **4 cm³** doesn't fit with the other results, so you need to ignore it when drawing the line of best fit.

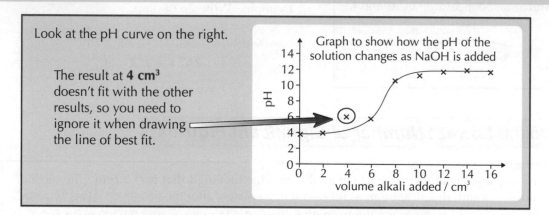

Graph to show how the pH of the solution changes as NaOH is added

Scatter Graphs *Show How Two Variables are* **Correlated**

Correlation describes the **relationship** between the independent variable and dependent variable. Data can show:

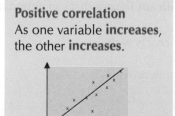

Positive correlation
As one variable **increases**, the other **increases**.

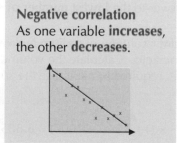

Negative correlation
As one variable **increases**, the other **decreases**.

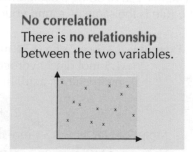

No correlation
There is **no relationship** between the two variables.

Correlation **Doesn't** Mean **Cause** — Don't Jump to Conclusions

1) Ideally, only **two** quantities would **ever** change in any experiment — everything else would remain **constant**.

2) But in experiments or studies outside the lab, you **can't** usually control all the variables. So even if two variables are correlated, the change in one may **not** be causing the change in the other. Both changes might be caused by a **third variable**.

For example, some studies have found a correlation between drinking **chlorinated tap water** and the risk of developing certain cancers. Some people argue that this means water shouldn't have chlorine added.

BUT it's hard to design a study that **controls all the variables** between people who drink tap water and people who don't. The risk of getting different cancers is affected by many lifestyle factors. Or there could be some other risk factor present in the tap water (or in whatever the non tap water drinkers drink instead).

Analysing Results

*Don't Get **Carried Away** When Drawing Conclusions*

1) The **data** should always **support** your conclusion. This may sound obvious but it's easy to **jump** to conclusions.
2) Also, conclusions have to be **specific** — you can't make sweeping generalisations.

For example: the **rate** of an enzyme-controlled reaction was measured at **10 °C**, **20 °C**, **30 °C**, **40 °C**, **50 °C** and **60 °C**. All other variables were kept constant. The results of this experiment are shown in the graph below.

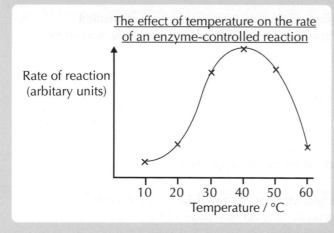

The effect of temperature on the rate of an enzyme-controlled reaction

Rate of reaction (arbitary units)

Temperature / °C

1) A science magazine **concluded** from this data that the enzyme used in the experiment works best at **40 °C**.
2) The data **doesn't** support this exact claim. The enzyme **could** work best at 42 °C or 47 °C, but you can't tell from the data because **increases** of **10 °C** at a time were used. The rate of reaction at in-between temperatures **wasn't** measured.
3) All you can say for certain is that this particular reaction was faster at **40 °C** than at any of the other temperatures tested.

4) Also you can't be sure that if you did the experiment under **different conditions**, e.g. at a **different pressure**, you wouldn't get a **different optimum temperature**.
5) It's also worth remembering that this experiment **ONLY** gives you information about this particular reaction. You can't conclude that **all** enzyme-controlled reactions happen fastest at this temperature — only this one.

*You Can Find **Rate** By Finding the **Gradient** of a Graph*

Rate is a **measure** of how much something is changing over time.
Calculating a rate can be useful when analysing data, e.g. you might want to the find the **rate of a reaction**.

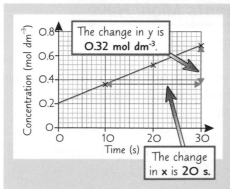

The change in y is **0.32 mol dm⁻³**.

Concentration (mol dm⁻³)

Time (s)

The change in x is **20 s**.

For a **linear** graph you can calculate the **rate** by finding the **gradient of the line**:

$$\text{Gradient} = \frac{\text{Change in } y}{\text{Change in } x}$$

So in this **example**:

$$\text{rate} = \frac{0.32 \text{ mol dm}^{-3}}{20 \text{ seconds}} = 0.016 \text{ mol dm}^{-3} \text{ s}^{-1}$$

The **equation** of a **straight line** can always be written in the form $y = mx + c$, where **m** is the **gradient** and **c** is the **y-intercept** (this is the **value of y** when the line crosses the **y-axis**).
In this example, the equation of the line is $y = 0.016x + 0.2$.

For a **curved** graph you find the **gradient** by drawing a **tangent**:

1) Position a ruler on the graph at the **point** where you want to know the **rate**.
2) **Angle** the **ruler** so there is **equal space** between the **ruler** and the **curve** on **either** side of the point.
3) **Draw** a **line** along the ruler to make the tangent. Extend the line right across the graph — it'll help to make your gradient calculation **easier** as you'll have **more points** to choose from.
4) **Calculate** the **gradient** of the **tangent** to find the **rate**: rate = 55 °C ÷ 44 s = **1.25 °C s⁻¹**

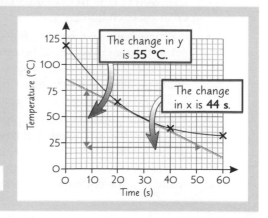

The change in y is **55 °C**.

The change in x is **44 s**.

Temperature (°C)

Time (s)

Evaluating Experiments

So you've planned an experiment, done the practical work, collected lots of data and plotted it all on a beautiful graph. Now it's time to sit back, relax and... work out everything you did wrong. That's science, I'm afraid.

You Need to Look **Critically** at Your Results

Here are a few terms that will come in handy when you're evaluating how convincing your results are...

Valid

Valid results are results that answer the **original question**. For example, if you haven't **controlled all the variables** your results won't be valid, because you won't be testing just the thing you wanted to.

Accurate

Accurate results are results that are **really close** to the **true** answer.

You might see results that fulfil all of these being called <u>reliable</u>.

Precise

The smaller the amount of **spread** of your data around the **mean** (see page 108), the more **precise** it is.

Calculating a **mean** (average) result from your repeats will **increase** the **precision** of your result, because it helps to reduce the effect of **random errors** on the answer (see page 113).

Repeatable

Your results are **repeatable** if **you** get the same results when you repeat the experiment using the same method and the same equipment. You really need to repeat your readings **at least three times** to demonstrate that your results really are repeatable.

Reproducible

Your results are **reproducible** if **other people** get the same results when they repeat your experiment.

You Need to Think About the **Error** Your **Measurements** Might Have

1) Any measurements you make will have **errors** (or **uncertainties**) in them, due to the limits of the **sensitivity** of the equipment.

2) Errors are usually written with a ± sign, e.g ±0.05 cm. The ± sign tells you the **actual value** of the measurement lies somewhere between your reading **minus** the error value and your reading **plus** the error value.

3) The error will be different for different pieces of equipment. For example:

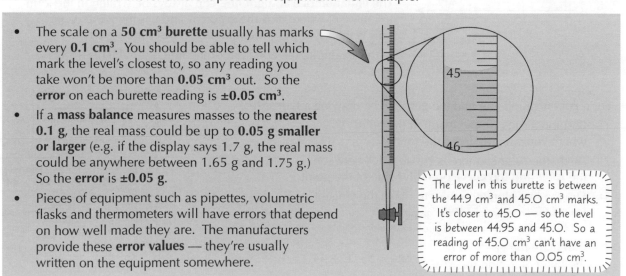

- The scale on a **50 cm³ burette** usually has marks every **0.1 cm³**. You should be able to tell which mark the level's closest to, so any reading you take won't be more than **0.05 cm³** out. So the **error** on each burette reading is **±0.05 cm³**.

- If a **mass balance** measures masses to the **nearest 0.1 g**, the real mass could be up to **0.05 g smaller or larger** (e.g. if the display says 1.7 g, the real mass could be anywhere between 1.65 g and 1.75 g.) So the **error** is **±0.05 g**.

- Pieces of equipment such as pipettes, volumetric flasks and thermometers will have errors that depend on how well made they are. The manufacturers provide these **error values** — they're usually written on the equipment somewhere.

The level in this burette is between the 44.9 cm³ and 45.0 cm³ marks. It's closer to 45.0 — so the level is between 44.95 and 45.0. So a reading of 45.0 cm³ can't have an error of more than 0.05 cm³.

Evaluating Experiments

You Can Calculate The **Percentage Error** in a Result

If you know the **error** (uncertainty) in a reading that you've taken using a certain piece of equipment, you can use it to calculate the **percentage error** in your measurement.

$$\text{percentage error} = \frac{\text{error}}{\text{reading}} \times 100$$

Example: 2.00 g of solid $CaCl_2$ is measured out on a balance with an error of ±0.005 g. Calculate the percentage error on this reading.

$$\text{percentage error} = \frac{0.005}{2.00} \times 100 = \textbf{0.25\%}$$

Example: In a titration a burette with an error of ±0.05 cm^3 is used. The initial reading on the burette is 50.0 cm^3. The final reading is 28.8 cm^3. Calculate the percentage error on the titre value.

Titre value = 50.0 cm^3 – 28.8 cm^3 = 21.2 cm^3

Error on each burette reading = ±0.05 cm^3

Two burette readings have been combined to find the titre value, so total error = 0.05 + 0.05 = ±0.1 cm^3

Percentage error on titre value = $\frac{0.1}{21.2} \times 100 = \textbf{0.47\%}$

Percentage error is useful because it tells you how **significant** the error in a reading is in comparison to its **size** — e.g. an error of ±0.1 g is more significant when you weigh out 0.2 g of a solid than when you weigh out 100.0 g.

You Can **Minimise** the Percentage Error

1) One obvious way to **reduce errors** in your measurements is to use the most **sensitive equipment** available. There's not much you can do about this at school or college though — you're stuck with whatever's available.

2) But there are other ways to **lower the uncertainty** in experiments. The **larger the reading** you take with a piece of equipment, the **smaller the percentage error** on that reading will be. Here's a quick example:

- If you measure out **5.0 cm^3** of liquid in a burette with an error of **±0.05 ml** then the percentage error is (0.05 ÷ 5.0) × 100 = **1%**.
- But if you measure **10.0 cm^3** of liquid in the same burette, the percentage error is (0.05 ÷ 10.0) × 100 = **0.5%**. Hey presto — you've just halved the percentage error.
- So you can reduce the percentage error of this experiment by using a **larger volume** of liquid.

3) You can apply the same principle to other measurements too. For example, if you weigh out a small mass of a solid, the **percentage error** will be larger than if you weighed out a larger mass using the same balance.

Errors Can Be **Systematic** or **Random**

1) **Systematic errors** cause each reading to be different to the true value by the same amount, i.e. they shift all of your results. They may be caused by the **set-up** or the **equipment** you're using. If the 10.00 cm^3 pipette you're using to measure out a sample for titration actually only measures 9.95 cm^3, your sample will be 0.05 cm^3 too small **every time** you repeat the experiment.

2) **Random errors** cause readings to be spread about the true value due to the results varying in an **unpredictable** way. You get random error in all measurements and no matter how hard you try, you can't correct them. The tiny errors you make when you read a burette are random — you have to estimate the level when it's between two marks, so sometimes your figure will be **above** the real one and sometimes **below**.

3) **Repeating an experiment** and finding the mean of your results helps to deal with **random errors**. The results that are a bit high will be **cancelled out** by the ones that are a bit low, so your results will be more **precise**. But repeating your results won't get rid of **systematic errors**, so your results won't get more **accurate**.

This should be a photo of a scientist. I don't know what happened — it's a random error...

PRACTICAL SKILLS

Exam Structure and Technique

Passing exams isn't all about revision — it really helps if you know how the exams are structured and have got your exam technique nailed so that you pick up every mark you can.

Make Sure You Know the **Structure** of Your **Exams**

The AQA A-Level Chemistry course is split into three units: **Physical Chemistry** (Unit 1), **Inorganic Chemistry** (Unit 2) and **Organic Chemistry** (Unit 3).

For AQA A-Level Chemistry you're going to have to sit **three exams** — Paper 1, Paper 2 and Paper 3.

- **Paper 1** will test you on most of Physical Chemistry and all of Inorganic Chemistry.
- **Paper 2** will test you on some of Physical Chemistry and all of Organic Chemistry.
- **Paper 3** can test you on any of the material covered in the course.
- All three papers could include questions on **practical skills**.

If you want more detail on what could come up in each paper, look at the table below:

If you haven't got a copy of the AQA specification, you can download it from the AQA website (or ask your teacher).

Paper	Content Assessed
1	• Unit 1: Physical chemistry. (Year 2 content covered in Unit 1 of this book.) AQA specification references 3.1.1.1 to 3.1.4.4 (Year 1), 3.1.6.1 to 3.1.7 (Year 1), 3.1.8.1 to 3.1.8.2 (Year 2) and 3.1.10 to 3.1.12.6 (Year 2). • Unit 2: Inorganic chemistry. (Year 2 content covered in Unit 2 of this book.) AQA specification references 3.2.1.1 to 3.2.3.2 (Year 1) and 3.2.4 to 3.2.6 (Year 2). • Relevant practical skills. (Covered in the Practical Skills section of this book.)
2	• Unit 1: Physical chemistry. (Year 2 content covered in Unit 1 of this book.) AQA specification references 3.1.2.1 to 3.1.6.2 (Year 1) and 3.1.9.1 to 3.1.9.2 (Year 2). • Unit 3: Organic chemistry. (Year 2 content covered in Unit 3 of this book.) AQA specification references 3.3.1.1 to 3.3.6.3 (Year 1) and 3.3.7 to 3.3.16 (Year 2). • Relevant practical skills. (Covered in the Practical Skills section of this book.)
3	• Any content from Units 1, 2 and 3. • Relevant practical skills. (Covered in the Practical Skills section of this book.)

All the exams are **2 hours** long. Papers 1 and 2 are each worth **105 marks**, which is **35%** of your total mark. Paper 3 is worth **90 marks**, which is **30%** of your total mark.

- Paper 1 and Paper 2 are made up of **short and long answer questions**.
- Paper 3 will be made up of 40 marks of questions relating to **practical techniques** and **data analysis**, 20 marks of **general questions** from all parts of the specification, and 30 marks of **multiple choice** questions.

Manage Your Time Sensibly

1) **How long** you spend on each question is important in an exam — it could make all the difference to your grade.

2) The **number of marks** tells you roughly how long to spend on a question. Some questions will require lots of work for only a few marks but other questions will be much quicker.

> **Example:** Q1 Define the term 'enthalpy change of solution'. [2 marks]
>
> Q2 Draw the structures of the two monomers that react to form the condensation polymer shown above. [2 marks]
>
> Question 1 only asks you to write down a **definition** — if you can remember it this shouldn't take too long.
>
> Question 2 asks you to **work out and draw** the structures of two monomers used to make a condensation polymer — this may take longer than writing down a definition.
>
> If you're running out of time, it makes sense to do Q1 first and come back to Q2 if you have time at the end.

3) Don't spend ages struggling with questions that are only worth a couple of marks — **move on**. You can come back to them later when you've bagged loads of other marks elsewhere.

4) If you get really stuck on a question, it's also probably best to move on and come back to it later.

Exam Structure and Technique

Make Sure You *Read the Question*

1) **Command words** are just the bit of the question that tell you what to do.
2) You'll find answering exam questions much easier if you understand exactly what they mean, so here's a summary of the most common command words.

Not all of the questions will have a command word — they may just be a which / what / how type of question.

Command word:	What to do:
Give / Name / State	Write a concise answer, from fact recall or from information that you've been given in the question.
Identify	Say what something is.
Describe	Write about what something is like or how it happens.
Explain	Give reasons for something.
Suggest / Predict	Use your scientific knowledge to work out what the answer might be.
Outline	Give a brief description of the main characteristics of something.
Calculate	Work out the solution to a mathematical problem.
Draw	Produce a diagram or graph.
Sketch	Draw something approximately — for example, draw a rough line graph to show the main trend of some data.

Elsie worked hard on making perfect points in her Chemistry exams.

Some Questions Will Test Your Knowledge of *Practical Skills*

At least 15% of the marks in your A-Level Chemistry exams will focus on practical skills.

This means you will be given questions where you're asked to do things like comment on the design of experiments, make predictions, draw graphs, calculate percentage errors — basically, anything related to planning experiments or analysing results. These skills are covered in the Practical Skills section of this book on pages 106 to 113.

Be *Careful* With *Calculations*

1) In calculation questions you should always **show your working** — you may get some marks for your **method** even if you get the answer wrong.
2) Don't **round** your answer until the **very end**. Some of the calculations in A-level Chemistry can be quite **long**, and if you round too early you could introduce errors to your final answer.

At least 20% of the marks up for grabs in A-level Chemistry will require maths skills, so make sure you know your stuff.

Remember to Use the *Exam Data Booklet*

When you sit your exams, you'll be given a data booklet. It will contain lots of useful information, including:

- the characteristic infrared absorptions, ^{13}C NMR shifts and ^{1}H NMR shifts of some common functional groups,
- the structures of some biologically important molecules, such as the DNA bases, some amino acids, common phosphates and sugars and Heme B.
- a copy of the periodic table.

I'd put a joke here, but there's just nothing funny about exams...

The real key to preparing for your exams is to get as much practice as possible. Get hold of some practice papers and try doing them in two hours so you can be sure you've got the timing right. It'll help you get used to the different types of questions that might pop up too. And it'll flag up any topics that you're a bit shaky on, so you can go back and revise.

DO WELL IN YOUR EXAMS

Answers

Unit 1: Section 6 — Thermodynamics

Page 5 — Lattice Enthalpy and Born-Haber Cycles

1 a)

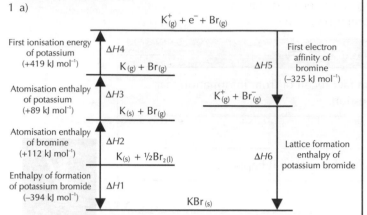

[1 mark for all enthalpy changes correct. 1 mark for all formulas correct. 1 mark for correct directions of arrows.]

b) Lattice formation enthalpy, $\Delta H6$
$= -\Delta H5 - \Delta H4 - \Delta H3 - \Delta H2 + \Delta H1$
$= -(-325) - (+419) - (+89) - (+112) + (-394)$ **[1 mark]**
$= \textbf{-689 kJ mol}^{-1}$ **[1 mark]**

You can still have the first mark here if you wrote out any calculation that's equivalent to the one shown.

2 a)

[1 mark for all enthalpy changes correct. 1 mark for all formulas correct. 1 mark for correct directions of arrows.]

There are often a couple of steps in a Born-Haber cycle that you can do in any order. For example, you could swap round $\Delta H2$ and $\Delta H3$ here and still be right.

b) First ionisation energy (aluminium), $\Delta H4$
$= -\Delta H3 - \Delta H2 + \Delta H1 - \Delta H8 - \Delta H7 - \Delta H6 - \Delta H5$
$= -3(+122) - (+326) + (-706) - (-5491) - 3(-349)$
$\quad - (+2745) - (+1817)$ **[1 mark]**
$= \textbf{+578 kJ mol}^{-1}$ **[1 mark]**

You can still have the first mark here if you wrote out any calculation that's equivalent to the one shown.

Page 7 — Enthalpies of Solution

1 a)

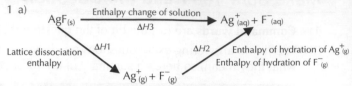

[1 mark for a complete correct cycle, 1 mark for correctly labelled arrows.]

b) $\Delta H3 = \Delta H1 + \Delta H2$
$= 960 + (-506) + (-464) = \textbf{-10 kJ mol}^{-1}$ **[1 mark]**

2 Enthalpy change of solution ($SrF_{2(s)}$)
$=$ lattice dissociation enthalpy ($SrF_{2(s)}$)
$\quad +$ enthalpy of hydration ($Sr^{2+}_{(g)}$)
$\quad + [2 \times$ enthalpy of hydration ($F^-_{(g)}$)] **[1 mark]**
$= 2492 + (-1480) + (2 \times -506) = \textbf{0 kJ mol}^{-1}$ **[1 mark]**

Don't forget — you have to double the enthalpy of hydration for F^- because there are two in SrF_2.

3 By Hess's law:
Enthalpy change of solution ($MgCl_{2(s)}$)
$= -$lattice formation enthalpy ($MgCl_{2(s)}$)
$\quad +$ enthalpy of hydration ($Mg^{2+}_{(g)}$)
$\quad + [2 \times$ enthalpy of hydration ($Cl^-_{(g)}$)] **[1 mark]**

You've been given a negative lattice enthalpy value, so it must be the lattice formation enthalpy.

So enthalpy of hydration ($Cl^-_{(g)}$)
$= [$enthalpy change of solution ($MgCl_{2(s)}$)
$\quad +$ lattice formation enthalpy ($MgCl_{2(s)}$)
$\quad -$ enthalpy of hydration ($Mg^{2+}_{(g)}$)] $\div 2$
$= [(-122) + (-2526) - (-1920)] \div 2$ **[1 mark]**
$= -728 \div 2 = \textbf{-364 kJ mol}^{-1}$ **[1 mark]**

Page 9 — Entropy

1 You would expect the entropy change to be positive, because there are more moles of products than moles of reactant **[1 mark]** and the reactant is a solid while one of the products is a gas **[1 mark]**.

2 $\Delta S = S_{products} - S_{reactants}$
$= 26.9 - (32.7 + (\frac{1}{2} \times 205))$ **[1 mark]**
$= -108.3$ J K^{-1} mol^{-1} = $\textbf{-108 J K}^{-1}\textbf{ mol}^{-1}$ (3 s.f.) **[1 mark]**

3 $\Delta S = S_{products} - S_{reactants}$
$= ((2 \times 69.9) + 205) - (2 \times 110)$ **[1 mark]**
$= 124.8$ J K^{-1} mol^{-1} = $\textbf{125 J K}^{-1}\textbf{ mol}^{-1}$ (3 s.f.) **[1 mark]**

Page 11 — Free-Energy Change

1 a) i) $\Delta G = \Delta H - (T \times \Delta S)$
$= 117\,000 - (500 \times 175)$
$= \textbf{+29 500 J mol}^{-1}$ **[1 mark]**
You can have the mark here if you gave your answer in kJ mol^{-1}.

ii) $\Delta G = \Delta H - (T \times \Delta S)$
$= 117\,000 - (760 \times 175)$
$= \textbf{-16 000 J mol}^{-1}$ **[1 mark]**
You can also have the mark here if you gave your answer in kJ mol^{-1}.

b) The reaction is feasible at 760 K **[1 mark]** because the free energy change at this temperature is negative **[1 mark]**.

2 a) $\Delta S = \Delta S_{products} - \Delta S_{reactants}$
$= [214 + (2 \times 69.9)] - [186 + (2 \times 205)]$
$= -242.2$ J K^{-1} mol^{-1} **[1 mark]**
$\Delta G = \Delta H - (T \times \Delta S)$
$= -730\,000 - (298 \times -242.2)$
$= \textbf{-658 000 J mol}^{-1}$ (3 s.f.) **[1 mark]**
You can have the mark here if you gave your answer in kJ mol^{-1}.

b) $T = \Delta H \div \Delta S$
$= -730\,000 \div -242.2$ **[1 mark]**
$= \textbf{3010 K}$ (3 s.f.) **[1 mark]**

Unit 1: Section 7 — Rate Equations and K_p

Page 14 — Rate Equations

1 a) E.g.

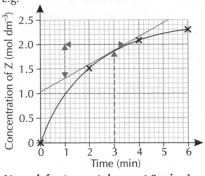

[1 mark for tangent drawn at 3 mins.]
rate of reaction = gradient of tangent at 3 mins
gradient = change in y ÷ change in x
e.g. = (2.0 – 1.3) ÷ (3.4 – 1.0)
= **0.29 mol dm^{-3} min^{-1}**
[1 mark for an answer correctly calculated from the tangent, 1 mark for units.]
Different people will draw ever-so-slightly different tangents and pick different points on their tangent to do the gradient calculation. So as long as you've drawn the tangent accurately, any answer that you've calculated from it correctly gets the mark.

b) rate = k[X][Y] *[1 mark]*

2 a) rate = k[NO]^2[H$_2$] *[1 mark]*

b) $0.00267 = k \times 0.00400^2 \times 0.00200$
So $k = 0.00267 ÷ (0.00400^2 \times 0.00200) = 8.34 \times 10^4$
Units: mol dm^{-3} s^{-1}/((mol dm^{-3})$^2 \times$ (mol dm^{-3})) = dm^6 mol^{-2} s^{-1}
$k = \mathbf{8.34 \times 10^4}$ **dm^6 mol^{-2} s^{-1}**
[1 mark for the correct value of k, 1 mark for units]

Page 17 — Rate Experiments

1 a) 1st order *[1 mark]*
[D] doubles between experiments 1 and 2 and the initial rate doubles (with [E] remaining constant).

b) 0 order *[1 mark]*
[E] and [D] both halve between experiments 1 and 3 and the initial rate halves. Halving [D] alone would halve the rate, so changing [E] cannot affect the rate.

c) $1.30 \times 3 = \mathbf{3.90 \times 10^{-3}}$ **mol dm^{-3} s^{-1}** *[1 mark]*
[D] is tripled and [E] is halved between experiments 1 and 4. The rate is proportional to [D] (and [E] doesn't affect the rate), so the initial rate is tripled.

Page 19 — The Rate Determining Step

1 H$^+$ is acting as a catalyst *[1 mark]*. You know this because it is not one of the reactants in the chemical equation, but it does affect the rate of reaction/appear in the rate equation *[1 mark]*.

2 a) One molecule of H$_2$ and one molecule of ICl (or something derived from these molecules) *[1 mark]*. If the molecule is in the rate equation, it must be in the rate determining step *[1 mark]*. The orders of the reaction tell you how many molecules of each reactant are in the rate determining step *[1 mark]*.

b) Incorrect *[1 mark]*. H$_2$ and ICl are both in the rate equation, so they must both be in the rate determining step OR the order of the reaction with respect to ICl is 1, so there must be only one molecule of ICl in the rate determining step *[1 mark]*.

Page 21 — The Arrhenius Equation

1 a)

T (K)	k	1/T (K^{-1})	ln k
305	0.181	0.00328	–1.709
313	0.468	**0.00319**	**–0.759**
323	1.34	**0.00310**	**0.293**
333	3.29	0.00300	1.191
344	10.1	**0.00291**	**2.313**
353	22.7	0.00283	3.122

[1 mark for all three 1/T values correct, 1 mark for all three ln k values correct]

b)

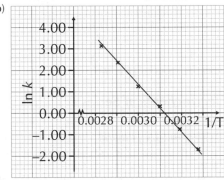

[1 mark for correct axes, 1 mark for correctly plotted points, 1 mark for line of best fit]

c) E.g. gradient = (2.313 – (–0.759)) ÷ (0.00291 – 0.00319)
= **–11 000** *[1 mark]*
You can have the mark here for any gradient correctly calculated from two points on your graph.
$\frac{-E_a}{R}$ = –11 000
E_a = 11 000 × 8.31 = **91 400 J mol^{-1}** OR **91.4 kJ mol^{-1}** *[1 mark]*
Again, you can have the mark here for any value of E_a correctly calculated from your value for the gradient of the graph.

d) By substituting values into the expression ln $k = \frac{-E_a}{RT} + $ ln A
E.g. 2.313 = (–11 000 × 0.00291) + ln A
ln A = 34.3
A = e$^{34.3}$ = **8 × 10^{14}** *[1 mark]*
You've guessed it — you get the mark here for a value of A correctly calculated using your value for the gradient from part c) and values for ln k and 1/T from a data point in the table or on the graph.

Page 23 — Gas Equilibria and K_p

PQ3 $K_p = \dfrac{(p_{NH_3})^2}{p_{N_2} \times (p_{H_2})^3}$

1 a) $K_p = \dfrac{p_{SO_2} \times p_{Cl_2}}{p_{SO_2Cl_2}}$ *[1 mark]*

b) Cl$_2$ and SO$_2$ are produced in equal amounts so
$p_{Cl_2} = p_{SO_2}$ = 60.2 kPa *[1 mark]*
Total pressure = $p_{SO_2Cl_2} + p_{Cl_2} + p_{SO_2}$ so
$p_{SO_2Cl_2}$ = 141 – 60.2 – 60.2 = **20.6 kPa** *[1 mark]*

c) $K_p = \dfrac{60.2\,\text{kPa} \times 60.2\,\text{kPa}}{20.6\,\text{kPa}}$ = **176 kPa**
[2 marks — 1 mark for 176 correct, 1 mark for kPa correct]
The units are kPa because (kPa × kPa)/kPa = kPa.

d) Increasing the temperature favours the endothermic reaction, which in this case is the forward reaction *[1 mark]*.
The equilibrium will shift to the right, so there will be more SO$_2$ and Cl$_2$ produced *[1 mark]*. The partial pressures of the products will increase and the partial pressure of the reactant will decrease, so the value of K_p will increase *[1 mark]*.

2 a) p_{O_2} = ½ × p_{NO} = ½ × 36 = **18 kPa** *[1 mark]*

b) p_{NO_2} = total pressure – p_{NO} – p_{O_2}
= 99 – 36 – 18 = **45 kPa** *[1 mark]*

Answers

c) $K_P = \dfrac{(p_{NO_2})^2}{(p_{NO_2})^2 p_{O_2}}$

$= \dfrac{(45\,kPa)^2}{(36\,kPa)^2 \times (18\,kPa)} = \textbf{0.087 kPa}^{-1}$

**[3 marks — 1 mark for K_p expression correct,
1 mark for 0.087 correct, 1 mark for kPa^{-1} correct]**
The units are kPa^{-1} because kPa^2/(kPa^2 × kPa) = kPa^{-1}.

Unit 1: Section 8 — Electrode Potentials and Cells

Page 25 — Electrode Potentials

1   Iron *[1 mark]* as it has a more negative electrode potential/ it loses electrons more easily than lead *[1 mark]*.

2 a) $Zn_{(s)} + 2Ag^+_{(aq)} \rightarrow Zn^{2+}_{(aq)} + 2Ag_{(s)}$ *[1 mark]*

   b)   The silver half-cell. It has a more positive standard electrode potential/it's more easily reduced *[1 mark]*.

Page 27 — The Electrochemical Series

1 a) $Zn_{(s)} + Ni^{2+}_{(aq)} \rightleftharpoons Zn^{2+}_{(aq)} + Ni_{(s)}$

     $E^\ominus = (-0.25) - (-0.76) = \textbf{+0.51 V}$ *[1 mark]*
This reaction takes places because Zn^{2+}/Zn has a more negative electrode potential so this half-reaction will go in the oxidisation direction. So Ni^{2+}/Ni will go in the reduction direction *[1 mark]*.

   b) $2MnO_4^-_{(aq)} + 16H^+_{(aq)} + 5Sn^{2+}_{(aq)} \rightleftharpoons$
                   $2Mn^{2+}_{(aq)} + 8H_2O_{(l)} + 5Sn^{4+}_{(aq)}$

     $E^\ominus = (+1.51) - (+0.14) = \textbf{+1.37 V}$ *[1 mark]*
This reaction takes places because MnO_4^-/Mn^{2+} has a more negative electrode potential, so this half-reaction will go in the oxidisation direction. This means that Sn^{4+}/Sn^{2+} must go in the reduction direction *[1 mark]*.

   c)   No reaction *[1 mark]*. Both reactants are in their oxidised form *[1 mark]*.

2   KMnO$_4$ *[1 mark]* because it has a more positive/less negative electrode potential *[1 mark]*.

3 a)   i) $Fe_{(s)} \mid Fe^{2+}_{(aq)} \mid\mid O_{2(g)} \mid OH^-_{(aq)}$ *[1 mark]*

     ii) $E^\circ_{cell} = E^\circ_{reduced} - E^\circ_{oxidised} = 0.40 - (-0.44) = \textbf{+0.84 V}$ *[1 mark]*
The EMF of a functional cell should be a positive value. If you get a negative value, check you've done the subtraction the right way round.

   b)   The iron half-cell has a more negative electrode potential than the oxygen/water half-cell, so iron is oxidised *[1 mark]*.

Page 29 — Batteries and Fuel Cells

1 a)   i) and ii)

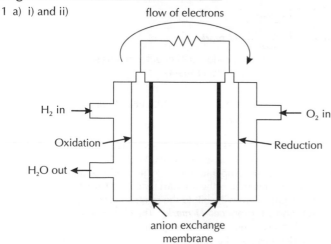

[1 mark for labelling the sites of reduction and oxidation correctly. 1 mark for drawing the arrow showing the direction of electron flow correctly.]

b)   Positive electrode: $H_{2(g)} + 4OH^-_{(aq)} \rightarrow 4H_2O_{(l)} + 4e^-$ *[1 mark]*
     Negative electrode: $O_{2(g)} + 2H_2O_{(l)} + 4e^- \rightarrow 4OH^-_{(aq)}$ *[1 mark]*

c)   It only allows the OH$^-$ across and not O$_2$ and H$_2$ gases *[1 mark]*.

2 a)   negative electrode: $Li_{(s)} \rightarrow Li^+_{(aq)} + e^-$ *[1 mark]*
     positive electrode: $Li^+_{(aq)} + CoO_{2(s)} + e^- \rightarrow Li^+[CoO_2]^-_{(s)}$ *[1 mark]*

   b)   A current is supplied to force the electrons to flow in the opposite direction to when the cell is supplying electricity *[1 mark]*.

   c)   They are reversed *[1 mark]*.

Unit 1: Section 9 — Acids, Bases and pH

Page 31 — Acids, Bases and K_w

1 a) $HSO_4^- \rightarrow H^+ + SO_4^{2-}$ <u>or</u> $HSO_4^- + H_2O \rightarrow H_3O^+ + SO_4^{2-}$
     [1 mark]

   b) $HSO_4^- + H^+ \rightarrow H_2SO_4$ <u>or</u> $HSO_4^- + H_2O \rightarrow H_2SO_4 + OH^-$
     [1 mark]

2 a)   Weak acids dissociate (or ionise) a small amount to produce hydrogen ions (or protons) *[1 mark]*.

   b) $HCN \rightleftharpoons H^+ + CN^-$ *[1 mark]*

3   Moles of NaOH = mass ÷ M_r
               $= 2.50 ÷ 40.0 = 0.0625$ mol *[1 mark]*
   1 mol of NaOH gives 1 mol of OH$^-$.
   So [OH$^-$] = [NaOH] = **0.0625 mol dm^{-3}** *[1 mark]*.

Page 33 — pH Calculations

1 a)   HBr is a strong monoprotic acid,
     so [H$^+$] = [HBr] = 0.32 mol dm^{-3}.
     pH = $-\log_{10}(0.32)$ = **0.49** *[1 mark]*

   b)   HBr is a stronger acid than ethanoic acid, so will be more dissociated in solution. This means the concentration of hydrogen ions will be higher, so the pH will be lower *[1 mark]*.

2 a)   A monoprotic acid means that each molecule of acid will release one proton when it dissociates OR each mole of acid will produce one mole of protons when it dissociates *[1 mark]*.

   b)   [H$^+$] = 10^{-pH} = $10^{-0.55}$ = **0.28 mol dm^{-3}** *[1 mark]*.
A strong acid will ionise fully in solution — so [H$^+$] = [Acid]. That's why the question tells you that HNO$_3$ is a strong acid.

3 a)   Moles of KOH = m ÷ M_r
               $= 11.22 ÷ 56.1 = 0.200$ mol *[1 mark]*
   1 mol of KOH gives 1 mol of OH$^-$.
   So [OH$^-$] = [KOH] = **0.200 mol dm^{-3}** *[1 mark]*.

   b) $K_w = $ [H$^+$][OH$^-$]
     [H$^+$] = $(1.0 \times 10^{-14}) ÷ 0.200 = 5.0 \times 10^{-14}$ *[1 mark]*
     pH = $-\log_{10}(5.00 \times 10^{-14})$ = **13.3** *[1 mark]*
If you got the answer to part a) wrong, you can have the mark for part b) if you used your wrong value in the right calculation.

Page 35 — More pH Calculations

1 a) $K_a = \dfrac{[H^+][A^-]}{[HA]}$ or $K_a = \dfrac{[H^+]^2}{[HA]}$ *[1 mark]*

   b) $K_a = \dfrac{[H^+]^2}{[HA]}$
     [HA] is 0.280 because only a small amount of HA will dissociate
     [H$^+$] = $\sqrt{(5.60 \times 10^{-4}) \times (0.280)} = 0.0125$ mol dm^{-3} *[1 mark]*
     pH = $-\log_{10}$ [H$^+$] = $-\log_{10}(0.0125)$ = **1.90** *[1 mark]*

2 a)   [H$^+$] = $10^{-2.64} = 2.3 \times 10^{-3}$ mol dm^{-3} *[1 mark]*
     $K_a = \dfrac{[H^+]^2}{[HX]} = \dfrac{(2.3 \times 10^{-3})^2}{0.150}$ = **3.5×10^{-5} mol dm^{-3}** *[1 mark]*

   b) $pK_a = -\log_{10} K_a = -\log_{10}(3.5 \times 10^{-5})$ = **4.46** *[1 mark]*

3   $K_a = 10^{-pK_a} = 10^{-4.2} = 6.3 \times 10^{-5}$ mol dm^{-3} *[1 mark]*

   $K_a = \dfrac{[H^+]^2}{[HA]}$ so [H$^+$] = $\sqrt{K_a \times [HA]}$

       $= \sqrt{(6.3 \times 10^{-5}) \times (1.6 \times 10^{-4})} = \sqrt{1.0 \times 10^{-8}}$

       $= 1.0 \times 10^{-4}$ mol dm^{-3} *[1 mark]*

   pH = $-\log_{10}$ [H$^+$] = $-\log_{10}(1.0 \times 10^{-4})$ = **4.0** *[1 mark]*

Answers

Page 37 — pH Curves and Indicators

1 Nitric acid:

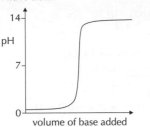

[1 mark]

Ethanoic acid:

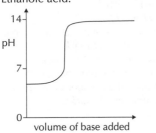

[1 mark]

2 Thymol blue *[1 mark]*. It's a weak acid/strong base titration so the equivalence point/end point is above pH 8 *[1 mark]*.

3 a)

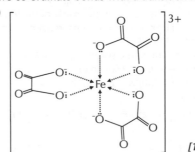

[1 mark]

   b) In a weak acid/weak base titration, the change in pH is gradual, not sharp *[1 mark]*. This makes it very difficult to determine the exact point the acid is neutralised, using an indicator *[1 mark]*.

Page 39 — Titration Calculations

1 a) $HCl_{(aq)} + NaOH_{(aq)} \rightarrow NaCl_{(aq)} + H_2O_{(l)}$ *[1 mark]*
   b) i) $(25.60 + 25.65 + 25.55) \div 3 = \mathbf{25.60\ cm^3}$ *[1 mark]*
      ii) Moles NaOH = $(0.10 \times 25.60) \div 1000 = \mathbf{2.560 \times 10^{-3}}$ *[1 mark]*
   c) Conc. HCl = $((2.56 \times 10^{-3}) \times 1000) \div 25 = \mathbf{0.102\ mol\ dm^{-3}}$ *[1 mark]*
2 a) $H_2SO_{4(aq)} + 2NaOH_{(aq)} \rightarrow Na_2SO_{4(aq)} + 2H_2O_{(l)}$ *[1 mark]*
   b) i) Moles NaOH = $(0.100 \times 35.6) \div 1000 = \mathbf{3.56 \times 10^{-3}}$ *[1 mark]*
      ii) Moles H_2SO_4 = Moles NaOH $\div 2 = \mathbf{1.78 \times 10^{-3}}$ *[1 mark]*
      iii) $[H_2SO_4] = ((1.78 \times 10^{-3}) \times 1000) \div 25.0$
              $= \mathbf{0.0712\ mol\ dm^{-3}}$ *[1 mark]*

Page 41 — Buffer Action

1 a) $K_a = ([H^+] \times [CH_3CH_2COO^-]) \div [CH_3CH_2COOH]$ *[1 mark]*
      So, $[H^+] = K_a \times ([CH_3CH_2COOH] \div [CH_3CH_2COO^-])$
          $= (1.3 \times 10^{-5}) \times (0.40 \div 0.20)$
          $= 2.6 \times 10^{-5}\ mol\ dm^{-3}$ *[1 mark]*
      pH = $-\log_{10}(2.6 \times 10^{-5}) = \mathbf{4.59}$ *[1 mark]*
   b) Adding H_2SO_4 increases the concentration of H^+ *[1 mark]*. This will cause more propanoic acid in the buffer to dissociate / shift the $C_6H_5COOH \rightleftharpoons H^+ + C_6H_5COO^-$ equilibrium in the buffer to the left *[1 mark]*.
2 a) $CH_3(CH_2)_2COOH \rightleftharpoons H^+ + CH_3(CH_2)_2COO^-$ *[1 mark]*
   b) $[CH_3(CH_2)_2COOH] = [CH_3(CH_2)_2COO^-]$ *[1 mark]*
      so $[CH_3(CH_2)_2COOH] \div [CH_3(CH_2)_2COO^-] = 1$
      and $K_a = [H^+]$ *[1 mark]*.
      pH = $-\log_{10}(1.5 \times 10^{-5}) = \mathbf{4.8}$ *[1 mark]*
      If the concentrations of the weak acid and the salt of the weak acid are equal, they cancel from the K_a expression and the buffer pH = pK_a.

Unit 2: Section 3 — Period 3 Elements

Page 43 — Period 3 Elements and Oxides

1 a) Compound X is SO_3 *[1 mark]*.
      $SO_3 + H_2O \rightarrow H_2SO_4$ *[1 mark]*
   b) i) Compound Y is Na_2O *[1 mark]*.
          $Na_2O + H_2O \rightarrow 2\ NaOH$ *[1 mark]*
      ii) Na_2O/compound Y has a giant lattice structure with strong ionic bonds *[1 mark]* that take a lot of energy to break *[1 mark]*.

Unit 2: Section 4 — Transition Metals

Page 45 — Transition Metals — The Basics

1 a) $1s^2\ 2s^2\ 2p^6\ 3s^2\ 3p^6\ 3d^{10}$ or $[Ar]3d^{10}$ *[1 mark]*
   b) No *[1 mark]*. Cu^+ ions have a full 3d subshell *[1 mark]*.
   c) copper(II) sulfate $(CuSO_{4(aq)})$ *[1 mark]*

Page 47 — Complex Ions

1 a) i) A species (atom, ion or molecule) that donates a lone pair of electrons to form a co-ordinate bond with a metal atom or ion *[1 mark]*, such as NH_3 in $[Ag(NH_3)_2]^+$ *[1 mark]*.
      ii) A covalent bond in which both electrons come from the same species *[1 mark]*. In the $Ag–NH_3$ bond, both electrons come from nitrogen *[1 mark]*.
      iii) The number of co-ordinate bonds formed with the central metal atom or ion *[1 mark]*. In $[Ag(NH_3)_2]^+$, the co-ordination number is 2 because two NH_3 ligands are bonded to Ag^+ *[1 mark]*.
   b) Linear *[1 mark]*
2 a) Co-ordination number: 6 *[1 mark]*
      Shape: octahedral *[1 mark]*
   b) Co-ordination number: 4 *[1 mark]*
      Shape: tetrahedral *[1 mark]*
      Formula: $[CuCl_4]^{2-}$ *[1 mark]*
   c) 109.5° *[1 mark]*
   d) Cl^- ligands are larger than water ligands *[1 mark]*, so only 4 Cl^- ligands can fit around the Cu^{2+} ion *[1 mark]*.

Page 49 — More on Complex Ions

1 a) A bidentate ligand is an atom, ion or molecule that can form two co-ordinate bonds with a transition metal ion *[1 mark]*.
   b) i)

[1 mark]

[1 mark]

Answers

ii) Optical isomerism *[1 mark]*.

2

[1 mark]

Page 51 — Formation of Coloured Ions

1 a) Energy is absorbed from visible light when electrons move from the ground state to a higher energy level *[1 mark]*.

b) Change in oxidation state *[1 mark]*, ligand *[1 mark]* or co-ordination number *[1 mark]*.

2 Prepare a range of dilutions of known concentrations *[1 mark]*. Measure the absorbance of the solutions *[1 mark]*. Plot a graph of concentration versus absorbance *[1 mark]*.

3 a) ΔE is the energy absorbed when an electron moves from the ground state to a higher energy level/excited state *[1 mark]*. OR ΔE is the difference between the ground state energy and the energy of an excited electron *[1 mark]*.

b) i) [Ar] $3d^{10}$ *[1 mark]*

ii) [Ar] $3d^9$ *[1 mark]*

c) Cu^{2+} because it has an incomplete d-subshell *[1 mark]*.

Page 53 — Substitution Reactions

1 a) $[Fe(H_2O)_6]^{3+}$ + $EDTA^{4-}$ → $[FeEDTA]^-$ + $6H_2O$ *[1 mark]*

b) The formation of $[FeEDTA]^-$ results in an increase in entropy, because the number of particles increases from two to seven *[1 mark]*.

2 a) $[Co(H_2O)_6]^{2+}$ + $6NH_3$ → $[Co(NH_3)_6]^{2+}$ + $6H_2O$ *[1 mark]*
You can fit the same number of H_2O and NH_3 ligands around a Co^{2+} ion because they are a similar size and both uncharged.

b) $[Co(H_2O)_6]^{2+}$ + $3NH_2CH_2CH_2NH_2$ →
$[Co(NH_2CH_2CH_2NH_2)_3]^{2+}$ + $6H_2O$ *[1 mark]*

c) $[Co(H_2O)_6]^{2+}$ + $4Cl^-$ → $[CoCl_4]^{2-}$ + $6H_2O$ *[1 mark]*

Page 55 — Variable Oxidation States

1 a) i) $[Ag(NH_3)_2]^+$ *[1 mark]*

ii) Silver is in the +1 oxidation state *[1 mark]*.

b) Aldehydes are oxidised by Tollens' reagent in the following redox reaction:
$RCHO_{(aq)}$ + $2[Ag(NH_3)_2]^+_{(aq)}$ + $3OH^-_{(aq)}$ →
$RCOO^-_{(aq)}$ + $2Ag_{(s)}$ + $4NH_{3(aq)}$ + $2H_2O_{(l)}$ *[1 mark]*
This causes a silver mirror to form on the inside of the test tube *[1 mark]*. Ketones aren't oxidised by Tollens' reagent, so no silver mirror is formed *[1 mark]*.

2 a) Zinc metal *[1 mark]* and an acidic solution *[1 mark]*.

b) The blue solution is due to the presence of $VO^{2+}_{(aq)}$ ions *[1 mark]*, and the green solution is due to the presence of $V^{3+}_{(aq)}$ ions *[1 mark]*.

c) $2VO_2^+_{(aq)}$ + $Zn_{(s)}$ + $4H^+_{(aq)}$ → $2VO^{2+}_{(aq)}$ + $Zn^{2+}_{(aq)}$ + $2H_2O_{(l)}$
[1 mark]
$2VO^{2+}_{(aq)}$ + $Zn_{(s)}$ + $4H^+_{(aq)}$ → $2V^{3+}_{(aq)}$ + $Zn^{2+}_{(aq)}$ + $2H_2O_{(l)}$
[1 mark]
$2V^{3+}_{(aq)}$ + $Zn_{(s)}$ → $2V^{2+}_{(aq)}$ + $Zn^{2+}_{(aq)}$ *[1 mark]*

3 B *[1 mark]*

Page 57 — Titrations with Transition Metals

1 a) Moles of MnO_4^- added = $\frac{0.0100 \times 29.4}{1000}$
= **2.94×10^{-4} moles** *[1 mark]*

b) 5 moles of Fe^{2+} react with 1 mole of MnO_4^-.
So moles of Fe^{2+} reacted = $2.94 \times 10^{-4} \times 5$
= **1.47×10^{-3} moles** *[1 mark]*

c) Mass of Fe = A_r × moles = $55.8 \times 1.47 \times 10^{-3}$
= **0.0820 g** *[1 mark]*

d) % Fe = $\frac{0.0820}{0.100} \times 100$
= **82.0%** *[1 mark]*

2 Moles of MnO_4^- added = $\frac{0.0200 \times 18.30}{1000}$
= 3.66×10^{-4} moles *[1 mark]*.
5 moles of $C_2O_4^{2-}$ react with 2 moles of MnO_4^-
so moles of $C_2O_4^{2-}$ added = $\frac{(3.66 \times 10^{-4}) \times 5}{2}$
= 9.15×10^{-4} moles *[1 mark]*.
M_r of $Na_2C_2O_4$ = (23.0 × 2) + (12.0 × 2) + (16.0 × 4)
= 134.0 *[1 mark]*.
Mass of $Na_2C_2O_4$ = M_r × moles
= 134.0 × 9.15 × 10^{-4}
= **0.123 g** *[1 mark]*.

3 Add dilute sulfuric acid to the iron(II) sulfate solution *[1 mark]*. Titrate with potassium manganate(VII) *[1 mark]*. The remaining Fe^{2+} will be oxidised to Fe^{3+} *[1 mark]*. Calculate the number of moles of potassium manganate(VII) that react and use this to calculate the number of moles of iron(II), and hence the concentration *[1 mark]*.

Page 59 — Catalysts

1 a) Vanadium(V) is reduced to vanadium(IV) and oxidises SO_2 to SO_3: V_2O_5 + SO_2 → V_2O_4 + SO_3 *[1 mark]*
Vanadium(IV) is oxidised to vanadium(V) by oxygen gas:
V_2O_4 + ½O_2 → V_2O_5 *[1 mark]*

b) i) Impurities are adsorbed onto the surface of the catalyst *[1 mark]*. For example, sulfur in hydrogen poisons the iron catalyst in the Haber Process *[1 mark]*.

ii) E.g. Reduced efficiency *[1 mark]*, increased cost *[1 mark]*.

2 The overall equation for the reaction is:
$2MnO_4^-_{(aq)}$ + $16H^+_{(aq)}$ + $5C_2O_4^{2-}_{(aq)}$ →
$2Mn^{2+}_{(aq)}$ + $8H_2O_{(l)}$ + $10CO_{2(g)}$ *[1 mark]*.
This is slow to begin with, because the MnO_4^- and $C_2O_4^{2-}$ ions are both negatively charged, so repel each other and don't collide very frequently *[1 mark]*. The Mn^{2+} product, however, is able to catalyse the reaction. It reduces MnO_4^- to Mn^{3+}:
$MnO_4^-_{(aq)}$ + $4Mn^{2+}_{(aq)}$ + $8H^+_{(aq)}$ → $5Mn^{3+}_{(aq)}$ + $4H_2O_{(l)}$ *[1 mark]*.
The Mn^{3+} ions are reduced back to Mn^{2+} by reaction with $C_2O_4^{2-}$:
$2Mn^{3+}_{(aq)}$ + $C_2O_4^{2-}_{(aq)}$ → $2Mn^{2+}_{(aq)}$ + $2CO_{2(g)}$ *[1 mark]*.
This means the reaction is an autocatalysis reaction. As more Mn^{2+} is produced, there is more catalyst available and so the reaction rate will increase *[1 mark]*.

Page 61 — Metal-Aqua Ions

1 Fe^{3+} has a higher charge density than Fe^{2+} *[1 mark]*. This means Fe^{3+} polarises water molecules more, weakening the O–H bond more and making it more likely that H^+ ions are released into the solution *[1 mark]*.

2 a) $[Fe(H_2O)_6]^{2+}_{(aq)}$ + $CO_3^{2-}_{(aq)}$ → $FeCO_{3(s)}$ + $6H_2O_{(l)}$ *[1 mark]*

b) The CO_3^{2-} ions remove H_3O^+ from the solution:
$CO_3^{2-}_{(aq)}$ + $2H_3O^+_{(aq)}$ → $CO_{2(g)}$ + $2H_2O_{(l)}$ *[1 mark]*.
This causes the following two equilibrium reactions to shift to the right:
$[Fe(OH)(H_2O)_5]^{2+}_{(aq)}$ + $H_2O_{(l)}$ ⇌ $[Fe(OH)_2(H_2O)_4]^+_{(aq)}$ + $H_3O^+_{(aq)}$
$[Fe(OH)_2(H_2O)_4]^+_{(aq)}$ + $H_2O_{(l)}$ ⇌ $Fe(OH)_3(H_2O)_{3(s)}$ + $H_3O^+_{(aq)}$
[1 mark].

Answers

Page 63 — More on Metal-Aqua Ions

1. A blue precipitate *[1 mark]* of copper(II) hydroxide forms in the blue solution of copper sulfate:
$[Cu(H_2O)_6]^{2+}{}_{(aq)} + 2H_2O_{(l)} \rightleftharpoons Cu(OH)_2(H_2O)_{4(s)} + 2H_3O^+{}_{(aq)}$
[1 mark]
On addition of excess ammonia, the precipitate dissolves to give a deep blue solution *[1 mark]*:
$Cu(OH)_2(H_2O)_{4(s)} + 4NH_{3(aq)} \rightleftharpoons$
$[Cu(NH_3)_4(H_2O)_2]^{2+}{}_{(aq)} + 2H_2O_{(l)} + 2OH^-{}_{(aq)}$ *[1 mark]*

2. a) i) $[Al(H_2O)_6]^{3+}$ *[1 mark]*
   ii) $Al(OH)_3(H_2O)_3$ *[1 mark]*
   iii) $[Al(OH)_4(H_2O)_2]^-$ *[1 mark]*
   b) $Al(OH)_3(H_2O)_{3(s)} + OH^-{}_{(aq)} \rightleftharpoons [Al(OH)_4(H_2O)_2]^-{}_{(aq)} + H_2O_{(l)}$
   [1 mark]

3. a) i) Formation of a brown precipitate *[1 mark]*.
   ii) Formation of a green precipitate *[1 mark]*.
   b) $[Fe(H_2O)_6]^{2+}{}_{(aq)} + CO_3{}^{2-}{}_{(aq)} \rightarrow FeCO_{3(s)} + 6H_2O_{(aq)}$ *[1 mark]*
   c) i) Formation of a brown precipitate *[1 mark]*.
   ii) Fe^{2+} has been oxidised to Fe^{3+} by the oxygen in the air *[1 mark]*.

Unit 3: Section 5 — Isomerism and Carbonyl Compounds

Page 65 — Optical Isomerism

1. a) The property of having stereoisomers, which are molecules with the same molecular formula and with their atoms arranged in the same way *[1 mark]*, but with a different orientation of the bonds in space *[1 mark]*.
   b) i)

   [1 mark for each correctly drawn structure]
   Your isomers don't have to be orientated in the same way as in the diagram above, just as long as the molecules are mirror images of each other.
   ii) Shine (monochromatic) plane-polarised light through a solution of the molecule *[1 mark]*. The enantiomers will rotate the light in opposite directions *[1 mark]*.

2. a)

   [1 mark for chiral carbon clearly marked]
   b) A mixture of equal quantities of each enantiomer of an optically active compound *[1 mark]*.

3. a) E.g. Pentanal has a planar C=O bond *[1 mark]*. Depending on which direction the CN^- ion attacks the δ+ carbon from, two different enantiomers can be formed *[1 mark]*. The CN^- ion is equally likely to attack from either direction *[1 mark]*, so equal amounts of each enantiomer are formed, giving an optically inactive racemic mixture *[1 mark]*.
   b) The reaction of pentan-3-one would not produce an optically active product *[1 mark]* as it is a symmetrical ketone/ the product does not contain a chiral centre *[1 mark]*.

Page 67 — Aldehydes and Ketones

1. a) Propanal *[1 mark]*

   [1 mark]
   Propanone *[1 mark]*

   [1 mark]
   b) i) Nucleophilic addition *[1 mark]*.
   ii)

   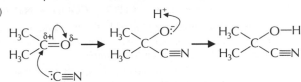

   [1 mark for arrow showing attack of ⁻:CN on δ+ carbon, 1 mark for arrow showing electrons moving from the C=O double bond to the oxygen, 1 mark for correct structure of charged intermediate, 1 mark for arrow showing O:⁻ attacking an H+, 1 mark for correct structure of product.]
   c) $CH_3CH_2CHO + 2[H] \rightarrow CH_3CH_2CH_2OH$ *[1 mark]*
   $[H]$ = e.g. $NaBH_4$ *[1 mark]* dissolved in water with methanol *[1 mark]*.

2. a) Butanal *[1 mark]* and butanone (or butan-2-one) *[1 mark]*
   b) EITHER: Tollens' reagent *[1 mark]* gives a silver mirror with butanal *[1 mark]* but no reaction with butanone *[1 mark]*
   OR Fehling's solution *[1 mark]* gives a brick-red precipitate with butanal *[1 mark]* but no reaction with butanone *[1 mark]*.

Page 69 — Carboxylic Acids and Esters

1. a) $2CH_3COOH_{(aq)} + Na_2CO_{3(s)} \rightarrow 2CH_3COONa_{(aq)} + H_2O_{(l)} + CO_{2(g)}$
   [1 mark for CH_3COONa, 1 mark for CO_2, and 1 mark for correctly balancing the equation.]
   b) methanol *[1 mark]*, esterification (or condensation) *[1 mark]*.
   Substance X is a carboxylic acid (ethanoic acid) and substance Y is an ester (methyl ethanoate).

2. a)

   [1 mark]
   b) Flavouring / perfume / plasticiser *[1 mark]*

3. a) $CH_3COOH + CH_3CH(CH_3)CH_2CH_2OH \rightleftharpoons$
   $CH_3COOCH_2CH_2CH(CH_3)CH_3 + H_2O$ *[1 mark]*
   Heat OR warm OR reflux *[1 mark]*
   and (concentrated sulfuric) acid catalyst *[1 mark]*.
   b) ethanoic acid *[1 mark]*

Page 71 — More on Esters

1. a) 2-methylpropyl ethanoate *[1 mark]*
   b) Ethanoic acid *[1 mark]*

   [1 mark]
   2-methylpropan-1-ol *[1 mark]*

   [1 mark]
   This is acid hydrolysis *[1 mark]*

c) With sodium hydroxide, sodium ethanoate/ethanoate ions are produced, but in the reaction in part b), ethanoic acid is produced *[1 mark]*.

2 a)

H—C—OH
|
H—C—OH
|
H—C—OH
|
H   *[1 mark]*

b) $CH_3(CH_2)_7CH=CH(CH_2)_7COONa + H^+ \rightarrow$
$CH_3(CH_2)_7CH=CH(CH_2)_7COOH + Na^+$ *[1 mark]*

c) Shake with bromine water *[1 mark]*. The bromine water will turn from orange to colourless with oleic acid, but not with stearic acid, $CH_3(CH_2)_{16}COOH$ *[1 mark]*.

You might never have heard of these two fatty acids, but you are told in the question that one of them has a double bond — and you already know from Year 1 how to test for unsaturation...

Page 73 — Acyl Chlorides

1 a) Ethanoyl chloride:
$CH_3COCl + CH_3OH \rightarrow CH_3COOCH_3 + HCl$ *[1 mark]*
Ethanoic anhydride:
$(CH_3CO)_2O + CH_3OH \rightarrow CH_3COOCH_3 + CH_3COOH$ *[1 mark]*
methyl ethanoate *[1 mark]*

b) Vigorous reaction OR (HCl) gas/fumes produced *[1 mark]*

c) Irreversible reaction OR faster reaction *[1 mark]*

2 a) $CH_3COCl + CH_3CH_2NH_2 \rightarrow CH_3CONHCH_2CH_3 + HCl$
[1 mark]
N-ethylethanamide *[1 mark]*

b)

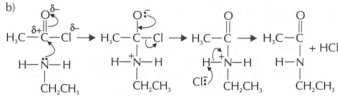

[1 mark for each curly arrow on first diagram, 1 mark for curly arrows on second diagram, 1 mark for correct curly arrows on third diagram, 1 mark for correct structures and charges.]

Page 75 — Purifying Organic Compounds

1   B *[1 mark]*

2 a) The scientist used the minimum possible amount of hot solvent to make sure that the solution would be saturated *[1 mark]*.

b) Filter the hot solution through a heated funnel to remove any insoluble impurities *[1 mark]*. Leave the solution to cool down slowly until crystals of the product have formed *[1 mark]*. Filter the mixture under reduced pressure *[1 mark]*. Wash the crystals with ice-cold solvent *[1 mark]*. Leave the crystals to dry *[1 mark]*.

c) The melting point range of the impure product will be lower and broader than that of the pure product *[1 mark]*.

Unit 3: Section 6 — Aromatic Compounds and Amines

Page 78 — Aromatic Compounds

1 a) Conditions: non-aqueous solvent (e.g. dry ether), reflux *[1 mark]*

b) The acyl chloride molecule isn't polarised enough/isn't a strong enough electrophile to attack the benzene *[1 mark]*. The halogen carrier makes the acyl chloride electrophile stronger *[1 mark]*.

c) H_3C-C^+ 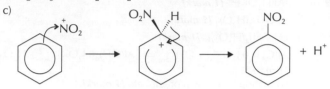 *[1 mark]*

2 a) A: nitrobenzene *[1 mark]*
B + C: concentrated nitric acid and concentrated sulfuric acid *[1 mark]*
D: warm, not more than 55 °C *[1 mark]*
When you're asked to name a compound, give the name, not the formula.

b) $HNO_3 + H_2SO_4 \rightarrow H_2NO_3^+ + HSO_4^-$ *[1 mark]*
$H_2NO_3^+ \rightarrow NO_2^+ + H_2O$ *[1 mark]*

c)

[2 marks — 1 mark for each correct step.]

Page 81 — Amines and Amides

1 a) It can accept protons/H^+ ions, or it can donate a lone pair of electrons *[1 mark]*.

b) Methylamine is stronger, as the methyl group/CH_3 pushes electrons onto/increases electron density on the nitrogen, making the lone pair more available *[1 mark]*. Phenylamine is weaker, as the nitrogen lone pair is less available — nitrogen's electron density is decreased as it's partially delocalised around the benzene ring *[1 mark]*.

2 a) You get a mixture of primary, secondary and tertiary amines, and quaternary ammonium salts *[1 mark]*.

b) i) $LiAlH_4$ and a non-aqueous solvent (e.g. dry ether), followed by dilute acid *[1 mark]*.
   ii) It's too expensive *[1 mark]*.
   iii) Hydrogen gas *[1 mark]*, metal catalyst such as platinum or nickel and high temperature and pressure *[1 mark]*.

3 $2CH_3CH_2NH_2 + CH_3CH_2Br \rightarrow (CH_3CH_2)_2NH + CH_3CH_2NH_3Br$
[1 mark]

Mechanism:

[1 mark]

Then:

[1 mark]

Unit 3: Section 7 — Polymers

Page 83 — Condensation Polymers

1 a) A polyamide *[1 mark]*.

b) A dicarboxylic acid and a diamine *[1 mark]*.

c) Hydrolysis *[1 mark]*.

2

H\
   N—(CH_2)_6—N
H/   \
[1 mark]

[1 mark]

3 a)

$$-\overset{O}{\underset{\|}{C}}-(CH_2)_4-\overset{O}{\underset{\|}{C}}-O-(CH_2)_6-O-$$

or

$$-O-(CH_2)_6-O-\overset{O}{\underset{\|}{C}}-(CH_2)_4-\overset{O}{\underset{\|}{C}}-$$

[1 mark]

b) For each link formed, one small molecule (water) is eliminated *[1 mark]*.

Page 85 — Disposing of Polymers

1 a) E.g. heat energy produced can be used to generate electricity / saves on space in landfill *[1 mark]*
   b) Burning plastics that contain chlorine produces toxic gases/ HCl gas *[1 mark]*. Waste gases from combustion can be passed through scrubbers which neutralise the gases/HCl by allowing them/it to react with a base *[1 mark]*.
2   Any sensible advantage e.g. it is cheap and easy / it doesn't require waste plastics to be separated or sorted *[1 mark]*. Any sensible disadvantage e.g. it requires large areas of land / decomposing waste may release methane/greenhouse gases / leaks from landfill sites can contaminate water supplies *[1 mark]*.
3 a) Polymer A *[1 mark]*. Polymer A is more reactive than polymer B because it has polar bonds in its chain, so it can be attacked by nucleophiles/hydrolysed *[1 mark]*.
   b) hydrolysis *[1 mark]*.

Unit 3: Section 8 — Amino Acids, Proteins and DNA

Page 87 — Amino Acids

1 a)
$$\begin{array}{c}CH_3\\|\\H_3C-CH\\|\\H_2N-\overset{*}{C}-COOH\\|\\H\end{array}$$

[2 marks — 1 mark for the correct structure and 1 mark for labelling the chiral carbon]

b) 2-amino-3-methylbutanoic acid *[1 mark]*

2 a)
$$\begin{array}{c}CH_3\\|\\H_3C-C-H\\|\\CH_2\\|\\H_2N-C-COOH\\|\\H\end{array}$$

[1 mark]

b)
$$\begin{array}{c}CH_3\\|\\H_3C-C-H\\|\\CH_2\\|\\H_3\overset{+}{N}-C-COO^-\\|\\H\end{array}$$

[1 mark]

c)
$$\begin{array}{c}CH_3\\|\\H_3C-C-H\\|\\CH_2\\|\\H_2N-C-COO^-\\|\\H\end{array}$$

[1 mark]

Page 90 — Proteins and Enzymes

1
$$\begin{array}{c}OH\\|\\CH_2\ O\\|\ \|\\H_2N-C-C-N-C-COOH\\|\quad\ H\ H\\H\end{array}$$
[1 mark]

$$\begin{array}{c}OH\\|\\CH_2\\H\ O\quad\ |\\|\ \|\\H_2N-C-C-N-C-COOH\\|\quad\ H\ H\\H\end{array}$$
[1 mark]

The amino acids can join together in either order — serine first then glycine, or glycine first then serine. That's why there are two possible dipeptides that can be made here.

2 a) inhibitors *[1 mark]*
   b) i) A drug molecule may have a very similar shape to the enzyme's substrate and fit into its active site *[1 mark]*. This blocks the active site, preventing the substrate from entering *[1 mark]*.
      ii) The active site of an enzyme is stereospecific *[1 mark]* so only one of the enantiomers will be able to fit into the active site of the enzyme *[1 mark]*.

Page 93 — DNA

1 a)

[1 mark for phosphate group correctly attached to 2-deoxyribose. 1 mark for guanine correctly attached to 2-deoxyribose.]

b) E.g.

[3 marks — 1 mark for each hydrogen bond correctly shown.]
The bonds between the bases are hydrogen bonds *[1 mark]*.

Answers

Unit 3: Section 9 — Further Synthesis and Analysis

Page 95 — Organic Synthesis

1 a) Heat under reflux *[1 mark]*
   b) $K_2Cr_2O_7$/potassium dichromate and H_2SO_4/sulfuric acid *[1 mark]*.
   Heat and reflux *[1 mark]*.
2 Step 1: The methanol is refluxed *[1 mark]* with $K_2Cr_2O_7$ *[1 mark]* and sulfuric acid *[1 mark]* to form methanoic acid *[1 mark]*.
   Step 2: The methanoic acid is reacted under reflux *[1 mark]* with ethanol *[1 mark]* using an acid catalyst *[1 mark]*.
3 Step 1: React propane with bromine *[1 mark]* in the presence of UV light *[1 mark]*. Bromine is toxic and corrosive *[1 mark]* so great care should be taken. Bromopropane is formed *[1 mark]*.
   Step 2: Bromopropane is then refluxed *[1 mark]* with sodium hydroxide solution *[1 mark]*, again a corrosive substance so take care *[1 mark]*, to form propanol *[1 mark]*.

Page 98 — NMR Spectroscopy

1 a)

[1 mark]

4 peaks *[1 mark]*
This molecule has no symmetry — each carbon is joined to different groups and in a unique environment. So its ^{13}C NMR spectrum has four peaks.

   b)

[1 mark]

3 peaks *[1 mark]*
One peak is for the red carbon (joined to $H_2ClCH(CH_3)_2$), another is for the blue carbon (joined to $H(CH_3)_2CH_2Cl$), and the third is for both green carbons, which are in the same environment (both joined to $H_3C(CH_3)HCH_2Cl$).

   c)

[1 mark]

2 peaks *[1 mark]*
This molecule has three lines of symmetry — the three (blue) carbons with Cl atoms attached to them are all in the same environment, and the three (red) carbons that don't are all in the same environment. So its ^{13}C NMR spectrum has two peaks.

2 a)

[1 mark]

[1 mark]

   b)

OR propan-2-ol *[1 mark]*

There are only two peaks on the spectrum. So there must be exactly 2 different carbon environments in the isomer *[1 mark]*.
   c) Tetramethylsilane / TMS / $Si(CH_3)_4$ *[1 mark]*

Page 101 — ^1H NMR

1 a) A CH_2 group adjacent to a halogen / R–CH_2–X *[1 mark]*.
   You've got to read the question carefully — it tells you it's a halogenoalkane. So the group at 3.6 ppm can't have oxygen in it. It can't be halogen-CH_3 either, as this has 3 hydrogens in it.
   b) A CH_3 group / R–CH_3 *[1 mark]*.
   c) CH_2 added to CH_3 gives a mass of 29, so the halogen must be chlorine with a mass of 35.5 *[1 mark]*. So a likely structure is CH_3CH_2Cl *[1 mark]*.
   d) The quartet at 3.6 ppm is caused by 3 protons on the adjacent carbon. The $n + 1$ rule tells you that 3 protons give $3 + 1 = 4$ peaks *[1 mark]*. Similarly the triplet at 1.0 ppm is due to 2 adjacent protons giving $2 + 1 = 3$ peaks *[1 mark]*.
2 2 *[1 mark]*
   This molecule is symmetrical, so the hydrogens at opposite ends of the molecule are in the same environment:

3 a) $3:2:3$ *[1 mark]*
   b) A: singlet *[1 mark]*, B: quartet *[1 mark]*, C: triplet *[1 mark]*.

Page 103 — Chromatography

1 a) To prevent contamination from any substances on their hands *[1 mark]*.
   b) To prevent the solvent evaporating away *[1 mark]*.
   c) Place the plate in a fume cupboard and leave it to dry *[1 mark]*.
2 a) X *[1 mark]*
   b) 1 and 2 *[1 mark]* since the spots present in mixture Y are at the same height (and so would have the same R_f values) as 1 and 2 *[1 mark]*.
   c) R_f = spot distance ÷ solvent distance
   $= 5.6 ÷ 8 = \mathbf{0.7}$ *[1 mark]*
   There are no units as it's a ratio.

Page 105 — More on Chromatography

1 a) The mixture is injected into a stream of carrier gas, which takes it through a tube over the stationary phase *[1 mark]*. The components of the mixture dissolve in the stationary phase *[1 mark]*, evaporate into the mobile phase *[1 mark]*, and redissolve, gradually travelling along the tube to the detector *[1 mark]*.
   b) The substances separate because they have different solubilities in the mobile phase and retention to the stationary phase *[1 mark]*, so they take different amounts of time to move through the tube *[1 mark]*.
   c) The areas under the peaks will be proportional to the relative amount of each substance in the mixture / the area under the benzene peak will be three times greater than the area under the ethanol peak *[1 mark]*.
2 a) gas chromatography *[1 mark]*
   b) Different substances have different retention times *[1 mark]*. The retention time of substances in the sample is compared against that for ethanol *[1 mark]*.
   c) It is unreactive/does not react with the sample *[1 mark]*.
3 B *[1 mark]*

Index

Index